the
vocat
georg

weber and simmel

studies in vocational and continuing education

vol. 9

edited by
philipp gonon & anja heikkinen

peter lang

bern · berlin · bruxelles · frankfurt am main · new york · oxford · wien

philipp gonon

the quest for modern vocational education – georg kerschensteiner between dewey, weber and simmel

peter lang

bern · berlin · bruxelles · frankfurt am main · new york · oxford · wien

Bibliographic information published by Die Deutsche Bibliothek
Die Deutsche Bibliothek lists this publication in the Deutsche
Nationalbibliografie; detailed bibliographic data is available on the
Internet at <http://dnb.ddb.de>.

A catalogue record for this book is available from The British
Library, Great Britain.

Library of Congress Cataloging-in-Publication Data

Gonon, Philipp, 1955-
The quest for modern vocational education : Georg Kerschensteiner
between Dewey, Weber and Simmel / Philipp Gonon.
p. cm. — (Studies in vocational and continuing education,
ISSN 1660-3443 ; v. 9)
Includes bibliographical references and index.
ISBN 978-3-03-430026-1 (alk. paper)
1. Vocational education—Philosophy. 2. Kerschensteiner, Georg,
1854-1932. 3. Dewey, Melvil, 1851-1931. 4. Weber, Max, 1864-1920.
5. Simmel, Georg, 1858-1918. I. Title.
LC1042.5.G66 2009
370.11'301—dc22

                                        2009023176

ISSN 1660-3443
ISBN 978-3-0343-0026-1

© Peter Lang AG, International Academic Publishers, Bern 2009
Hochfeldstrasse 32, CH-3012 Bern, Switzerland
info@peterlang.com, www.peterlang.com, www.peterlang.net

Printed in Germany

Table of Contents

Preface 11

1. Introduction 13
   1.1   Kerschensteiner's approach – conservative
         modernisation 15
   1.2   The literature on Georg Kerschensteiner 17
   1.3   The structure of the book 18
   1.4   The modernity of vocational education or the
         rediscovery of the German classical period of
         vocational pedagogy 20

Part 1

Kerschensteiner as an Educator

2. The Pedagogue Georg Kerschensteiner: A Brief Biography 25

3. The German Concept of *Bildung* and School Reform
   in the 19th Century 31
   3.1   Humboldt and Condorcet 32
   3.2   The Philanthropists and the Neo-humanists 36
   3.3   Conclusion 39

4. Joy in Work – Germany's Educational Debates in the
   Industrial Age 41
   4.1   The 'horrors of the dominant industrial state'
         and how pedagogy failed to perceive them 41
   4.2   Educational institutions as contributing to the
         labour question (social reform as a means to
         forestall socialism) 45
   4.3   Joy in work through education for arts and crafts
         in the age of industry 50

4.4   Pedagogical conversion and implementation 57
4.5   Conclusions 59

5.   Georg Kerschensteiner's Concept of the *'Arbeitsschule'* –
     A Plea for Work as a Foundation for Education 63
     5.1   Organisation and structure of *Begriff*
         der Arbeitsschule 63
     5.2   The state, vocation and work 72
     5.3   The *Arbeitsschule* as school reform: from Herbart
         to Pestalozzi and Dewey 79
     5.4   Personality, character and work 83
     5.5   Work and education 87
     5.6   Topicality and effects 90
     5.7   Conclusion 91

6.   Kerschensteiner as the 'Pestalozzi of Our Time' –
     A Pedagogical Hero and His Tragedy 93
     6.1   Pestalozzi as Counter-Herbart (the Natorpian turn) 94
     6.2   Pestalozzi *redivivus* in the German Länder –
         Spranger's approach to Kerschensteiner 103
     6.3   The faded heroes 111

Part 2

Kerschensteiner in Relation to Dewey, Weber and Simmel

7.   School Reform and Pragmatism: John Dewey's
     Ambiguous Impact on Modernisation in Germany 115
     7.1   Dewey as school reformer – Kerschensteiner's view 116
     7.2   Dewey as the father of teaching through projects:
         the Petersen Foundation 121
     7.3   Dewey as a psychologist of learning:
         more Herbartian than the Herbartians 126
     7.4   Dewey and the generation of 1968 130
     7.5   Conclusions 133

8. Education as Self-guidance – Max Weber's Alternative
    to Liberal Education..137
    8.1   Max Weber and Georg Kerschensteiner..........................138
    8.2   Education and vocation as pedagogical topics:
          Kerschensteiner and Spranger 140
    8.3   Vocation and education as sociological topics 142
    8.4   Weber's understanding of education between
          professionalism and life reform 144
    8.5   Weber's and Kerschensteiner's lectures on the
          topic of 'vocation' in Munich 145
    8.6   Politics as a vocation 147
    8.7   Professional politicians without a profession –
          Weber's paradox of the non-learnable vocation 150
    8.8   Education as a vocation 151
    8.9   The educator as a gifted shaper of souls –
          Kerschensteiner's paradox of the non-learnable
          vocation 154
    8.10 Science as a vocation...155
    8.11 Science as a modern vocational paradigm.....................158
    8.12 Vocational education between calling and
          bureaucracy...159
    8.13 Charisma and conduct of life: education between
          passion and self-limitation..160
    8.14 Conclusion: education as self-management....................162

9. Georg Simmel's Discourse of Life and Form as a Blueprint
    for Georg Kerschensteiner's Theory of Education 165
    9.1   Goethe's 'full personality' and cultural criticism...........166
    9.2   Life and "the tragedy of culture" 170
    9.3   Pedagogy and the discourse of life 172
    9.4   Contemporary criticism on *Lebensphilosophie* 173
    9.5   Kerschensteiner's approach: work as a means to
          overcome the contrast between life and form.................177
    9.6   Spranger and Simmel as central points of reference
          for Kerschensteiner's theory of education 180
    9.7   The Simmel-Kerschensteiner controversy.....................185

Part 3

Kerschensteiner in Relation to Systems of Vocational Education and Vocational Educational Reform

10. Apprenticeship, Vocational Education and the Rise of the Dual System...193

    10.1 Education and vocational education as a contribution to the uplifting of the lower classes............193

    10.2 Adam Smith's critique of apprenticeship 197

    10.3 The role of education and vocational education in Bastiat's and Hayek's theory...................................202

    10.4 Vocational education as a contribution to the solution of the social question 204

    10.5 The social question and pedagogy..................................207

    10.6 Conclusion...208

11. Efficiency and Vocationalism as Structuring Principles of Vocation-oriented Education in the USA 209

    11.1 Introduction 209

    11.2 Efficiency and vocationalism as focal points 210

    11.3 Efficiency as a parallel of academic education and industrial production...211

    11.4 Efficiency as a historical argument of reform pedagogy..212

    11.5 Manual work in elementary school as a contribution to external efficiency...................................214

    11.6 Vocationalism and vocational schools as contributions to 'social efficiency' 215

    11.7 Vocational schools as alternatives and complement to comprehensive high schools 216

    11.8 Examination of the German apprenticeship system 217

    11.9 Vocationalism as a constitutive element in school curricula: how vocational education found its way into the schools 218

    11.10 Spread and ambivalence of vocationalism.....................219

11.11 Efficiency as an argument against vocationalism:
Snedden's utopia "1960" 221
11.12 Conclusion 222

12. The Development of Vocational Pedagogy in Germany 225
12.1 The institutional basis and historical-scientific
premises of vocational pedagogy....................................225
12.2 Vocational pedagogy in the early 1960s........................231
12.3 The critique of the theory of vocational education 243
12.4 Fading out – the paradox legacy of the classics.............247

Notes on the Chapters..249

References 251

Index of Names..275

Preface

To write a book on Georg Kerschensteiner is a task I have brought onto myself. In 1992 I wrote my dissertation on the history of the idea of the activity school (*Arbeitsschule*), and half of that publication was necessarily dedicated to Kerschensteiner. After I had received my PhD, I thought that I had done with him and with the topic of the activity school. But I was wrong. I had barely finished that piece of work when experts from Japan and later from England, the USA and Norway contacted me, inviting me to give lectures on the prominent pedagogue and founder of the successful 'Dual System' of vocational education.

This international interest in Kerschensteiner was not matched by an equal interest in the German-speaking countries. Here, Kerschensteiner was perceived as a representative of a long-gone epoch whose ideas were of antiquarian interest at best. Just like Kerschensteiner and the reform pedagogues had distanced themselves from the Herbartians, educationalists and pedagogues after 1968 distanced themselves from the 'classics'. My task now became a matter of preserving Kerschensteiner's ideas from sinking into oblivion and of highlighting their topicality, but also of deconstructing some of the myths that had grown around him, especially with regard to the extent of his influence on the shaping of the German system of vocational education.

The present book too is a contribution to this examination of education and its modernisation in the age of globalisation, demonstrating as it does how 'classical' approaches to educational issues can be useful even today. At different times and for different occasions, I wrote individual papers on Kerschensteiner and his work; these papers have now been merged to form the publication at hand. Numerous colleagues have been of help in this process, offering criticism, encouragement, advice and active support. In particular, I would like to mention those two who have directly collaborated with me in the creation of this book, first of all Bill Templer, who courageously translated a majority of the texts and who surprised me time and again by adding relevant references and suggestions. With his dedication he contributed more to the text than the mere translation into another language. Dr. Lukas Rosenberger translated the remaining German texts and urged me to rephrase or elaborate whenever he considered this to be in the interest of an English readership. His influence on the texts therefore goes beyond mere translation, too. It goes without saying, though, that all remaining errors are my own. I am deeply grateful to both of them since their work has made a vital contribution to the goal I pursue with this book: to demonstrate why it is worthwhile to look into the subject of the foundations of modern vocational education even today.

Philipp Gonon, Zurich, 21.1.2009

1. Introduction

In most European countries, compulsory schooling was introduced in the 19th century and answered one of the fundamental claims of the Enlightenment, namely to spread knowledge in order to foster democracy through education, and to foster education through democracy. This claim was summed up by the liberal Johann Heinrich Zschokke in the formula "popular education is liberation" (*"Volksbildung ist Volksbefreiung"*) (Zschokke 1859: 171). Zschokke already included the idea of continuing education, including adult education, after compulsory schooling.

In addition, education was also meant to foster economic prosperity. In this conception, education was not reserved for the elite of society but for the masses. In turn, these masses had to adapt to new developments in economic production. Apart from the ambition to popularise the achievements of culture and science there was the question of how the rural population, the middle classes and the industrial workers could qualify for employment. How could the elementary school impart further useful knowledge apart from the four Rs reading, writing, arithmetic and religion? And how could youths be integrated into modern society after compulsory schooling? These were some of the questions which educational policy had to deal with at the turn of the 19th century. The focus had shifted to the aspiring working class and the middle classes who felt threatened by the newly established freedom of trade; the answers to their claims – often connected to the so-called 'social question' – necessarily included educational measures.

The same problems appeared in similar forms in every nation with industrial ambitions. Since 1875, elementary schooling was being supplemented by instruction in handicrafts (for both sexes) in all of Europe and in the USA. Libraries and museums of arts-and-crafts should serve the purpose of further education for the workforce. Specific institutions for the needs of commercial and industrial, but also agricultural, home economics and mercantilist education were created. These were schools specifically intended for the training of skilled workers. Additionally, there was a first wave of legislation to regulate in-firm apprentice training and the creation of vocational educational institutions (Gonon 2008). In other words, there were a number of issues that indicated a need for reform in order to contribute to a modernisation of society:

- The existing elementary school was in need of reform. Instruction and curricula should take into account the latest developments in science and the arts. In particular, manual work and personal experience relating to modern culture – understood as revaluation and reform of industrial culture – should be included.
- In political discourse, a new concept of education was to be established, one which took heed of economic, industrial and social realities. In fact, it could even be said that educational policy at that time actually depended on such a new concept of education. For example, the natural sciences and 'realistic' contents quite generally needed to be re-valued vis-à-vis classical philology.
- Vocation-oriented and work-oriented education should be allowed room by acknowledging its educational value next to classical education and by accepting it as an independent area of education. These demands anticipated the development towards parity of esteem of general and vocational education.
- Until the end of the 19th century, pedagogy had normally been a sub-discipline of philosophy. At the beginning of the 20th century, pedagogy was to be established as a legitimate and independent university discipline in order to deal with educational issues, especially relating to school matters. Around the same time, psychology and sociology also became established as independent disciplines.
- The professionalisation of teacher-training was of particular importance. This was to be achieved by a more pronounced orientation towards scientific disciplines and by designing teacher-training at least in part as university education, though the practical components of the training were to be retained.

14

- In addition, specific post-elementary educational institutions had to be established. The vocationally oriented continuation schools that had developed out of optional local institution were to be redesigned in order to provide youths with further necessary skills and attitudes for their professional and social lives.

1.1 Kerschensteiner's approach – conservative modernisation

Georg Kerschensteiner took an active part in all of these issues, which becomes apparent already in his 1907 essay collection *Grundfragen der Schulorganisation* on basic questions of school organisation (cf. Kerschensteiner 1914 for an English translation). These essays deal with such topics as general and vocational education, the educational value of manual work, continuation schools and teacher-training (Kerschensteiner 1910).

Kerschensteiner's pedagogy provided specific answers to these basic questions insofar as for him it was not a matter of merely modernising the methods of knowledge transfer or of supplementing infirm training with theoretical training for apprentices. He rather wanted education to be oriented towards everyday life and the world of work. Furthermore, he considered vocational education – which he wanted to be recognised as an essential component of education – to be an important requisite for citizenship.

Kerschensteiner was ambivalent towards social and economic change. In his view, all the rights that were valued most highly in the modern state, i.e. freedom of speech, freedom of press, right of association, right of assembly, universal suffrage and freedom of trade, led to excessive and state-threatening individualism. In his essay *Das Problem der Volkserziehung* ("The Problem of National Education") he therefore argued that "the old forms and formulae of education" were no longer sufficient (Kerschensteiner 1910a: 1).

Kerschensteiner's reform concept was not the result of a scientific analysis or of deliberate educational planning, but it developed pragmatically over a period of time, in part motivated by fear of social upheaval. His ideas were influenced by an idealistic conception of society as had already been sketched by Plato. In his essay *Begriff der staatsbürgerlichen Erziehung* ("The Idea of Education for Citizenship") he argued that the realisation of an ethical, virtue-based community represented the ideal of the constitutional state and of national culture (Kerschensteiner 1912a: 27, 32). Character building that granted every individual a role in the state organism should contribute to this same end. Regarding his educational reforms, Kerschensteiner modelled himself on the astute Prussian politician Bismarck and on the Swiss pedagogue Pestalozzi.

This comprehensive perspective on reform was pivotal also for vocational education. In an essay on the system of continuation schools he argued that the neglect of education and training for craftsmanship had led to the establishment of a versatile and thorough education in apprenticeship workshops as an alternative, for example in France, but later on also in Austria and Switzerland. Even though he lauded the advantages of these institutions, he nevertheless pleaded for the enhancement and 'vocationalisation' of continuation schools in order to foster vocational education on a larger scale (Kerschensteiner 1912b: 288). Note that Kerschensteiner did not speak of a 'dual system of vocational education'; this term was introduced only in the 1960ies (Bohnenkamp/Dirks/Knab 1966: 429). He considered the continuation school for apprentices to be the right means to fulfil the tasks of education and strengthening of a sense of community (Kerschensteiner 1912b: 289). He argued that it was a shortcoming of existing continuation schools to be geared only towards economic benefit, while the ultimate goal of education in a modern state could not be limited to a purely vocational goal (ibid.: 295).

Kerschensteiner was obviously not the only one concerned with these issues. He shared the reform pedagogues' enthusiasm for Pestalozzi, and like the Neo-Kantian philosopher and pedagogue Paul Natorp he chose a social-pedagogical approach. Together with his younger friend Eduard Spranger he furthermore glorified Pestalozzi as a pedagogical classic, and with his colleague Aloys Fischer he established pedagogy as a discipline at the University of Munich.

From a contemporary point of view, Kerschensteiner was impressively powerful and influential, which in his first phase as an educational politician allowed him to implement the changes he deemed necessary. He was soon famous for his school reforms, and the fact that he was an exceptionally gifted speaker and gave many lectures in Germany as well as abroad added to his high profile. He received a host of prominent visitors who praised the "Munich Model" (Best/Ogden 1914: 21) as an example of educational reform because it had been possible to convert youths into "capable workmen" and "good citizens" (ibid.: 2). It is thus Kerschensteiner's merit that the German educational reforms at the beginning of the 20th century, in particular with regard to elementary school and vocational education, became internationally visible.

1.2 The literature on Georg Kerschensteiner

There are a large number of publications in German on many different aspects of Kerschensteiner's work. His lectures and some of his important texts have been edited by Gerhard Wehle (Wehle 1966, 1982). Most publications focus on one single aspect of his work, for example, on his role as vocational pedagogue, as educational theorist, or as an exponent of reform pedagogy. For a long time he had been portrayed very favourably, even with a lack of critical distance (but cf. also Wilhelm 1957; Walder 1992). Since the 1960s, however, a critical view on Kerschensteiner has developed, focussing on his backwardness regarding his stance on political and technological developments (Stratmann 1999, 1999a).

As far as publications in the English-speaking world are concerned, there is a detailed portrait and well-informed presentation of his work by Diane Simons (Simons 1966). In this monograph, she traces Kerschensteiner's impact in many areas and especially his pioneer work for educational reform in England (Simons 1966: 136).

Christopher Winch mainly focuses on the topic of vocational education and the German 'Dual System' of vocational education, in close connection with Kerschensteiner's concept of education. Like other authors too, he refers to Kerschensteiner's rather backward understanding of occupational work, although this understanding did not exclude the development of highly qualified work or the conveying of 'civic virtues'. Winch therefore considers a "re-examination of Kerschensteiner's philosophy of education" to be very useful (Winch 2006: 395).

In the present book these views will be taken up, yet they will be put into perspective by demonstrating that the German system of vocational education is not a deliberately planned concept, let alone planned by a single person, as has sometimes been claimed. By presenting the ken and the reform ideas of the then prominent activist and pedagogue Kerschensteiner it is possible to reveal the questions and problems which the educational reformers had to deal with at the turn of the 19th century. It was the shared concern for educational reform in modern times and for the preservation of the social contract that led to a historical compromise in educational matters. It is the remarkable achievement of German vocational pedagogy – and of Kerschensteiner as one of its prominent exponents – to have successfully met diverse demands in a new concept and system of education.

1.3 The structure of the book

Part I of the book starts off with a presentation of biographical characteristics (Chapter 2). The remainder of Part I explores Kerschensteiner's close ties with pedagogues and school reformers of his time. Beyond the distinction between a player in educational politics in his early years and an educational theorist in his later years (cf. Gonon 1994: 3134), the main focus will be on Kerschensteiner's references to education and work in the context of the German discourse at the turn of the 19th century (Chapters 3 and 4), followed by a presentation of his concept of the activity school (Chapter 5). Kerschensteiner saw himself as a follower of Pestalozzi; therefore, Part I closes with an examination of the pedagogical heroising of Pestalozzi in connection with Kerschensteiner's work (Chapter 6).

Part II of the book focuses on Kerschensteiner's relation to three important thinkers of his time. Especially the early, politically active Kerschensteiner referred to concepts of reform pedagogy and also, although not very extensively, to John Dewey's pragmatism (Chapter 7). However, it can be considered rather typical for a German thinker to react rather sceptical to philosophical rationales from the New World (cf. Gonon 2005).

Kerschensteiner's (non-)relationship to Max Weber is more complex in comparison. It seems that Weber's understanding of modernisation and vocation was difficult to grasp for pedagogues at the time (Chapter 8). Furthermore, it is little known that Kerschensteiner picked up the sociologist Georg Simmel's ideas on philosophy of life (*Lebensphilosophie*) and used them in the development of his concept of education (Chapter 9).

Kerschensteiner as well as other pedagogues were very reluctant to consider education from a modernisation point of view. This remark is important insofar as from an international perspective the German concept of education – in particular vocational education – is generally considered to be very up to date.

Part III deals with questions of system formation of vocational education in more concrete terms. As has already been hinted at, the Dual System was not deliberately planned as a pedagogical concept (Chapter 10). Particularly when contrasted to the reforms in the USA, the main foci in Germany can be clearly showed (Chapter 11). Finally, a brief presentation of the development of vocational pedagogy until the present day will illustrate today's significance of the classics, including Kerschensteiner (Chapter 12).

1.4 The modernity of vocational education or the rediscovery of the German classical period of vocational pedagogy

At the beginning of the 20th century, Georg Kerschensteiner was considered a highly respectable reform pedagogue not only in the German- and English-speaking world, but also in Eastern Europe and in Russia. In addition, he was considered to be the founder of the Dual System of vocational education, an opinion that can still be heard today. Yet his terminology and statements regarding the concept of education or educational reform have clearly become outmoded. For this reason, in the 1960s the German tradition of vocational pedagogy and especially Kerschensteiner's approach was sharply criticised as being obsolete, backward, apologetic, and as legitimising the current capitalistic regime. Furthermore, the historical exponents of vocational education were known to be politically right-wing, tending towards nationalism and later even National Socialism. The critical examination of the role of the classics of vocational pedagogy and their followers in the 1960s was thus fully justified. For a long time, these classics, including Kerschensteiner, were disregarded in the social-scientific research on vocational education.

Why is it still worthwhile to study Georg Kerschensteiner today? Vocational education that includes more than simply technical training is a model that successfully balances different interests. Even if Kerschensteiner's genuine influence is sometimes overestimated, the curricula of vocational schools and the general orientation of the German system of vocational education is still marked by Kerschensteiner and his colleagues. This orientation is of interest not only historically but also as a basis for future educational reforms. Therefore, two elements that were of central concern to Kerschensteiner and are still relevant today are worth stressing again:

(1) The reformation of the concept of education, i.e. the redefinition of the relation of general and vocational education:

In his 1904 essay *Vocational or general education?* Kerschensteiner presented vocational education as an important component of human development. According to him, the path to the ideal man leads via the useful man (Kerschensteiner 1910b: 30). The gap between general and vocational education was said to be artificial and to lead to one-sidedness and philistinism; vocational education was therefore a necessary part of true education. Referring to the great German classic Johann Wolfgang Goethe he furthermore claimed that vocational education was to be anchored in the handicrafts (ibid.: 32). It has rightly been pointed out that the respective comments by Goethe are taken from a novel, are of an allegorical nature and not really related to any sort of educational theory (Zabeck 2003: 79 ff.), yet the strategic approach of the argument – which indeed succeeded in convincing the educational elite and the ruling class of his time – is still remarkable. Apart from a technical or functional justification, vocational education is thus furthermore attributed a cultural legitimacy. This wider scope should also be considered in future educational reforms as a cultural component next to technical qualification.

(2) The combination of regulated in-firm training with expanded and strengthened vocational schools:
Adam Smith, author of *The Wealth of Nations*, had argued against an apprenticeship system (cf. Smith 1904b: 249 ff.). His arguments were discussed in Germany at the end of the 19th century with regard to educational reforms. Smith wanted to abolish the apprenticeship system for four reasons: He argued that the guilds prevented competition, that the apprenticeship model was little effective and better results could be achieved within a shorter period of training. Moreover, apprenticeships were not only too much of a constraint for young people but they also abetted the economic exploitation of apprentices (Rothschild 2001: 87 ff.). The economists of the German *Verein für Socialpolitik* revised Smith's theses, as did the classical thinkers of German vocational pedagogy later on. They argued for a more concise regulation of the apprenticeship system instead of its abolishment. In addition, apprenticeships should be comple-

mented by instruction in vocational schools. It was claimed that in such a "combined system" the apprentices would finally learn something (Brentano 1875: 68). This approach, based on regulated vocational education and training in schools and in the firm, prevailed in the reforms of the apprenticeship system in the German-speaking countries in the 20th century. The combination of different learning environments is still regarded as a model for future reforms of vocational education (cf. Gonon 2008a) because it allows to link theory with practical experience and to integrate youths who have not gained access to the *Gymnasium* (general education on the upper secondary level) or to a completely school-based vocational education.

Especially in this age of globalisation it is of prime importance that education is not understood as being limited to school-based education or even as referring to general education exclusively. Correspondingly, it is vital for the educational system to pay heed to the fragile relation between school and workplace, not to establish a monoculture of exclusively school-based vocational education or to submit squarely to a regime of economic exigencies. In this sense, the ideas of the classics of vocational education, and notably those of Kerschensteiner, are still surprisingly modern.

Part 1

Kerschensteiner as an Educator

2. The Pedagogue Georg Kerschensteiner: A Brief Biography

Georg Kerschensteiner was an educator who rose to great prominence during his lifetime. He was a much sought after speaker, an impressive figure, a spirited Bavarian with great rhetorical gifts and a well-developed sense for the spirit of the times, which he adroitly knew how to adapt to in setting forth his ideas. He gained a public profile as an energetic and vigorous school reformer, which was the foundation of his fame far beyond his native city of Munich.

There are three quite informative biographies of Kerschensteiner: an autobiography, one by his second wife Marie Kerschensteiner, and one by his granddaughter Gabriele Fernau-Kerschensteiner. It is only natural that descriptions of a person's life from his own perspective or from the perspective of close relatives and friends tend to be biased. In particular, such a close vantage contains the potential to construct a story of unmitigated success, and to exclude the dark or inglorious aspects in the subject's life. Nonetheless, for educators and a broader readership, these three biographies remain key reference points, especially since no critical biography has been published yet. They convey to the reader the ethos of a pedagogue who was endowed with the talent of a 'classic' educator, a paramount quality that contemporary fellow educators already recognised. Kerschensteiner was ranked with Pestalozzi, even by the doyen of German educational theory Eduard Spranger, and his granddaughter went so far as to dub him the "Newton of pedagogy" in regard to his keen intellect. It is apparently unavoidable that there will be some heroic idolising and exaggeration in the sense of models associated with a kind of hagiography of the discipline and its luminaries (cf. Chapter 6).

Georg Michael Kerschensteiner was born in 1854 in Munich. He was the second youngest child in a large family that lived in relative poverty in the city's tenements. He was a good pupil, and for that reason after finishing elementary school, he decided to become a teacher.

He was sent to the preparatory teachers' training school in Freising, which he left in 1871 to work as a teacher's assistant in a country school, hired on at the meagre salary of a servant. After a short interval in Lechhausen, he was transferred to the city of Augsburg. In 1873, he requested to leave school service in order to further his formal education.

Earning his living as a private tutor and piano teacher, he was able to prepare for admission to an academic high school. He was accepted into the sixth form, and in 1877 passed the school-leaving exam, the *Abitur*. He then went on to study mathematics and physics at the Technological University in Munich. After passing his state exams in 1881, he worked for a short time at the central meteorological station in Munich, and then became an assistant teacher at an academic high school on Nuremberg. His niece claims that at that time he was actually a university teaching assistant in mathematics and had no idea about pedagogy (Fernau-Kerschensteiner 1954: 39). In any event, even then he criticised the encyclopaedic nature of the curriculum. In 1883, he submitted a doctoral dissertation on "The Criteria for the Singularities of Rational Curves of the Fourth Order"; one of his examiners in the orals was none other than Max Planck. In 1885, he was appointed to the teaching staff of the Commercial Academy in Nuremberg, and five years later became a teacher at the *Gymnasium* (academic high school) in Schweinfurt, before he landed a post in 1893 at the Ludwig *Gymnasium* back in his native Munich.

During that period, Kerschensteiner was also engaged in survey work on glaciers in the Bavarian Alps. In the view of several descriptions, these experiences during his own time at high school, as a pupil and teacher who had come "late" to the calling, had a formative impact on his subsequent views about pedagogical reform. Even then, he was inclined to favour instruction in the natural sciences grounded on living and manual activity, and oriented to the outside real world. He was convinced that schools should not convey 'education' as something done to pupils; rather they could only stimulate a 'hunger for education' (cf. Kerschensteiner 1939: 105 ff.). When teaching in Schweinfurt, Georg Kerschensteiner was opposed to a newly instituted curriculum in the natural sciences based solely on imparting knowledge. However, it then turned out that this curriculum had been designed by his older brother Anton, a member of the school board, an excellent medical specialist but not a pedagogue (Kerschensteiner 1982: 122).

Now a high school teacher, Kerschensteiner married Sophie Müller in 1886. There is little known about her. Her niece Gabriele Fernau-Kerschensteiner has little flattering to tell about Sophie: She notes that since the time Georg was in Augsburg, Sophie had been his faithful "tin soldier", naive, insignificant, taking little part in his intellectual life. She bore him three sons, and he left the entire gamut of domestic chores to her, from "cooking the geese to bringing up the kids" (Fernau-Kerschensteiner 1954: 77).

Up until that time there was no indication whatsoever of the special character that would distinguish Georg Kerschensteiner as a classic pedagogue. Quite on the contrary, his life was marked by a rather unconventional career as a high school teacher after his somewhat difficult childhood and youth. He was an ambitious self-taught individual who had managed to gain access to higher education, and was evidently endowed with a number of talents. But in 1895, at the age of 41, an important chance occurrence catapulted Kerschensteiner out of this predictable trajectory as a civil servant and *Gymnasium* teacher in Munich. One of his neighbours was to be appointed as a school inspector and royal school commissioner, but he had to withdraw his candidacy because he was too controversial a candidate for political reasons. This unfortunate candidate then proposed Kerschensteiner as a "compromise candidate", and Kerschensteiner was indeed elected to this influential post.

This was the beginning of Kerschensteiner's pedagogical career and fame. For the present, the position provided him with a huge opportunity to influence educational policy far beyond the boundaries of Munich. First he set about reforming the curricula for the *Volksschule*, or more specifically, the concrete materials in syllabi used in class instruction and the teaching of drawing. Then he introduced reforms in the schools for further education (so-called *Fortbildungsschulen*), adding an obligatory 8th year of instruction. Particularly striking was the construction of new school buildings, in art deco *Jugendstil*, with attached workshops and school gardens, and a restructuring of vocational education in Munich. In addition, Kerschensteiner's fame spread through his trips to neighbouring countries, and he attended conferences on art education and on the *Arbeitsschule* of the day. He also lectured in England and the United States, awakening a broad international interest in the Munich reforms he had been instrumental in introducing.

His role thus shifted from a classroom teacher to an educational administrator and reformer, and then to an influential figure in educational theory. His manifest success in this shift in career trajectory was grounded on considerable publication activity. During his tenure as a school inspector, he drafted a theory of curriculum (1899) presented to a competition of the Erfurt Academy of Sciences, whose first prize he was awarded in 1901. According to his own statement, he analysed 'a million drawings' by schoolchildren. Based on these analyses he published *Die Entwicklung der zeichnerischen Begabung* ("The Development of Talent in Drawing") in 1905, along with a book on basic issues in school organisation. In this period he also published his classic volume *Begriff der Arbeitsschule* ("The Concept of the Activity School") and another volume entitled *Wesen und Wert des naturwissenschaftlichen Unterrichts* ("The Essence and Value of Instruction in the Natural Sciences").

In 1911, at the age of 58, he was convinced by friends to become a deputy in the *Reichstag* in Berlin, representing the Liberal People's Party (*Freisinnige Volkspartei*). He had close connections to the circle around Friedrich Naumann, a Liberal who originally espoused socialist and Christian ideas, and later also exercised a certain influence on modern political Liberalism in the Federal Republic, as personified by Theodor Heuss and the Free Democrats. But at that time, Liberalism was a very broad and diffuse phenomenon, and thus did not prevent Kerschensteiner from combining some politically reactionary views with his Liberal outlook. For example, he was in favour of strict cultural censorship and considered individualism – which he saw as closely akin to egoism – as great a danger as Social Democracy. He was also very sceptical of "pedagogical individualism" and saw himself standing more in the tradition of Plato than Humboldt (Fernau-Kerschensteiner 1954: 105). During the First World War, he placed himself in the service of a militaristic and extremely questionable nationalism, though at the time these were political sentiments widely shared by many segments of society.

He utilised his travels and tenure as a Reichstag deputy for further publications. In addition, further volumes were to appear from his lecture trips abroad: on the education of character, the German school system and the fundamental axiom of the process of education. His wife Sophie died in 1915, and that same year Kerschensteiner married the widow Maria Barst, who later was herself to write a biography of the man.

At the age of 64, he began his career as a university teacher. This compensated for the waning of his influence in, and ultimately virtual exclusion from the sphere of educational policy in Munich, the result of a rather turbulent phase in Munich politics that accompanied Germany's defeat after the First World War (cf. Walder 1992: 15). Intellectuals, the independent Social Democrat Kurt Eisner, and anarchist-socialist circles around Gustav Landauer had proclaimed a 'Council Republic' in Munich, which was bloodily suppressed a few days later. As an opponent of the revolution, Kerschensteiner too had to go into hiding for a short time. In 1920, after the situation had calmed, he was appointed to a professorship at the University of Munich. Only a short time before, he had declined a similar offer from Leipzig.

His influential work on teacher training, *Die Seele des Erziehers* ("The Soul of the Educator"), was published during this period. In 1924, he was celebrated as a distinguished educator, even though his writings on educational theory remained controversial and were only partially accepted. In 1926, his most extensive work was published, the *Theorie der Bildung* ("Theory of Education"), followed posthumously by his *Theorie der Bildungsorganisation* ("Theory of Educational Organisation") in 1933. Kerschensteiner died in 1932 in Munich.

3. The German Concept of *Bildung* and School Reform in the 19th Century

The concept of Bildung *(education) is not as genuinely German as it seems to be, since its development was in part based on French ideas. Initially,* Bildung *was virtually centred on a school curriculum at a higher educational level. This chapter aims to illustrate the close relation between the concept of* Bildung *and the idea of transforming schools into curricula-based learning institutions, i.e., the process generally referred to as school reform.*

In the following discussion of the concept of *Bildung* and the rise of schools as they exist today, the focus will be mainly on Germany and Switzerland. These countries and especially also Prussia have considerable experience in school reforms. In the 19th century they witnessed lengthy discussions concerning why and how people had to go to school and why they had to become educated. German-speaking countries were not only well known for their educational experience of mass schooling for the lower ranks, but also for their particular way of reflecting on education. The German concept of *Bildung* and a great many novels on education – such as Pestalozzi's charming Swiss novel *Lienhard und Gertrud* – were the products of the cultural elite. Their views on educational matters made an impact on other countries, as they were regarded as the crucial perspective which guaranteed the obvious success of schooling in Germany. In what follows I will show that there is a high degree of correlation between school reform and the new definition of education as *Bildung*.

The discussion about *Bildung* is an element in the argument for school reforms; however, there is no *direct* link between *Bildung* and school reform. Prussian bureaucracy and the milieu of the German philosophers and poets who dealt with educational matters belonged to two different worlds in this regard. It could also be argued that the success of German schooling emerged despite the rather strange ways in which educational matters were discussed. In fact, it was not the philosophers, novelists and poets who instituted the school reform, but the bureaucracy. Yet, it is true that the former had a considerable influence, especially in Prussia, by creating the secondary schools and the universities, although they could neither have foreseen nor intended all the effects that resulted from this reform. In all these developments, the concept of *Bildung* was not as unique as it may seem, but was mainly used as a discussion slogan. There was no specifically German concept of *Bildung*, but there were concepts of *Bildung* which referred to a relation between an individual and an objective culture, a world which had to be transformed and reconstructed in each individual personality. In was this process in particular which was labelled *Bildung*.

It was a great step forward when the Prussian state introduced its own education policy in the 18th century. Earlier on, there had been a wide variety of local and regional school systems, in which the church or the local rulers had been responsible for school matters. The extensive and well-known reforms, however, only started in the decade after 1800. It was not the education of the lower ranks that provoked a hard fight among school reformers and out of which a new understanding of education as *Bildung* emerged, but the *Abitur* and the *Gymnasium* (grammar school). *Bildung* was considered to be opposed to vocational training and a curriculum, both of which were directly oriented to state affairs.

3.1 Humboldt and Condorcet

In order to explain such a view it is very helpful to compare the ideas of Wilhelm von Humboldt, one of the main protagonists of school reform in Prussia, with those of the French mathematician and philosopher Marie-Jean-Antoine-Nicolas Caritat, Marquis de Condorcet. The distance to a form of education which leads to civic virtues was already mapped out in the young Wilhelm von Humboldt's early essay *Ideen zu einem Versuch die Grenzen der Wirksamkeit des Staates zu bestimmen* (Ideas on an attempt at determining the limits of state power). The state should not be obliged to ensure happiness for its citizens, but should guarantee individual freedom: The highest aim of humanity was to obtain *Bildung*, and freedom was the most important condition necessary to achieve this aim. Even the slightest amount of state intervention into educational matters would limit the enormous potential inherent in human education. As a first step, Humboldt claims that one should get a liberal and not a state- and civic-centred education. According to him, any man educated in this way could afterwards enter into the state. In all public education, however, one would find the ethos of a governing power, which influences the individual. Only free men could really enhance commercial and industrial success, perfect the arts and the sciences, acquire better educators, and so on (Humboldt 1987). With these claims Humboldt stands in explicit opposition to the French endeavours to build a national education system.

In the first of *Cinq mémoires sur l'instruction publique*, Condorcet claimed that public instruction was a duty of society in order to achieve true justice, to reduce the inequality of moral feelings and to enhance "*la masse des lumières utiles*" (Condorcet 1989a: 38). Public education was also needed for democracy to function well and not to become the concern of professionals only; furthermore, public education should guarantee that the division of labour does not leave people's minds dull (51). However, it was not Condorcet's aim to turn education into a state affair. Moreover, Condorcet would have liked the duty of public education to be limited. The state should only "*regler l'instruction*" and leave the rest of education to the family (Condorcet 1989a: 61). But the state has to ensure that a minimal amount of material is covered in schools to enable people to participate in the spheres of common life in a democratic way. *L'opinion publique* is the result of a rational discourse which in turn requires a minimal knowledge base. Only public instruction where the sciences and the know-how for republican behaviour can be learned provides the basis for this integral part of citizenship. Schools are the means by which *les lumières* could be taught to the people.

Condorcet emphasised what he perceived to be an important difference between *opinion* and *savoir*. Schools had to be the disseminators of knowledge, but they were not allowed to impart political or personal judgment. Condorcet's analysis identified a clear enemy, namely the French Jacobines, who defined school and education as a matter of getting a *volonté générale*. The Reign of Terror proved this understanding of education to be too narrow.

The French vision of Condorcet and, later, that of the *'Idéologues'* schools were centrally orientated to their concept of science. In this regard, *l'education publique* combined political and scientific development. Schools had to enable the transformation of knowledge and should in fact be *"encyclopédies vivantes"* (cf. Nieser 1992).

The ideas of Condorcet contained the seeds of impressive projects, but their realisation was not easy because of the prevailing political instability. *'Les idéologues'* built a school system which emphasised in particular *"les sciences morales et les sciences physiques"*. They put up so-called Central Schools, special schools and the great *École polytechnique*, where the best scientists of France instructed young teachers, technicians and scientists. Destutt de Tracy, Cabanis, Degerando and others tried to apply the concept of enlightenment by spreading scientific knowledge via schooling throughout the whole society (cf. Picavet 1972).

The political instability in France put an end to the energies of the *philosophes* (Condorcet died in prison), and the *'idéologues'*, who represented this tradition, had to pay their contribution to the political restoration. When Napoleon gained power he changed the educational system. Yet, as Picavet said in 1891, *"en pédagogie comme en philosophie les idéologues ont ouvert les voies ou nous nous essayons à marcher"* (Picavet 1972: 68). Besides this mainly science-based school system there was another important shift: The new curriculum was very empiricist and anti-dogmatic, and it furthermore reduced the canon of classical language teaching. A few years later, Humboldt, too – despite his earlier reflections on attempts at determining the limits of state power – developed a plan for a public school system. It is known that Humboldt was aware of the ideas of the *'Idéologues'* and Condorcet, yet, his concept was quite different. Humboldt's ideas of reform were oriented to antiquity, to a school with a critical distance to society. He argued that studying the classics, especially the Greeks,

34

essentially served the purpose of character building. In his later works he emphasised the study of grammar and language.

In contrast, Condorcet's view was much more dynamic and oriented towards the progress of science, i.e., towards the progress of the epistemological view, which provides the basis of a higher moral (cf. Baker 1975). In the 10th, posthumously added chapter to Condorcet's *Esquisse*, in which he sketched the progress of the human mind, he pointed out that up until the latest epoch, access to the sciences was reserved for a small elite. He went on to claim that everybody now had the possibility of gaining access to the sciences (Condorcet 1981: 330), that equal access to schooling would liberate the masses and would enable everyone to be guided by his own mind. According to his understanding, progress in science would lead to a progress in school instruction, and this would again benefit the progress of science. In its totality, this process of reciprocal reinforcement would lead to the perfection of humanity (ibid.: 215). In Condorcet's time, when a young man left school, he knew more than Newton knew in his time, and the *verités* were growing in other sciences as well. In his last sentences, Condorcet – who wrote this quasi testament in prison – argued that it was a nice prospect for a philosopher to know that humanity was on the way to greater virtue, truth and happiness (ibid.: 221).

Humboldt's view of state and education was much more sceptical. The question of sciences does not appear as a crucial element in his reflections on education. In his early writings (*Ideen*) he made a distinction between man and citizen. Education or, as it is now referred to, *Bildung* is centred on the individual; the world around him and also state affairs should just provide the impetus for the formation of a human being from the organic inside. He specified this view in other writings, such as in his *Theorie der Bildung*. In particular, he saw language as an ideal medium to build and rebuild humanity.

Another crucial aspect is history, which in Humboldt's sense is not a *magister vitae* as traditional concepts suggest, but a way of presenting and building one's own personality by learning and organising historical facts and views. Ideas and concepts are accommodated by researching their historical understanding. History is not a mere technique without relevance outside the boundaries of a purely scientific understanding, but it is the central idea of *Bildung*. This evolutionist perspective by Humboldt simultaneously shows his greatness and his weakness. By emphasising individual behaviour he does not take into account the development of the sciences in its empiric reality. *Bildung* is a romantic concept which leads to entity and totality. This is the very opposite of a scientific perspective, which is based on differentiation and empirical research. This historical and anthropocentric view marks the crucial difference between Humboldt's perspective and that of the French philosophers such as Condorcet.

Humboldt's view of education and educational system entails a confrontation of the pupil and the world as a result of history. This is why the Greek antiquity and the great endeavour to learn the Greek language are important for the formation of a new and ethical man. Both Condorcet and Humboldt build their educational systems starting from the highest educational institution, the university or academy. But there are different orientations in the two approaches. It is not the great antiquity that is central to Condorcet's model of education, but the dynamic of science itself. To the founders of the University of Berlin, among them Humboldt, mathematical and other sciences based on experience were assigned lower status than history or philosophy (cf. Habel 1990: 34). Their main emphasis was on formal learning, which was considered crucial in the development of individual powers (*Kräftebildung*) (Habel 1990: 65). Thus, at first glance Condorcet's and Humboldt's references to a higher education based on the sciences, including the humanities, sounds very similar. Yet, Humboldt's view was much more anthropocentric, whereas Condorcet's concept was based on a dynamic understanding of society and the sciences, which he thought would flourish best in a public and republican climate.

3.2 The Philanthropists and the Neo-humanists

As has been shown, the German and French discussions about education differed crucially, and these differences left their mark on the design of higher education in particular. However, in Germany the influence of French ideas was much stronger than is generally acknowledged. German observers – and some of them were also admirers – of the French Revolution, such as Johann Heinrich Campe, the teacher of the two brothers Wilhelm and Alexander von Humboldt, imported 'French' ideas on education into Germany. The *Revisionswerk*, edited by Campe (1979), includes a copy of the great encyclopaedia by D'Alembert and Diderot on educational matters. The aim was to collect all the available knowledge on education. It also includes a translation of Mary Wollestonecraft's pamphlets and John Locke's thoughts, as well as other sensualistic statements.

However, the Germans were especially fascinated by the writings of Rousseau. Thus, the *Revisionswerk* also contains a translated version of *Emile*. The philanthropists did not read the work of Rousseau primarily as a critique of culture or as a sceptical view of enlightenment, but derived from it the duty to build schools and to improve education quite generally. Philanthropists, such as Christian Heinrich Trapp, the first German professor of pedagogy in Halle, were familiar with the French debates and referred to them in their reflections. But their influence was reduced when Trapp's successor, Friedrich August Wolf, the famous philologist, began to teach at the University of Halle. He was much more orientated towards the classics than the sciences: he agreed with Trapp and the philanthropists that school reform was necessary, he was against Latin drill and the exclusive Bible studies, but not in the way the philanthropists suggested. Instead, he preferred the learning of languages.

In his *Concilia scholastica*, Wolf (1835) points out his problems with the philanthropic method, which to him does not seem to be applicable to higher education and by which *Bildung* is linked to instruction (*Unterricht*) and follows education on a lower level. So he limits the problem of *Bildung* to a higher degree of schooling and restrictively defines the matter of instruction as a philological study of the classics. The "neo-humanists", Paulsen's (1897) term for this movement in opposition to the philanthropists, also had an idea of reform, but their approach was not as methodical and 'realistic' as the philanthropists' attempt at adapting French theories on psychological sensualism and socially orientated utilitarianism.

Reducing the role of Latin and classical literature by lending more weight to the 'realistic' subjects served to provoke their activities as an intellectual elite. It was Friedrich Immanuel Niethammer, a friend of Hegel's, who constructed an alternative which very effectively undermined the early dominance of the philanthropist discussion. In the introduction to his pamphlet *Der Streit des Philantropinismus und Humanismus in der Theorie des Erziehungsunterrichtes unsrer Zeit* ("The struggle between philanthropy and humanism in the theory of education of our times") edited in 1808, Niethammer demonstrated that the centre of controversy was the grammar school (*Gymnasium*), but that the principles of the philanthropists extended even to primary school. He argued that a critique of the old Latin school methods, which he seemed to share, did not evoke a predominance of "realistic subjects". The central duty of a school should be to provide general education (*allgemeine Bildung*) and not applied or practical knowledge derived from the sciences.

Niethammer mainly attacked the spirit of the philanthropists because he thought that it could endanger the school system as a whole, since the focus of the curricula was reduced to a mere preparation for a business or industrial profession (Niethammer 1968: 23). For Niethammer, the difference between humanism and philanthropy was an anthropological difference, namely the difference between rationality and animalism (ibid.: 37)! Furthermore, in his understanding philanthropists were close to a materialist view, because the mind is determined by the body (ibid.: 59). Real *Bildung* is not linked to the knowledge of *how* to do something, i.e., to applied reason (*Kunstverstand*), but rather to general reason (ibid.: 63). Humanism needs to be concerned with the classical form, whereas the philanthropists prefer technical and physical knowledge – things that were unknown in antiquity (ibid.: 81).

The duty of education and instruction at school (*Erziehungsunterricht*) should be the education of reason, i.e., the education of humanity (*Humanitätsbildung*; Niethammer 1968: 93). At least, this kind of *Bildung* is more effective in making people fit for life. This is why the education of the mind should be the crucial concern of instruction (ibid.: 119). The fault of the old humanism was not its idea of humanity but the confusion of education with vocation for the higher ranks.

Like other humanists, Niethammer argues that there is a special value in learning Greek or classical languages, although he acknowledges that there is also a value in learning mathematics (ibid.: 228).

All the same, Niethammer was not such a terrible anti-modernist as his polemic against the philanthropists may suggest. However, his attack was very effective in the ongoing educational discussions. It not only discredited the endeavours of the philanthropists, but also marginalised the idea of establishing a realistic curriculum at a higher level of education. The result of this controversy was that schools – and especially grammar schools – emphasised the literary and classical studies, while in the beginning the sciences were virtually excluded. *Bürgerschulen, Realschulen* or the *Realgymnasien*, schools which included or preferred vocational, technical or scientific subjects, faced considerable difficulties in building a reputation as institutions, which would allow their alumni to gain access to higher studies. Thus the term '*Bildung*' was closely connected to literary and philological or historical studies, while protagonists of physics and other realistic subjects had to struggle for their reputation. It was not until the end of the 19th century that they were officially accepted (cf. Jeismann 1974).

3.3 Conclusion

In the 19th century, school reformers in Prussia, Bavaria, Switzerland and France had similar problems in creating a system of educational institutions. Pestalozzians centred their attention on a particular method, Pietists on religious matters, philanthropists on a 'real curriculum' and the neo-humanists on an idea of *Bildung*. *Bildung* represented a concept in opposition to vocational education. Blankertz (1985) correctly observes that although Humboldt and the neo-humanist opponents of utilitarianism were not *in concreto* as dogmatically opposed to a realistic curriculum, they were biased in favour of classical learning. Nevertheless, the sciences found a place in the curricula, because the grammar schools could simply not ignore the development of sciences.

This was also the result of linking the grammar schools to universities or polytechnics. For industrial regions the *Bürgerschulen* with their realistic subjects became more and more popular, so that by creating a polytechnic school in Switzerland the way was open to define a new branch in the grammar schools, which could no longer marginalise the natural sciences.

Despite this bias towards classical teaching and learning, which was very strongly criticised in Germany later on, Litt (1955) deplored the exclusion of the whole industrial world. His crucial point in the present context was to link education to curriculum reform. It is not primarily the methods – as was thought, for example, by the Pestalozzi followers – but the material aspect that is central to successful learning. *Bildung* is, secondly, also a concept that opposes vocationalism that is in danger of ignoring general aspects of culture. However, it needs to be kept in mind that this concept of *Bildung* ignores the dynamics of scientific and social development, which is why *Bildung* seems to be a privilege for the elite even today.

4. Joy in Work – Germany's Educational Debates in the Industrial Age

The prime trigger for the discussion on the topic of work in the fin de siècle was a "one-sided and excessive industrialism" (cf. Seiferle 1984: 147), which led to new and sundry consequences in society. "The horrors of the dominant industrial state" (Brentano 1901) had to be critically examined. For that reason, one dominant approach was social and political in thrust and, after the turn of the century, culminated in the idea of restoring 'joy in work' as part of a pedagogical agenda.

4.1 The 'horrors of the dominant industrial state' and how pedagogy failed to perceive them

In the introduction to his book *Die conventionellen Lügen der Kulturmenschheit* ("The Conventional Lies of Civilised Mankind", first published in 1883), the influential essayist Max Nordau cast the workers in a strikingly negative metaphor:

> In Germany, socialism is gnawing with a hundred thousand mouse teeth at the pillars of all government and social institutions. Neither the luring notes of the pied piper of state socialism, academic socialism and Christian socialism can deflect these indefatigable rodents even for a moment from their uncannily quiet, subterranean enterprise of destruction, nor do the wastefully installed traps of the emergency laws, the state of siege and police action have any effect. (Nordau 1909: 2)

This pessimistic assessment of the situation sums up the mood in the bourgeois establishment before the turn of the century regarding future developments if nothing were done to effect a "reordering of the economic organisation of society" (Nordau 1909: 253 f.). Even if we leave aside the culture-critical and conservative undertones that reverberate through the book as a whole, i.e. with a description of society as a huge edifice of lies, the author's insolent comparison between industrial workers and rodents is rather disconcerting from a contemporary perspective.

Nordau believed that there were indeed serviceable remedies, though not among the broad range of proposals for a solution as offered by socially engaged groups and individuals. In order to break free from the bind of potential internal conflict, he believed that there should be a return to a state of childhood. Like Indian Nirvana, this stage could rest either on lack of knowledge or absolute knowledge. Since it was no longer possible to return to childlike innocence, the necessary goal had to be human uplift, although all the while following the light of natural morals. In keeping with the instinct for self-preservation of the species, those morals instinctively evoked the good (ibid.: 341 ff.). From this analysis, in which economic and social problems are reduced to individual yardsticks for behaviour, it is possible to formulate a pedagogical program, and this is what was actually done at the time of reform pedagogy.

Initially, however, it is instructive to identify the above quote as a component in the discussion on the 'labour question', the famous *Arbeiterfrage*. As animal-like creatures decomposing the foundations of the state, the picture of the workers evoked here is reminiscent of thoughts in Friedrich Albert Lange's book *Die Arbeiterfrage – Ihre Bedeutung für die Gegenwart und Zukunft* ("The Labour Question. Its Importance for the Present and the Future", first ed. 1865). In the chapter on the "struggle for survival", which is evidently influenced by Darwinism, he warns about the physical degeneration of the human race (Lange 1879: 58 f.). Industrial workers are considered the strongest and most decisive stratum of society. They are exposed to the "exhausting burden" of their work, and thus long for a possible change (ibid.: 11). In order to ban wild thoughts, hatred and revenge, their situation should be enriched by "intellectual work" (ibid.: 389). Their desire to establish associations and educational societies should be supported.

A different approach was taken by Heinrich Herkner. He believed that the labour question could be solved in the ambit of life in the rural community. In any event, it necessitated social reform in order to increase the economic and social independence of the individual via intervention by the state. Herkner, who later became a professor of economics in Zurich and was a member of the *Verein für Socialpolitik* ("Association for Social Policy"), concluded his book *Die Arbeiterfrage* (1894) by propagating an alternative situated between liberalism and communism, emphasising the cultivation of patriotism and dedication to the common welfare, as was common in smaller independent social formations at the time (Herkner 1894: 282 f.).

These references are but a small sliver of opinion from a comprehensive debate on labour and its development in industrial society. There was no country where the question of labour with regard to the economic and social future was debated in greater intensity and detail than Germany (cf. Campbell 1989). Despite that fact, German pedagogy of the time seemed to have been little affected by this debate. This is evident from the analysis of Theodor Litt, who showed that the pedagogues were quite chary of touching this whole issue. In his view, the "antinomy of education," or the "triumph of materialism" as a consequence of the division of labour, prevented education from becoming an enterprise that sought to "shape the personality as a work of art," as he once put it (Litt 1955: 111). Litt can also discern hesitance and ignorance on the part of pedagogy with regard to social, technical and economic problems. Indeed, Litt contended, even Georg Kerschensteiner, who had explicitly dealt with these topics, had been blinded by his affinity for German classicism, geared to "creativity in arts and crafts, so esteemed by Goethe, and its educative impact" (ibid.: 67). In the process, he had more or less forgotten about industrial labour and its role. That criticism can be supplemented by the contemporaneous critical voice of Anna Siemsen. She complained that vocational pedagogy had peopled a world of factories with naively imaginary types of human beings and vocations: knights, artists, artisans, monks, landed gentry, landed clergy, officers, foresters (Siemsen 1926: 65 f.).

Yet naiveté and daydreaming à la classicism were not solely a failing of pedagogy. The division of labour, which in 1921 Hans

Freyer called the "a priori of the liberal system" (Freyer 1966: 27), was giving German philosophical thought a great deal of trouble. In a tone of derision, Freyer noted:

> The poets describe it with love, the pedagogues look for the educational value of labour, the philosophers try to find its moral dignity, and the economists, animated by the spirit of classicism, endeavour to show what is truly human in the realm of economy. [...] But Gertrude's children, busy spinning cotton [...] are all so intellectually and emotionally energised, so strong and healthy, so happy and cheerful, as though they had not actually had a spinning wheel in their hand all day long. (Freyer 1966: 28 f.)

If we follow this analysis in its full reach we could make the striking assumption that pedagogy had innocently romanticised or totally ignored the modern world of labour and its myriad changes. Of course, pedagogy as a discipline was not alone in this, but our focus here is primarily on educational theory and its theorists. Though this assumption is not completely unfounded, the present chapter will advance arguments which seek to partially relativise such a 'naiveté' on the part of pedagogical reflection. I would argue, then, that even the pedagogues intended to press ahead the quest for an ethos of labour as discussed especially by economists and social reformers, independent from and even often counter to such social and technological developments.

Education for work and a vocation should not follow deductively from an a priori analysis of the industrial world of labour and its future. The concept of work as seen by pedagogy does not involve any kind of empirical stock-taking from which conclusions can be drawn. Rather, it is a project tied to social policy involving historical, political and economic discussion threads which then expand into pedagogy. Seen in this light, Kerschensteiner's thoughts on work, vocation and civic education are not to be understood as original achievements. Rather, they are best conceived as Wilhelmine common sense.

4.2 Educational institutions as contributing to the labour question (social reform as a means to forestall socialism)

Despite the visible distance between pedagogy and the world of work, education and its institutions were accorded an important role in any solution to the labour question, at least by the economy and the government. The state of discussion and its reflection in Kerschensteiner's first prize-winning treatise – with which he established his fame – *Staatsbürgerliche Erziehung der deutschen Jugend* ("Civic Education of German Youth", 1901) will be discussed first before we look at the concept of 'joy in work'.

The pioneer folk life scholar and historian Wilhelm Heinrich Riehl tried to fathom the problem of work and other matters in a comprehensive study of German society. His *Die bürgerliche Gesellschaft* characterises the rise of the workers as a "class consciousness of poverty", which had arisen as a result of the social sins of the other classes (Riehl 1907: 379, 390). Written between 1847 and 1851, this work can be seen as a precursor of the discipline of sociology.

The influential editor of the *Preussische Jahrbücher*, Heinrich von Treitschke, saw little value in such an analysis. In his eyes, the so-called fourth estate consisting of rural inhabitants, small artisans and workers of all kinds was a population group largely oriented to economic life and to be described not by the attribute of being poor but by physical activity alien to political and intellectual life. Therefore, this estate or class was not as historically unique as Riehl imagined (Treitschke 1859: 28). In Riehl, he continued, there was always some underlying reflection of a melancholic longing for the good old days, apparent likewise in his subjective preference for the idyllic unadorned character of the peasant, and Riehl's socio-political interest in stabilising the estates stood in contrast to the fact that they were actually in the process of dissolution (ibid.: 79). In his habilitation thesis, Treitschke argued in an open polemic against Riehl that a critical science of society was needed instead of dilettantism. For Treitschke, the state constituted society in its unified organisation, encompassing all of the life of the people and overcoming all sectionalism. Thanks to its power, it was able to order society and imbue it with morality by means of law (ibid.: 81). Treitschke rejected also Riehl's later work *Die deutsche Arbeit* with the same arguments and accused Riehl's concept of work of harbouring an inadmissible idealisation.

The dispute between Schmoller and Treitschke, on the other hand, had a different set of accents when it came to work and society. Gustav Schmoller made a huge claim for himself and the social scientific analysis pursued in the Association for Social Policy: He alleged to have found a link between the misery of the workers and laisserfaire capitalism (Schmoller 1918: 287). In contrast, Treitschke saw the Association's aim and perspective as something that aided and abetted a socialist upheaval. Such a criticism, apparently shared by many, was levelled not only at the members of this Association, who later provokingly appropriated for themselves the title of 'lectern socialists', in the sense of 'armchair socialists'. In an article on 'labour' in the famous encyclopaedia *Herders Konversationslexikon*, even Adam Smith was accused of having abetted socialism by excluding the moral question from his analysis (Herders Konversationslexikon 1902). In a response directed against Treitschke in 1875, Gustav Schmoller noted that already Smith clearly must have understood that the problem of the division of labour gave rise to social inequalities. Treitschke's criticism in the *Preussische Jahrbücher* that the Association for Social Policy, in which Schmoller played a key role, was to be regarded as a "benefactor of socialism", prompted Schmoller to reply that a revolution should be prevented by the introduction of proper reforms (Schmoller 1875: 91). Unlike Treitschke, he did not view Social Democracy as the result of demagogic politics but as the product of an unjust division of wealth and of low wages. He claimed to hold this view not as a socialist but as a "radical Tory" (ibid.: 128):

> The more monarchic I feel and the more I know that all my thoughts are united with the state of the Hohenzollern, the reestablishment of the German Reich and its struggle against the anti-state tendencies of ultramontanism and Social Democracy, the more I feel bound, with unconditional openness and honesty, to express my support for what I believe is justified in today's movement of the fourth estate, struggling for what in my view is the only thing that can guarantee

the normal further development of our free institutions, namely social reform.
(Schmoller 1875: IV f.)

Not only is this answer to Treitschke's criticism a statement of political principles, it also contains a program for the Association for Social Policy, which will not be further explored here. Moreover, an ethical concept of work is developed and at the same time an expansion of the cultural and educational realm to the workers is called for.

In this respect, Schmoller's approach followed Riehl's definition of work, though for other motives: The honour of work is central yet it serves not only the individual but also the "personality of the nation" (Riehl 1883: 55), and in this process, socialism is said to fade away "as a spectre devoid of substance" (ibid.: 209).

Schmoller launches a vehement attack on Treitschke's notion that the workers must be denied education, a plan that could have unforeseeable negative consequences. Contrary to the view that a person who lives by "rough labour" every day was not amenable to higher education, he replied that what was important were the schools available and the cultural influences a person was subject to (Schmoller 1875: 113). Since the time of ancient Greece, cultural progress had reduced the gap between the classes, i.e. between slaves and citizens.

> The great progress of our time is that the honour of labour is recognised, that governing, painting and scientific research are no longer thought to be the only worthy pursuits of a decent human being, that handicraft and education are no longer seen as contraries that are mutually exclusive. (Schmoller 1875: 117)

Schmoller added that the desire to exclude workers from advanced education and even to keep them away from obligatory attendance at schools for further education was economically absurd at a time when factory owners and master artisans were complaining about the lack of proper education of these same workers (ibid.: 120 f.).

In sum, he argued that Treitschke's theory amounted to a division not only of the functions in the process of labour but indeed of society, which reserved education and knowledge for the higher classes and emotion and religion for the lower ones (ibid.: 125). To what extent Treitschke actually stated his opposition to education for the lower social classes must remain an open question here. But the fact is that his essay *Freiheit* ("Freedom") contains statements which concede only religious education to the lower social classes. He argues that the demand for equality in the field of law should not stray onto the territory of education for the individual (Treitschke 1907: 13).

Yet, the labour question was certainly not just some debate about the workers' level of education, whether actual or desired. It was about the future of society as a whole, and education was therefore much influenced by social policy and its desiderata. It was certain that the industrial working class would grow, and with it the urgency of the question of the workers' social-political integration. For a confirmation of this estimation, all that was necessary was to take a closer look at the situation in England. England's industrial development was a terrain not only for testing and developing economic theories but also for estimating the effects of a planned set of social and educational policies.

An important work in this connection is the study *Zum socialen Frieden* ("On Social Peace") by Schulze-Gaevernitz, published in 1890. Its subtitle reads "A description of the social-political education of the English people in the 19th century". Carlyle is portrayed as a great educator who also called for a social attitude and altruism even under the conditions of large-scale industry (Schulze-Gaevernitz 1890: 272). As the author emphasised, the example of England showed that a peaceful resolution to the class struggle was possible. With large-scale industry as the dominant form of business, the centre of gravity of society shifted to the masses, and at the same time towards democracy. In the Anglo-Saxon world, this had led to a reconciliation of social contrasts, a process for which an increase in education, the legalising of organised trade unions and higher wages had been characteristic prerequisites (Vol. 2: 486 ff.).

Accordingly, a high level of wages, a well-developed set of laws for the protection of workers and a reduction in the number of working hours per day were the demands that Lujo Brentano educed from a study of the situation in Great Britain, as well as the demand for increased wages, improved legal protection for the workers and shorter working hours. "It is a happy fact," he wrote in the final sentence of his book *Über das Verhältnis von Arbeitslohn und Arbeitszeit zur Arbeitsleistung* ("On the Relation of Wages and Labour Time to Labour Output"), "that social reform, which is called upon to elevate millions to a higher level of civilised behaviour, is also the only means that can lead to a strengthening of the economic and political power of the nation and its role in the world!" (Brentano 1893: 55).

Hans von Nostitz' *Das Aufsteigen des Arbeiterstandes in England* ("The Rise of the Working Class in England", 1900) also seeks to explore ideas to solve the German labour question. His extensive study can be seen as the actual blueprint for Kerschensteiner's work on civic education of German youth, not only with regard to the frequency of quotes from Nostitz but also to the orientation in theme and content. All of Kerschensteiner's examples of education are taken from Nostitz, and his references to Carlyle likewise point to this source.

Nostitz, a Prussian official who spent six months in England, soberly notes that the essential feature of social development in the 19th century had been the rise of the working class (Nostitz 1900: 721). He viewed his report as a belated reply to Engels' *Zur Lage der arbeitenden Klasse in England* ("On the Situation of the Working Class in England", 1845). Marx's prediction of the deepening destitution of the workers and the subsequent violent revolution had not proven true (ibid.: 740), but only due to the implemented social reforms. Nostitz stressed the fundamental importance of social peace, which in turn was based on political maturity and education (ibid.: 777).

It was precisely in order to domesticate socialism and to defuse its dangerous dimension that a well-developed education system was necessary. Nostitz described such a system in detail and with numerous examples, and Kerschensteiner referred to Nostitz' descriptions of educational institutions in England a number of times in his treatise. Along with Nostitz, the discussion between Schmoller and Treitschke finds its distant echo in Kerschensteiner's conceptions concerning the civic education of German youth.

Like Schmoller, Brentano was also opposed to a bifurcation of society into a select few and a "more or less brutish majority" (Brentano 1897: 9). He called for a differentiation in society in order to bring about the "greatest possible development of all natural abilities and the skills of all individuals" (ibid.: 21). To that extent, Kerschensteiner was following the social reformers of the Association for Social Policy by stressing the value of education for the workers. He called for a democratisation of the 'aristocratic attitude' even for the workers. However, he remained a faithful disciple of Treitschke in his conception of civic education, which in his view had to overcome all particularism and diversity for the sake of a higher unity and order.

4.3 Joy in work through education for arts and crafts in the age of industry

Not only the mere existence of educational institutions was of relevance to the labour question; it was also a matter of channelling the dynamics of industrial development and the connected potential for discontent into peaceful pathways. Riehl's notion of the 'honour of labour' had to be applied in new contexts. In particular vis-à-vis the working class and its tendency to basic materialism, it was important to cultivate ideals which would protect the workers and their stratum from "English-French enlightenment garbage" (Bang 1924: 65). In contrast, the far more sober economist Brentano stressed that ideals were necessary "in order to overcome the negative side effects of our economic development" (Brentano 1902: 37). In his view it was necessary to reconcile industrial labour with the needs of the respective workers. Anticipating this debate in 1846, Lorenz von Stein had also called for intellectual and physical education for the workers, since this would give them the capacity for a higher level of work and competence. At the same time, every effort should be made to develop plant and machinery to the highest possible level of perfection (Stein 1846: 289). This concern culminated in the postulate of 'joy in work', which was transposed from outside into the industrial labour sphere in order to bring education and personality into harmony alongside industrial output (Ferber 1959: 52). One suitable realm for cultivating such pleasure in work was the realm of arts and crafts. After all, despite the transition from wood to iron as the quintessential industrial material, experience and manual dexterity and creativity had retained

50

considerable importance in industrial production (Radkau 1989: 63). As Rein's *Enzyklopädisches Handbuch für Pädagogik* consistently noted, training for handicrafts was valuable not just for handicraft proper but for industry as well (Beyer 1904: 575). Work had to be imbued with a new dignity, and this was to be anchored and secured pedagogically and aesthetically. The potential threat emanating from machinery had of course to be downplayed. In literary fiction, however, such aspects were foregrounded far more explicitly: Industrial work was depicted as monotonous, and 'the machine' was even portrayed as a force able to literally bury the human being, as described in Julius Lerche's tale *Der Riese vom Spinnhof* (Lerche 1919).

Notwithstanding the asserted acceptance of machines, industrialism and large-scale factories, critical stances towards this development emerged, as a leitmotif or more tacitly under the surface, shaped in part by an idealisation of handicrafts. This becomes evident from Herkner's 1905 publication that deals with the topic of 'joy in work'. He noted that modern industrialism was characterised by a concentration of ever more professions in large-scale factories. For that reason, a new discussion of the question of 'joy in work' was imperative. Such joy or pleasure was greater in agricultural and craft vocations than in industry (Herkner 1905: 14). Joy in work could be fostered by ensuring that the specific activity to be performed took on the character of a professional specialty (ibid.: 16). Work must not become monotonous. This meant that the machine had to serve and assist the worker and allow latitude for his or her individuality, for example, in such a way that the final product was then seen as "the result of the worker's hands and his craftsmanship, dexterity, and professional competence" (ibid.: 19). To enhance pleasure in work thus demanded an upgrading in professional training and skill levels. With reference to Goethe, Pestalozzi and Ruskin, he claimed that professional activity formed an "infinitely valuable means for education, one that shaped character. In the interest of our national future, we cannot do without its growing application and utilisation" (ibid.: 32). Furthermore, the search for genuine 'joy in work' also awakened the spirit for inquiry and discovery.

Karl Bücher did not hesitate to go into great detail, looking at the function of music and poetry in the world of work in classical Greece as well as in 'indigenous peoples', such as in the Sudan. He stressed that work had of course become more productive by the division of labour, but was now also more sober and drab. A cheerful playfulness and joyous delight on the job had been supplanted by deadly earnestness and an often painful resignation. Nonetheless, he advised, we should cling to the hope that "technology and art would someday meld in a higher rhythmic unity" (Bücher 1896: 117).

That longing for 'joy in work' with regard to changes in working conditions was already present in the writings of Charles Fourier: In his *De l'anarchie industrielle et scientifique* (anarchy here is meant in a negative sense), he calls industrialisation an insidious gift to humankind because industry leads to the desperation of the "salaried classes" (Fourier 1847: 4). He argued that even the primitive in his state of sluggishness had a better life than these workers, and his senses were not perpetually being goaded, stimulated and irritated by luxury products (ibid.: 5). Industrial anarchy was spreading, even into Switzerland, a country famous for its freedom and morality. Even workers from St. Gallen and other Swiss factories were in a similar sorry state. In addition, Switzerland was providing workers to all countries and crowns, which would never be possible if the Swiss farmers were happy (ibid.: 19). So it was clear to Fourier that the *"masse d'une nation"* could not derive any benefit from such industrialism, aside from a few factory owners and mercantile Cossacks (ibid.: 21). A way had to be found out of this labyrinth and monstrous mechanism, not by destroying factories (ibid.: 22) but, as stated in his "plan for social reform", by passionate and hands-on creativity (Fourier 1925: 129). The prerequisite for this was a varied spectrum of small activities. Fourier mainly proposed to concentrate on agricultural work in groups, involving hunting, fishing, raising pheasants and growing vegetables. Industrial work was also scheduled but needed little time, since three times as much could be accomplished in an hour than by wage labourers who were slow, inept, bored and loved to stand around gaping (ibid.: 131). Since his envisioned new mode of work in what he called a Phalansterie – a kind of communal unit for labour and living – would not be exhausting, people would be able to gather to enjoy concerts, theatre and art of all kinds after dinner, and less time would be needed for sleep.

In Germany, this criticism of 'industrial feudalism', the rural Phalansterie as its alternative and Fourier's visionary predictions made a
huge impression on August Bebel. He decided to make Fourier's
thought applicable to and fruitful for 'scientific socialism', and published a detailed presentation of his ideas for the German public (Bebel 1907: XVI). Following Fourier, he wrote that education for the
young sought to train and educate them for work (ibid.: 117). In the
Phalansterie, three-year-olds would be playfully introduced to light
work in the household and encouraged to do small tasks, though without enforcement. Purposefully appointed and nicely furnished playing
halls, kitchens, small workshops, equipped with small tools and machines, would give them an opportunity "to activate their abilities and
instincts" (ibid.: 124). Actual intellectual work would not begin until
they reached the age of nine.

Bebel put Fourier's work on a par with that of Goethe, since he
considered both their fantasies about human happiness to be related.
Still, Fourier was considered superior to Goethe in his knowledge of
the real situation of the masses and the natural history of humankind
(ibid.: 244 f.). In Bebel's view, the socialist future would be rich in
artists and scholars, since physical work would only take up a small
part of daily life (Schwarte 1980: 181).

This way of perceiving Fourier was also found outside the strict
perimeter of German Social Democracy, for example in thinkers such
as Gustav Landauer. In his *Aufruf zum Sozialismus* ("Call to Socialism") he stressed that socialism was a kind of re-fulfilment of society
and work with spirit, a combination of agriculture, industry and handicraft, intellectual and manual labour (Landauer 1978: 145 f.). Work
must become play again, in the economy and in the working community.

Even thinkers diametrically opposed to socialism were influenced
by Fourier when it came to the idea of 'joy in work'. Riehl, the author
of *Deutsche Arbeit*, was initially directly inspired by this idea (Campbell 1989: 36), although in later writings he scrupulously avoided any
'foreign' references (yet, cf. his reference to Fourier in Riehl 1883:
239). Following Fourier, Riehl stressed that ethical reform in connection with work was fully justified, complementing economic and political reform. The ethical motive and aim of work were distinguishing

traits of the true worker (ibid.: 222). Along with all reforms, the previous 'honour of the trade' should continue to be cultivated; hence every work should have its honour (ibid.: 26 f.).

There is no denying that all these proposals sprang from a handicraft-oriented or rather pre-modern concept of work. An additional fond hope was that industrial work would be located in rural environments, as was common in Switzerland (cf. Michels 1928: 160 f.).

The concept of 'joy in work' or 'joy in creation' contained a moral component in particular. Creating such a condition in industry and the large factories was no easy matter, as can be seen from a number of book titles that speak, for example, of the *Kampf um die Arbeitsfreude* ("Struggle for joy in work", De Man 1927). Drawing on ideas of Ruskin, the famous art historian Karl Scheffler thus called for an idealisation of the existing scheme of work. Ethical and even national ideas had to underpin labour, and such an ideal would elevate both the individual and the collective to a higher level of civilisation (Scheffler 1909: 77). The soul harboured a "quiet need for an idealism of labour"; this is why questions of how to make work more ethical should also become part of economics and its discourse (ibid.: 99 f.). Other authors too liked to link such ideas with nationalism. Work as an ethical act had to accentuate what was "truly German" (Lhotzky 1919: 64). Moreover, the will to high-quality work went hand in hand with 'joy in work':

> Every person should become productive in such a manner that he completely rejects the disgraceful botchy work that we are surrounded with on the street and at home and that we live with and accept as if there was no other choice. Instead we should demand high-quality work. (Scheffler, n.d.: 34 f.)

Idealism of work and joy in work also required a new simplicity and solidity which could likewise lead to a renewal of industrial work and handicraft. In the case of Scheffler, this reasoning was even connected with the hope that the old handicrafts could gain the upper hand over industrial work, serving as a kind of 'rebirth' of productive manufacture. He stressed that the culture of art was based on handicraft and high-quality artisanship. With the proper quality, it could replace a 'dazzling' but hollow commercial civilisation:

And precisely because we are able to do it, because moral exertion, diligence, intelligence, objectivity and self-limitation are sufficient to create high-quality work in handicrafts in all fields, it is our duty and obligation to work untiringly in this direction. (Scheffler, n.d.: 35)

Art and artistic handicrafts, indeed the "spirit of the Gothic" (Scheffler 1917) seemed to take on an educative role. The efforts to preserve and advance traditional crafts – exemplified, for instance, in the British Arts and Crafts Movement – were directed against industrialisation and its seemingly unavoidable side effects. These efforts had a broad impact and were met with interest even by protagonists of the German movement for the activity school, the *Arbeitsschule* (cf. Chapter 5).

The reformist Arts and Crafts Movement in Britain had been inspired by the writings of Ruskin and was at its height from 1880 to about 1910, with William Morris as one of its best-known practitioners. The movement began as a reaction to the 'soulless' machine-made production of the Industrial Revolution, and turned from the machine as the root cause of all evil to an emphasis on the revival of all manner of handicrafts.

That someone of the stature of William Morris, following in the footsteps of Ruskin, denounced the "ugliness of modern life", appeared to assign a new role to arts and crafts. This approach had an impact on the industrial world of work beyond art circles (Campbell 1989a).[1] In contrast to Morris, however, the accent here was not on banning the machine but on curbing its unimaginative and dull application. Along with representatives of art and crafts schools, such as Van de Velde, resolute advocates of an idealised understanding of work oriented to joyful creativity could also be found in social reform circles.

1   As Osthaus notes in his biography of Van de Velde, new perspectives were opened up for the plastic arts: "Now he saw the path stretching out before him: Plastic art had to become applied art, applied to life, from which the spirit had departed. And work on beauty had to return to humankind its lost nobility" (Osthaus 1920: 10 f.). The Belgian Henry Van de Velde was one of the first designers and architects to work in the abstract style that would become characteristic in design of Art Nouveau (Jugendstil). He founded the Kunstgewerbeschule in Weimar, the predecessor of the Bauhaus, and was closely associated with the Deutscher Werkbund.

As early as 1902, Friedrich Naumann had spoken of the ideal of a people imbued with the spirit of aesthetics and beauty in his *Kunst und Volk* ("Art and the People", 1902: 5). Industrial work, he alleged, led ever more people to carry out fragmentary tasks on the job instead of a holistic shaping of a product (ibid.: 6). "Education for the Personality in the Age of the Large Factory" – thus the title of another of his publications – should not just train workers to operate machines, because then both man and machine were nothing but a "sloppy piece of work". This request can surely be read as a criticism of Treitschke. Instead, human beings had to preserve a responsibility for their work even when using advanced machinery (Naumann 1907: 24, 37). For that reason, before people were sent to work in large factories, the school had the special task of preparing them by shaping their attitude and intellect (ibid.: 39).

The handicrafts could serve as a paradigm especially for the industry, because they might provoke a self-critical development and a revamp of its approaches. As Naumann noted in an allegorical vein in *Die Kunst im Zeitalter der Maschine*, "when the machine saw that it was only doing little work, it took up a position behind the artisan again, adopting [...] his art" (Naumann 1964: 189).

Unlike Scheffler, Naumann sees the ideal for Germany not in handicraft per se but rather in a "people working with machines, but thoroughly educated in the arts" (ibid.: 192). An absolute prerequisite for this was social peace. He reasoned that the orientation to the world market and the status of Germany as a world power must lead to a conciliation of management and labour.

It was not the machine that was the problem, but rather the concomitant depersonalisation of work, the draining and evisceration of its very soul and spirit. That was a tendency inherent in philosophical materialism and industrialism (Bang 1924: 89). The strong agreement of social reform and art regarding pedagogical consequences becomes evident in the quest for the "New Art" and "New Man" (Scheffler 1932). This quest peaked in an empathetic endorsement of work that could, in the form of a general task for education, serve as a useful slogan for any reform pedagogue: "We need work, work – nothing but selfless work, animated by joy" (Scheffler, n.d.: 40).

In keeping with this view, it was considered important to cultivate work and joy in work inside the school as well. Illustrative of that
turn was the call for "practical action" in Kerschensteiner's widely
read work *Begriff der Arbeitsschule* ("The Concept of the Activity
School", cf. Chapter 5). Such practical activity served not only to in-
culcate an "objective attitude" but also led to an "inward, soulful happiness". According to Kerschensteiner, "joy in work" in a pedagogical
sense was "nothing other than the joy in being the very origin of the
realisation of the value of objectivity" (Kerschensteiner 1957: 55).

4.4 Pedagogical conversion and implementation

The idealisation of work and imbuing it with "spirit," its *Vergeistung*,
along with joy in work had of course been topics in educational discourse even before the proponents of the activity school came on the
scene. For example, the Swiss writer Friedrich Graberg in *Die Erziehung in Schule und Werkstätte* ("Education in the School and Work-
shop", 1894) stressed that it was important not just to perfect steam
and electricity but also to cultivate "the intellectual powers of our
workers bestowed as a gift from their Creator" (Graberg 1894: 12).
Competence on the job had to be increased through education in order
to generate the level of respect for manual labour that was necessary
for cultural development as well as with regard to instruction in the
manual arts (Schenkendorff, n.d.: 13). As early as 1896, Ewald Haufe
had termed this reform an "activity school", and one can easily gain
the impression that he was directly anticipating Kerschensteiner a full
decade earlier when instead of book wisdom and knowledge he
stressed a more hands-on curricular framework: inquiry and active
learning, creative endeavours, artistic activity and productive work as
hallmarks of such an *Arbeitsschule* (Haufe 1896: 4, 28, 37 f.).

  With this focus on education for joy in work in the school, it was
possible to 'subjectivise' a social problem, translating it from social-
political analysis into a concept amenable to work in pedagogy. This
was precisely the achievement of proponents of manual arts and the

activity school: They accorded the school a role that promoted more manual dexterity, more activism in the classroom and active learning, joy in creativity, and education of character for the community and state. This is how Georg Kerschensteiner formulated it in 1901 in his festive address on the occasion of the 50th anniversary of the Bavarian Arts Association, referring there to Goethe and thus providing the necessary classical legitimation. "The industrial education of German youth" should not rely on an early groundwork of general knowledge; only "creative and industrious work can propel us forward" (Kerschensteiner 1901: 5). His 1904 essay *Berufs- oder Allgemeinbildung* ("Vocational or General Education") states that "true education" derives its power "solely from serious, intensive, practical and productive work." Only through independent creative activity oriented to specific tasks could the artisan, the peasant, the artist or scholar achieve a true peak of human perfection (Kerschensteiner 1910b: 42).

The role of manual-practical activity in education is especially prominent in the 1908 proceedings of the German Work Federation (*Deutscher Werkbund*). It is stressed there that such manual activity is not only useful for handicrafts but also for industry (Muthesius 1908: 143 ff.).[2]

Georg Kerschensteiner was a member of the Federation, and he also emphatically stressed that industrial education was beneficial for the entire education of the people and nation (Kerschensteiner 1908: 137). In his view, what was being neglected in particular was education for "joy in creativity." But education for "joy in work" entailed that the schools pay special attention to the productive powers of the pupils, because that was how workers could be won over to handicrafts and industrial labour (ibid.: 140 f.).

In addition, Kerschensteiner advocated the value of artistic education – one that did not stress a merely superficial semblance of beauty but the "honesty of all productive work" (Kerschensteiner

2   The German Work Federation was an association of architects, designers and industrialists, founded by Hermann Muthesius in Munich in 1907, and was an important precursor of the Bauhaus movement. It attempted to integrate traditional crafts and industrial mass-production techniques under the motto "from sofa cushions to the building of cities".

1905: 508). Such a moral aim demanded a proper form, careful and exacting implementation and solid material (ibid.: 508).

This was the paramount contribution of the school and of education more generally: to elevate manual dexterity and – far more importantly – to contribute to the national work ethos. This was the answer of the pedagogues to the challenge of socialism.

Kerschensteiner's demands for school reform were not original, but he followed the tenor of contemporary discourse as developed and laid out above. He endorsed further schooling primarily oriented to social integration. The strong emphasis on activity in the manual arts and crafts was furthermore intended as a contribution by the school to the promotion of "joy in work". A national work ethos that overcame particularism should draw on the myth of the past, be well-grounded in classicism and be able to morally integrate into contemporary Wilhelmine society. Drawing on Carlyle and Ruskin, industrial work was thus to receive the revitalising breath of a new soul; Freyer termed such efforts "radicalism with gilt edging" (Freyer 1921: 157 f.).

4.5 Conclusions

Behind the project of 'work and education' stood another project, oriented in particular to social policy. This means that industrial development and the development of technology were not central here. Rather, what mattered most was the productive integration of the working classes in society. The social question was conceived as an institutional issue. Motivation for work and a sense of community were to be stabilised by education in the school. In this respect, the criticism of Litt and Blonskij, which associated pedagogical ideas with the state of technology, was inadequate. Rather, it was far more important to conjure up a new vision of community by means of an aestheticised and moralised ethical conception of work. If need be, that vision took on a certain tint and tenor from nationalist and folkish ideas and agendas.

These motives could be effectively bundled together in the education for "joy in work." The longing for change was transformed from a wide-ranging socio-political project to something geared to everyday industrial reality. This small-scale romantic utopia did not necessitate any social unrest and upheaval. Rather, it required a new culture, mediated by the dominant classes. The image of the artisan offered itself as the most realistically adaptable project. The farmer was too far removed from the large industrial plant, the entrepreneur was too controversial a figure. But the artisan brought in an element of the old social estate and its sense of honour and community; he was furthermore sanctioned by German classicism and provided a projection screen where economic, artistic and political visions could be combined.

The 'achievement' of pedagogy thus consisted in the translation of this general discourse into pedagogical categories, not just into institutional vessels such as the school for further education, but also into school ethos and instructional methodology. Having said that, pedagogy revealed itself to be less original, more a kind of appendix to discourses in artistic circles and among social reformers. This is also evident in Kerschensteiner's works, which should be understood in the context of discourse and discussion in the 19th century. His interface was not the pedagogy of the 19th century but its economic journalism, a *Publizistik* with a conservative to social-reform-oriented touch. Treitschke's idea of the state, Riehl's conception of estate-anchored morality, Schmoller's gentle enthusiasm for reform and Nostitz's international perspective provided him with the necessary tools to team up with Naumann, Muthesius and the German Werkbund in a broader intellectual sense after the turn of the century in a re-adapted project of reform for the German workers, grounded in an ideal of handicrafts.

The question of work as a question of education is a concern that the socialist and pedagogue Robert Seidel tried to articulate in lines of lyric poetry in his *Lichtglaube und Zukunftssonnen* ("Faith in Light and Suns of the Future"):

Ihr ahnt die Leiden nicht des Armen,
Dem die Natur hat Geist beschert

Und dem das Elend ohn' Erbarmen
Am Born der Bildung Raum verwehrt.
Er muss als Kind schon Fäden drehen
An der Maschine Tag für Tag
Und kann erst dann nach Weisheit gehen,
Wenn alles ruht von Last und Plag.
(Seidel, n.d.: 27)[3]

In another one of his poems, where the worker is depicted as a modern Prometheus, the ending is as follows:

Und strahlend Licht und heilig Feuer,
Die tragen wir ins ärmste Haus
Und treiben alle Ungeheuer
Der Not und Dummheit ewig aus.
(Seidel, n.d.: 30)[4]

In order to prevent such vehemence, Kerschensteiner's plea for civic education (1901), later entitled *Staatsbürgerliche Erziehung der Deutschen Jugend* ("Civic Education of German Youth"), ends with the admonition drawn verbatim from Nostitz: For the sake of the development of the internal life of the state, the upper classes would have to surrender their absolute dominance in favour of a guidance and leadership role toward the lower classes (Kerschensteiner 1987: 77 f.).

Artisan idylls led by the bourgeoisie were to engender a process of pacification of the working classes. It may therefore be regarded as ironical that today this initiative and approach are interpreted from an international perspective as a contribution to the modern work ethos of the Federal Republic of Germany and as the prerequisite for a flexible system of general and vocational education that can cope astonishingly well with technological change (cf. Campbell 1989 and Lasserre/Lattard 1994).

---

3   "You do not imagine the suffering of the poor / whom nature has given sprit / and to whom misery without pity / denies space and place for education / Already as a child he has to spins threads / at the machine day after day / and can only pursue wisdom / when everything rests from its burden and worry."

4   "And shining light and holy fire / we shall carry into the poorest house / and drive out all monsters / of distress and stupidity for ever and all time."

5. Georg Kerschensteiner's Concept of the 'Arbeitsschule' – A Plea for Work as a Foundation for Education

In his path-breaking publication Begriff der Arbeitsschule *("The Concept of the Activity School"),[5] Kerschensteiner sought to lay out his views on school reform and to ground them on theory. As a slogan, the 'Arbeitsschule' had an international impact far beyond the borders of Germany, making Kerschensteiner into* the *proponent of the concern to make work a fertile, innovative source for education in general. This book was to prove one of his most successful, and in the course of its later revised editions, the intellectual and thematic development of the author also becomes clear. This chapter discusses the concept of the 'Arbeitsschule' in the light of Kerschensteiner's thoughts on the state, character and education, and in dynamic confrontation with prevalent conceptions of the day.*

5.1 Organisation and structure of *Begriff der Arbeitsschule*

Kerschensteiner's book on the concept of the *Arbeitsschule* was published together with two others: a slim volume entitled *Der Begriff der staatsbürgerlichen Erziehung* ("The Concept of Civic Education") and a more extensive work, *Charakterbegriff und Charaktererziehung* ("The Concept and Education of Character"). For Kerschensteiner, the year 1911 marked a recapitulation and more precise theoretical formulation of his views deriving from a diverse array of various occasions

---

5 Kerschensteiner's *Arbeitsschule* is also referred to as 'work school' or 'industrial school', the latter being a common translation in English pedagogical discourse at the time (cf. Kerschensteiner 1913).

and contexts. He stated that one view had necessarily given rise to the other and that the product was a "unified whole" (Kerschensteiner 1929: X). As he wrote in the foreword to his book on character, there was nothing more crucial "in the struggle for reshaping public schooling" than conceptual clarity, and therefore "complete clarity about the correct means, ways and goals" would render "most school battles" superfluous (ibid.: V).

His attempt to infuse his efforts with more theoretical dignity and stringency also becomes clear from his work *Begriff der Arbeitsschule*. It is concerned with the clarification of what is meant by 'activity school', and in particular with the signification of 'activity'. Already in his first pedagogical publication, *Betrachtungen zur Theorie des Lehrplans* ("Observations on the Theory of Curriculum", 1899), he used the expression "intellectual work", which he later elaborated in his essay *Produktive Arbeit und ihr Erziehungswert* ("Productive Work and its Educational Value"). That essay was published together with his address *Die Schule der Zukunft eine Arbeitsschule* ("The School of the Future. An Activity School"), given on the occasion of a Pestalozzi celebration in Zurich in 1908. It appears in his *Grundfragen der Schulorganisation* ("Basic Issues in School Organisation"), a collection of speeches, essays and examples of organisation. It was precisely the address he gave in Zurich which induced him to elaborate further on the concept of the *Arbeitsschule*. Kerschensteiner had made this a central and powerful new focus. His work on the concept was designed to contribute to furthering the notion of the activity school and its concrete development.

The publication of *Begriff der Arbeitsschule* remained quite stable in structure and organisation of argument even after several revisions. After introductory remarks, he develops the conception of the *Arbeitsschule* over some 100 pages, which are then supplemented by an annex nearly as long. The 6th edition (1925) contained a separate essay originally published in 1923, which accounts for the fact that later editions had seven chapters rather than six. In what follows, a brief overview of the sections of this work will be presented.

Kerschensteiner introduced his various editions by corresponding brief introductory remarks. They inform the reader about the changes that the concept of the activity school has undergone. Thus, the 1st edition (1911) refers to the circumstances of his formulation of the *Arbeitsschule* as a school of the future, which later became a slogan of reform education, while the 6th edition announces that there will be an additional chapter. The 7th edition (1928) points to improvements in presentation and a more economical line of reasoning.

It was the festive address on the occasion of the commemoration of the 162nd anniversary of Heinrich Pestalozzi's birth in Zurich in 1908 which made the concept of *Arbeitsschule* popular. Referring to Pestalozzi, he argued that the spirit of the *Arbeitsschule* had to infuse both elementary and secondary education. The preface to the first edition also refers to the controversies in which Kerschensteiner was involved. On the one hand, there was the move away from the traditional school, a topic over which he debated with the followers of Herbartian pedagogy. One the other hand, the book focuses on the 'correct' understanding of the *Arbeitsschule*, thus referring to a debate that arose in the context of a conference of the League for School Reform held in Dresden the same year of this publication. Finally, Kerschensteiner points out that the activity school stands in a tradition extending from Plato to Pestalozzi. This not only points up the eminent legacy of the concept but is also a barb directed against others who accused him of simple-mindedness, of "stealing ideas" and the like. He responded to remarks by the educator and politician Robert Seidel – without mentioning his name – who claimed that the idea of the *Arbeitsschule* was primarily his own innovation, by stressing that what was important was to reinvigorate and adapt an idea that was indeed as old as pedagogy itself.

Without basic changes to the original orientation, the preface of the 1st edition was supplemented by the author with an expanded preface in the 4th and 5th edition. This pointed to revisions and to the changing times. In the 6th edition in 1925, Kerschensteiner noted that "errors and a lack of clarity" which he had "noticed in the experimental implementation of the activity school in various German towns" had prompted him to a further "clarification" of the concept of work, which is why another chapter had been added. As a main reason for this effort he argued that there was a danger that in misunderstanding the concept, the idea of the *Arbeitsschule* itself could be discredited. He was apparently little satisfied with various practical realisations of the activity school when he remarked in the same preface that he would much prefer a "steel-hard and rigid old book-school" to a "wax-soft modern activity school." After all, he stressed, *Arbeitsschule* did not mean to "let things grow as they may". It meant subjecting "the will unconditionally to the law of the thing", as he formulated his program in a memorable pithy phrase. Kerschensteiner was extremely sceptical of 'expressionistic' or solely aesthetic variants of work in school. He preferred an understanding of work more in tune with modern science at the time, which correlated human power with its effect (Auerbach 1910: 120 ff.).

The reader can also sense a clear feeling of resignation in this preface when the author comments on the gap between the success of the book on the one hand, and the lack of success of concrete examples on the other. Thanks to the publication, translated in the meantime into 11 European and three Asian languages, he received constant requests to describe schools of this type in his city of Munich, but he notes that he had to refuse because there were no more any such schools. While there were welcome 'realisations' outside Germany, Kerschensteiner lamented that in Bavaria, the idea of the *Arbeitsschule* was "a kind of walking spectre". Already in his preface he points to a discrepancy that is painful for him: Though the *idea* of the activity school had found a certain acceptance, there were setbacks when it came to its realisation. He was unhappy both about the failure to implement the idea of the *Arbeitsschule* and about the actual concrete examples that had been created. Consequently, his book is directed both to opponents of the activity school as well as to supposed proponents of the idea.

"The Purpose of the State and the Tasks of Public Schooling"

In the first chapter, Kerschensteiner sketches the social aims of schools in their historical development. From this he then derives three primary tasks for public schooling. In his view, the foundation for the activity school derives from an aim of the state which he sees not as directly political but rather ethical. He refers here not to a concrete state but to an ideal state embodying in its goals and institutions the idea of a moral order. He proceeds on the assumption that in the course of history, many polities do indeed "move along the path to a state based on the rule of law and a state grounded on culture" (Kerschensteiner 1922: 3). The life of the individual is also integrated into this general development. For that reason, a state based on the rule of reason (*Vernunftstaat*) and the moral personality were correlated concepts and an ideal worth striving for.

"Vocational Education as a Primary Task"

Chapters two and three in the earlier editions then turn to elaborating on the three tasks of public education in detail. Derived from the purpose of the state, the first task of the school for Kerschensteiner is to guarantee or lay the groundwork for the vocational education of the individual. Referring to Pestalozzi, he stresses the importance of manual work for each individual in the process of education and the significant role of physical work by a majority of human beings in society. For this reason, he emphasises the importance of the activity school as a type of school which best prepares boys and girls for their later life in the world of work. The goal is not – as in the long-demanded handiwork instruction – to train pupils in skills and knowledge as a preparation for a future vocation. Rather, it centres on educating pupils to awaken and develop a 'joy in work' (cf. Chapter 4).

"The Pedagogical Concept of Work"

Kerschensteiner added this chapter in the 6th (1925) and later editions. In the 7th edition (1928) he also included additional comments in connection with his dispute with Aloys Fischer and his "psychology of work" (cf. Adrian 1998: 147). Kerschensteiner must have attributed special importance to this new chapter, since he was debating issues not only with his old opponents but now also with his colleagues from the universities: He placed this new chapter, previously published as a separate essay, right in the middle of his original line of argument. His dispute with Hugo Gaudig, which had already surfaces elsewhere in the 1st edition, was taken up again here. Kerschensteiner rejected expressionistic approaches as well as those he deemed too one-sided in stressing the personality or classroom instruction. Building on the neo-Kantian theory of values developed by Heinrich Rickert, he underscored objectivity and perfection as the central components in a pedagogical concept of work. To that extent, this chapter contains some of the reorientation in the theory of education springing from Kerschensteiner's late work.

"The Second and Third Tasks of the Public School"

Yet vocational education as the first task of public schooling, closely linked with civic education, is but one function of the school. In addition, vocational education itself needs to be imbued with morality. Only then there can be a moral transformation of society, both at the personal level and on a larger scale. Kerschensteiner refers here to the "community of work", the *Arbeitsgemeinschaft*. In instruction, this is related not just to the pupils but to the teachers as well. All should be "deeply imbued" with the spirit of the community of work, ready to sacrifice where needed (Kerschensteiner 1922: 50). From the spirit of the work community, the state and society undergo a process of becoming more moral. This notion elaborated by Kerschensteiner is reflected in Pestalozzi and is in agreement with John Dewey and Paul Natorp, the influential author of a conception of social pedagogy, and in critical confrontation with Hermann Lietz and Friedrich Wilhelm

Foerster, all contemporary proponents of educational reform. The pupils have an active hand in this development by "exercising their vocational activity as part of their lives" (ibid.: 51). At the micro scale, i.e. in the schools and particularly in the workshops, labs, school kitchens and school gardens, the seed must be planted for what will later benefit society as a whole. This orientation, Kerschensteiner argues, is precisely in keeping with the nature of the child, and this is why, in line with Dewey, a Copernican revolution is in the offing: Now the child shall become the sun around which the school revolves (Kerschensteiner 1910d: 37 f.).

The three tasks of public schooling, which flow into the demand for manual and intellectual work in the school and the creation of communities of work as a contribution to vocational education, lead to the demand for civic education for future citizens of the state.

"The Methods of the Arbeitsschule"

In contrast to prevailing views today, Kerschensteiner regarded 'methods' less as a set of recipes for school instruction and more as a conceptual frame that could best be understood as guidelines for 'working out', 'inducing' ideas and conceptions (*erarbeiten*).

This chapter too was changed from the 3rd edition on, incorporating new views from another of his publications, *Das Grundaxiom des Bildungsprozesses* ("The Fundamental Axiom of the Process of Education"), first published in 1917. The procedure of education described there is integrated into the chapter on methods, and the new formulations of the "fundamental axiom" are then included in the various subsequent editions (cf. Adrian 1998: 147).

From the tasks sketched above, Kerschensteiner posits an outline of the internal organisation of the German elementary school (*Volksschule*). The school should orient its influence to the ethical direction of the education of character in line with the three goals as described earlier. In order to enhance strength of will, clarity of judgment, sensitivity and the ability to be aroused and activated as valuable features of personal character – and he refers here to his book on the concept of character in which these elements are treated in greater detail – it is crucial that there be a freedom of activity and a multiplicity of relations. Ideas and conceptions should be worked out "as far as possible by means and on the basis of experience" (Kerschensteiner 1922: 55 f.).

By means of its "methods and the entire manner of its operation", the activity school is suited to triggering the educational values imminent in the respective assets ('goods') of culture and education. If earlier editions spoke of the objective spirit and subjective structures of the intellect, explicitly referring to Dilthey, Kerschensteiner later stresses the "experience of value" in connection with the sense of "working out an asset of education", its acquisition by hands-on activity. This "experience of value" takes place when a person enters into the spirit of an "asset of culture" (ibid.: 60 f.). Thus working out is more than rendering vivid through visual aids, and more than simple manual activity, though the latter is a central element of the *Arbeitsschule*. In elaborating certain elements of culture, manual activity must be put at the service of the formation of the will and the sharpening of judgment. Only then is a "new element of education" added to manual activity in the sense of the activity school.

"The Discipline of Work Instruction and the Technical Teacher"

In accordance with these notions, special demands were made of the teachers at activity schools. These went far beyond what was normally required in teacher training at that time. Kerschensteiner thus believed that along with the teachers being well-trained in theory and science, if manual work instruction was to be established as a discipline and not just a method, a second kind of instructor was needed: a technical teacher. The working out and acquisition of educational assets by means of purely intellectual work was only possible for a minority. Consequently, the moral education of the masses necessitated another category of instructor, namely a well-trained technical teacher.

"Summary and Final Observations"

In his summary and final observations, Kerschensteiner stresses once again the education of character in particular. In contrast to the traditional school, the activity school aims for a minimum of material; at the same time, however, it creates a maximum of skills, abilities and pleasure in work. He also stresses that the *Arbeitsschule* is not a break with the past, asking the impossible, but rather contributes to the further development of what is of value.

"Appendix"

In the extensive appendix, an example of organisation for a municipal class in the elementary school is sketched. Kerschensteiner presents experimental classes in Munich, looking at the way they arrange their periods of instruction, the elaboration of content, and the amount of resources available and their expenses. Naturally, what is striking here is visual instruction, female handicrafts and woodworking. The experiment lasted only four years and was marked by many unfavourable conditions. Class instruction was not allowed to deviate from the syllabus and was restricted by circumstances emanating from the war. In the beginning, boys and girls were given the same amount of work instruction, including work in the garden and domestic activities (ibid.: 83 ff.). In teaching composition, the experimental schools also integrated ideas from the pedagogy of Maria Montessori. On the whole, Kerschensteiner would have wanted his experimental schools in Munich to expand woodshop instruction and gardening in the more advanced experimental classes in order to promote autonomous activity and self-education among the pupils, proceeding on the basis of the primarily practical interests of the children (ibid.: 112 f.). Despite the limited experience, he assumes in closing that the activity school has a bright future and that better teacher training will be beneficial for such a development.

5.2 The state, vocation and work

The close linkage between civic education, activity school and vocation had already been spelled out in ideas published earlier on by Kerschensteiner. What was the source for his certainty that an existing state would develop in the direction of an ideal state if work was accorded a special significance in the elementary school? The idea of the *Arbeitsschule* as a contribution to making vocational education and society as a whole more moral was already developed in part in his first publication, generally known under the title *Die staatsbürgerliche Erziehung der deutschen Jugend* ("The Civic Education of German Youth"). In this treatise written in 1901, the key role of work and vocation is foregrounded with respect to the transformation of schools for further education. Kerschensteiner gained sudden fame with this plea for school reform precisely at the moment when his plans for reform had run up against vehement opposition from the teachers. It was at that time that he was awarded the coveted prize of the Royal Academic of Useful Sciences in Erfurt. On April 25, 1900 the following competition was announced: "How can our male youth, from the end of the *Volksschule* until their recruitment in the armed services, be most properly educated for civil society?" The prize money was 600 marks. In addition, the topic was explained in greater detail:

> The task is to present the aims of a more general moral and intellectual education of our male youth as contrasted with a specific vocational education. A description should be provided of the means that are deemed appropriate to protect these young men from the danger of being left helplessly to fend for themselves or falling prey to the revolutionary parties. (Wehle 1966b: 203 f.)

Until April 30, 75 submissions were received, and in June the commission in charge awarded Kerschensteiner with the prize. His answer was published in the Academy's yearbook for 1901; at the same time, Kerschensteiner published the essay as *Staatsbürgerliche Erziehung der deutschen Jugend*. It was reprinted 10 times during the next 30 years; the 4th printing in 1909 was a revised edition, with a new foreword and other changes. This 'prize essay', as it had later come to be referred to, made Kerschensteiner famous, since it is considered as the foundation for the later so-called 'vocational school' (*Berufsschule*) and its elaboration as a school type. In the literature on education, the 'prize essay', which basically called for a new, vocation-oriented curriculum in the schools for further education, is also known as the "foundation document" of the vocational school in Germany (cf. Müllges 1991b: 149–175).

From the original question it is evident that the problem at hand is one of social policy: How can young males be kept off the street and functionally integrated into civil society, instead of becoming dangerous to the state or criminals? This topic was a matter of intense public concern in that period, or more precisely to the elites in the Empire, given the steady growth in the labour movement and the political influence of Social Democracy. Political economy, politics and sociology, which established itself as an independent discipline, were kindled by the consequences of industrialisation, urbanisation and cultural upheaval within the matrix of a rapidly changing society. How could such a dynamic be channelled onto ordered paths? How could revolutions and social discontent be prevented? How could the working class be subdued and 'tamed'? Kerschensteiner's answer was simple: They should go to school! The key idea was to make the schools for further learning, as they were called at the time, accessible to the greater masses. These institutions had often arisen out of local initiatives that were open to a small number of youth after they finished their obligatory schooling. Along with this idea of pacification, Kerschensteiner was also optimistic that what had been learned in the elementary school could be repeated and deepened, so that more know-how would be available for later service in the armed forces. In this way, everyone had something to gain by schooling: the elites in the Wilhelmian Empire, the army, and the young men themselves – if only schooling could become something not just popular among young people, their parents and the broader society, but a source of genuine further qualification for the young, a basis for a livelihood. It was therefore necessary to revalue and revitalise the schools for further education and to modernise their curricula. The municipal schools for further education needed to be organised along revamped lines: First, an elementary department with three years of required schooling of eight to nine hours a week. This was to be followed by a more advanced department offering evening courses with voluntary attendance by all those who had completed the obligatory department. In other words, Kerschensteiner called for three years of additional obligatory education for all young people, since he also expanded his demands to school attendance by girls. Thus, this *Fortbildungsschule* (school for further education), later to be called vocational school (*Berufsschule*), is his response to the prize question from the Erfurt Academy. As he notes in the 'prize essay':

> The core and central point of the first civic education program is a purposeful (re)designing of the industrial (for example agricultural) school for further education, expanded in accordance with the various larger or smaller vocational groups. As insignificant as this force may appear to be, [...] it is governed by the law of the summation of an infinite number of smaller equal forces which are active, generation after generation. It is the means that affects all, without exception. (Kerschensteiner 1966: 43)

What kind of a curriculum did he recommend? It is not hard to discern here the abiding pattern that still stamps the vocational schools in Germany today:

- Practical-industrial instruction for the specific vocational group: drawing, modelling, commodity economics, tool-making, and if possible instruction in workshops conducted by qualified personnel.
- Theoretical-industrial instruction: This is the task of vocational school teachers. The curriculum includes business writing, arithmetic, book-keeping and reading of highly esteemed works of German literature along with a good library for students.
- Civic Education: Kerschensteiner includes civics, knowledge of life studies (*Lebenskunde*), and health studies. It also includes weekly gymnastics lessons, Sunday hikes, preferably in conjunction with local gymnastic clubs, along with voluntary "social evenings, imbued with the spirit of patriotism and moral earnestness" (Kerschensteiner 1966: 44).

74

The rest of this essay deals with a justification as to why civic education was necessary, particularly for the workers and young people who did not aspire to a higher career. Education had to be made accessible to as many as possible, as he makes clear in disagreement with conservative representatives, such as the influential national-conservative historian Treitschke, who regarded educated workers as a clear and present danger (cf. Chapter 4: 42 ff.). Yet Kerschensteiner's answer is a form of education clearly different from that offered at the *Gymnasium*. In his model, education for vocational competence as a contribution to civic education is paramount (Kerschensteiner 1912a: 17). It was important to lay the foundations for elementary civil virtues. He argued that "the value of our school education as enjoyed by the great masses is basically grounded less on the education of the circle of ideas" – this is a clear criticism of the followers of Herbart, who were openly opposed to Kerschensteiner – "than in consistent education to diligent, conscientious, thorough and precise work in constant habituation to unconditional obedience and faithful execution of one's obligation, and in the authoritative constant guidance to the willing performance of services" (Kerschensteiner 1912a: 34).

This statement shows that Kerschensteiner's 'idealistic rationale' penetrated to the very ground of social and political relations. Family, occupation and military discipline, along with school, are foci of authority where what is important for education is not one's own will but rather rules, law and instructions handed down by others. Only on such a foundation can autonomy develop, because work and adaptation (habituation) create the preconditions for the need to be good and moral to arise in the human soul. Habituation in action is necessary by means of "conscientious but joyous work". Kerschensteiner agrees with Carlyle, whom he quotes:

> Older than all preached Gospels was this unpreached, inarticulate, but ineradicable, forever-enduring Gospel: Work, and therein have well-being. […] All true work is sacred; in all true Work, were it but true hand-labour, there is something of divineness. (Carlyle 1843: 35)

The importance of the value of true work is for most *Volksschule* leavers not only the principal instrument for the education of the will, but the only secure point of reference and anchorage for the further development of knowledge as well as the anchorage for the character traits which in turn depend on insight and knowledge. As Kerschensteiner sees it, vocational work is the most appropriate means for civic education, both directly as the foundation for the education of many talents, and indirectly because it has the power to engage the mind of the pupil and lead to the development of a general interest and curiosity. Education should not begin with the general. Rather, its door is opened through the solid vestibule of the vocational (Carlyle 1843: 37). There is a need for insight into the value of good work. That is why competence in work, which grows from a joy in work, is of such great importance.

The comments in the 'prize essay' up to this point relate not only to the municipal schools for further education which he consistently developed in later years and can be learned from the annual reports of the Munich municipality. Rural schools for further education, workshops for apprentices and industrial technical schools were also to be restructured in line with the aims of civic education.

Kerschensteiner played a major role in the reform of local instruction in vocational schools. He gained inspiration and new ideas from numerous trips neighbouring countries, as reported in his work *Beobachtungen und Vergleiche über Einrichtungen für gewerbliche Erziehung ausserhalb Bayern* ("Observations and Comparisons Regarding Facilities for Industrial Education Outside Bavaria"), which was published the same year as the 'prize essay'.

Using the same rationale, workshops were also introduced in the elementary schools. He also appreciated rural boarding schools for children and youth (*Landerziehungsheime, Landschulheime*) and associations such as youth clubs, athletic associations, vocational associations – and in particular associations for popular education and libraries. In his view, they assisted in promoting and bolstering civic education. During this period, Kerschensteiner stressed education for 'joy in work' at many conferences and in various publications. He emphasised that such a basic ethical attitude was also manifested aesthetically in the product of work. In his view, the joy in work and creation generated in the process also benefited the state and society as a whole (cf. Chapter 4).

In the 'prize essay', we have come to know an educator who oriented the school system clearly towards social-political needs. It was the 'social question' so important at the time which induced him and others to come up with educational solutions for its pressing concerns. Social injustice, great social differences in income and living standards were to be 'ironed out' by corresponding social policies which Bismarck had pioneered in other spheres (such as state medical insurance), using the school as an instrument for amelioration and betterment. Here Kerschensteiner proceeds from an idealistic conception: the state as a *Kulturstaat*, a state of culture in which each individual finds his or her place by means of a relation to work and vocation, and is properly trained for this function. His conception bears some resemblance to Plato, to whose ideas he refers in this connection (Kerschensteiner 1912a: 27). But there is no transcendental, religious rationale that underpins and determines the need of the individual for education in this view. Rather, it is a question of living together in society, which is conceived as something civic, and not a political question.

Here Kerschensteiner does not engage in an exact empirical analysis of society, but rather attempts to argue in terms of an ideal conception. This point of departure made it easy for him to hold up the idea of civic education in various pedagogical contexts, inscribing it on his agenda banner through all the political confusion and turmoil of his era. Some of his views even found favour among Social Democrats. A dimension in the 'prize essay' worth emphasising is the notion of *social pacification through education*. Here Kerschensteiner relied primarily on the example of Great Britain. He based his comments on Heinrich von Nostitz, a Prussian civil servant who wrote a detailed study *Das Aufsteigen des Arbeiterstandes in England* ("The Rise of the Working Class in England", 1900). In this study, Nostitz asked why the prognosis of Marx und Engels had not come to pass in England, namely that a revolution of the working class would come upon the heels of immiseration, mass poverty and 'Manchester liberalism'. Nostitz concluded that it was the inclusion of the socialist forces and the workers in the system of education which helped solve the 'social question' in Britain. The elites there did not hinder the urge of the working class to improve its lot, but rather promoted this desire.

Kerschensteiner therefore concludes his comments on Germany with a question that quotes Nostitz: "Will the propertied classes remain the leaders after they have ceased to be the masters?" (Kerschensteiner 1966: 88).

We can readily identify the orientation of education to grand overarching aims in the concept of civic education. These are aims clearly rooted in a social context, not just a religious one. To that extent, a system of education is always bound up with and integrated into political contexts. Or, to phrase it differently: By the very process of education, one necessarily engages in social policy as well. Through civic education, the younger generations are equipped for social life by their relation to work and vocation. Society reproduces itself through such education. As he wrote in his treatise on the concept of civic education, in the ideal of the state of culture, the *Kulturstaat*, all citizens without exception would have to be active in accordance with their measure of talent (Kerschensteiner 1912a: 32). Today too we are confronted with demands pertaining to schools, calling on education to remedy social-political deficits in society, for example, to promote peace by peace education or health by health education.

Kerschensteiner's conception also aimed at remedying deficits. The school was to make a comprehensive and even the central contribution to the social integration of the working class. For this aim, the right type of school was required, namely an industrial school for further education, later called a vocational school, the right kind of curriculum, namely a mixture of general and vocational education, the right goal, namely vocational competence as a central contribution to civic education, and, as will be shown below, the right mode of psychology, namely one that took children and teens seriously in the context of their everyday life. From the matrix of 'work inspired by a joy in creation' sprang the social virtues, such as voluntary submission to self-elected leaders and a positive alacrity in the performance of dutiful service, which would then bear fruit in society (Kerschensteiner 1912a: 42).

Kerschensteiner oriented the activity school to such a transformed school for further education. In his view it was precisely the *Arbeitsschule* which was to assist children and teenagers to find their place in society. As these comments show, work is placed in an ethical and political context. The 'state grounded on reason' as the highest good derives from the moral forms of social communities, such as the family, community of profession and religious community. As he notes in conclusion in his treatise on civic education, it is the community work in the classroom that works against political passion and partisanship. Democratic constitutions can favour mob rule if the majority of citizens do not have an aristocratic frame of mind and sentiment (Kerschensteiner 1912a: 62). Kerschensteiner believed that civic education could serve as an instrument to foster and spread this aristocratic-ethical attitude in the broader population.

5.3 The *Arbeitsschule* as school reform: from Herbart to Pestalozzi and Dewey

At the beginning of the new century, it was particularly with the transformation of the existing model of the schools for further education that Kerschensteiner had made a public impact. Subsequently, questions of school organisation came ever more frequently to the fore, especially questions regarding the elementary school system. The most prominent contribution by Kerschensteiner in this regard was the address given in Zurich on the topic *Die Schule der Zukunft im Geiste Pestalozzis* ("The School of the Future in the Spirit of Pestalozzi"), which was published as *Die Schule der Zukunft eine Arbeitsschule* ("The School of the Future: An Activity School") (Kerschensteiner 1910d: 26–45).

Kerschensteiner stood firmly in the tradition and legacy of Pestalozzi when he stressed *Anschauung* (clarity, vivid illustration, visual experience) and self-activity of the pupil as the key principles for instruction in the school. In doing so, he criticised the followers of Ziller, who based their thinking in part both on Herbart and Pestalozzi, but promoted only attitudes of pupil passivity in the classroom. In his view, they were advocates of the 'book school'. What was needed was rather an 'activity school'. The productive forces of the pupils should not be allowed to atrophy. On the contrary, they needed to be actively developed.

Like the reformed schools in the United States, the schools in Germany should also be changed in such a way that they were not only geared to a school population of passive listeners. Not mere listening and passive absorption of alien knowledge were necessary, because the years of childhood and puberty were marked by living activity. Kerschensteiner stresses: "The essence of the human being in this period is work, creating, taking action, trying things out, experiencing, so as to learn ceaselessly in the medium of reality" (Kerschensteiner 1910d: 27 f.). The school should not let these active germs of creativity and traits of character wither, but should promote the courage to be independent, the desire to observe, examine and work. For that reason, the school of learning must become a school of work which follows directly and is linked to the school of play of the earliest years of childhood.

Kerschensteiner regarded the *Arbeitsschule*, which he expressly did not claim to have coined as a term, as a contribution to the reform of both the elementary and secondary schools. He pointed to the idea of morality (virtues) which arose from the purpose of the state. For Kerschensteiner, the state had a twofold aim, an egoistic one, oriented to care, social welfare and protection, and an altruistic one, which sought to achieve the gradual realisation of the kingdom of humanity through the development towards a moral polity. For that reason, the heart of reform consisted in the education of the useful active citizen. This gave rise to the following demands addressed to the activity school: Each person should be rendered capable of and prepared to fulfil a function in the state, i.e. to be active in a given vocation. The second task was to view this vocation as an office, not only for earning a living, but also for the moral self-assertion of the individual, while also providing a basis for services to society. The inclination needed to be awakened in the pupil to do his or her part to contribute to the development of the ideal of a moral community and polity, as Kerschensteiner had already written in the first chapter of his treatise on the concept of the *Arbeitsschule* (Kerschensteiner 1922: 16 ff.).

Kerschensteiner attributes to Pestalozzi the ideals of self-activity and *Anschauung*, connecting them with the idea of the ideal state. Pestalozzi and Plato are his classic reference points in this regard. If the productive power of the child is preserved and the school promotes this – instead of putting a brake on the child with book knowledge and paralysing its activity – then this also has consequences for society as a whole.

Reform pedagogy is necessary precisely in order to effect social renewal and moral reinvigoration. Over against the representatives of a Herbartian pedagogy along the lines of Ziller, who at the time claimed to represent scientific pedagogy, Kerschensteiner expressed a distance to these currents right from the start, based on his own experiences at school. In this connection, he referred to Pestalozzi's famous book *Wie Gertrud ihre Kinder lehrt* ("Leonard and Gertrude") and to John Dewey's *School and Society, The Child and the Curriculum* and *How we think*.

Curricula should, in contrast to the principles of the followers of Herbart, not be organised in so-called concentric circles, nor should they be structured in terms of cultural levels. Instead, Kerschensteiner argued, the pupils had to feel and recognise the intellectual bond that held together an area of instruction. Here Pestalozzi and Dewey proved useful, but not Herbart. In addition, Kerschensteiner referred to Ernst Mach and Richard Avenarius, two philosophers and theorists with inclinations toward Kantian positivism, who both espoused the principle of the economy of thought. Thus both his curriculum on visual aids and later his entire pedagogical work ran up against vehement opposition from adherents of Herbart and Ziller. This was not surprising: they contended that Kerschensteiner's curriculum and notion of school reform were devoid of thought and inane, and were evidence of the much regrettable demise of intellectual life in Bavaria (Kerschensteiner 1982a: 128). Zillig launched an especially strong attack against Kerschensteiner. Writing in the *Jahrbuch des Vereins für wissenschaftliche Pädagogik*, Zillig characterised the key orientation to work, occupation and citizenship, based on the principles of altruism and the natural sciences, as a dilettante construction, posing a major threat for the education of children (Zillig 1907: 2 ff.).

What did Kerschensteiner have to offer that was so different and awakened so much controversy? In brief, it was a reduction in systematic professional presentation of the object of instruction and a more powerful inclusion of the everyday interests of children in their own reality, i.e. a more student-cantered classroom. Kerschensteiner saw a danger in overburdening pupils in the elementary school with knowledge. Instead, it was important to further their desire and ability (Kerschensteiner 1899: 16). On the other hand, he also called for further development of natural science subjects in the elementary school, precisely because the adherents of Herbart were so keen to emphasise the need to awaken and heighten interests among the learners. Kerschensteiner grounded his arguments on psychology, though a different psychology from that of the Herbart school, for example when he mentioned Hans Cornelius' neo-Kantian *Psychologie als Erfahrungswissenschaft* ("Psychology as a Science of Experience", 1897).

Kerschensteiner was critical of existing conceptions of mediation and their methods, such as Kehr's concentric circles. He considered these as nothing more than a relatively unimaginative collection and expansion of a huge mass of individual bits of knowledge without any evident internal bond. Instead of awakening interest the effect was to stifle it. Concentration and ways of thinking had nothing to do with natural-scientific thought or the organic idea of progress (Kerschensteiner 1899: 99). Concentration, he argued, was not based solely on purely external arrangement but rather on a clear set of goals in content. In his critique of the traditional syllabus and curriculum, and in conjunction with his efforts for reform, Kerschensteiner referred to Paul Natorp as a source of inspiration. In his *Gesammelte Abhandlungen zur Sozialpädagogik*, Natorp had clearly rejected Herbartian pedagogy, instead holding up Kant and Pestalozzi as an alternative for the immediate tasks in educational theory (Natorp 1922).

In his autobiography, Kerschensteiner describes how he broke free from the dominant views of Herbart, stating that in preparing for teaching mathematics, he worked along psychological-methodological lines and not logical-methodological ones:

> The central point of all method, its logical aspect, was laid down for me as a preordained path by the material, and my never extinguishing love for the pupils

took care of the psychological aspect of method. [...] I have today no doubt that my later idea of the activity school as it developed, and the much later evolvement of the concept of work, sprouted from the soil of this instruction in mathematics. (Kerschensteiner 1982a: 119)

Thus, Kerschensteiner's conception of the activity school was nurtured by several sources. Along with a perspective oriented to social policy, there was also his background in the natural sciences and mathematics as a teacher, which was connected with a 'new' way of looking at children and teenagers.

5.4 Personality, character and work

Kerschensteiner distinguished already in the 'prize essay' between political and civic education. Later on, too, he sought to make plausible a concept of the state beyond partisan politics, coupled with a conception of education oriented to humanity, and drawing on Kant, Plato and Dewey (Kerschensteiner 1912a: 7). He argued that civic education was more than political education and social training, but it was the highest pedagogical ideal. The schools had to be geared to this ideal, in their content, their structure and in the idea of the community of work (*Arbeitsgemeinschaft*). In his *Charakterbegriff und Charaktererziehung*, the foundations of these overarching goals are explored. His concept of character can be linked with traditional notions, while the aims involved are transposed to the psychological level: It was a central concept in Herbart and among contemporary psychologists, and was also common in everyday discourse. Character was defined, in agreement with Herbart, as the "constant and definite way in which an individual approaches the external world", which was also the basic view of Pestalozzi (Kerschensteiner 1929: 168). But Herbart reduced character to the generation of many-sided interest(s) through instruction. In doing so, he overlooked or failed to take into proper account the inner drives of the individual. Only later did he see a closer bond between interest and self-activity.

In dealing with contemporary psychology and psychoanalysis (A. Adler and C. G. Jung), Kerschensteiner discussed various types of individuality, and then asked how something could develop within the envelope of an individuality that might, in an ethical and value-oriented sense, be called character. He came to speak of four elements: strength of will, clarity of judgment, sensitivity and the ability to be aroused and activated. He described the education of character in the family, in school, in 'self-education' and in trade unions. Education in the family is meant to serve the inculcation of respect. School – here building on Dewey – should create a society on a small scale, a community of living, and a community of work, an *Arbeitsgemeinschaft*. Kerschensteiner did not hesitate to question the traditional understanding of education when he notes that the path to the 'ideal individual' only is attained via the path to the 'useful individual'. But the useful person is one who knows his work and that of his people and who possesses "the will and the strength" to do that work (Kerschensteiner 1910b: 29 ff.). Work, vocation and the state are central elements for the education of character. In his conception, human education is based, in a kind of reversal of the previously rarely questioned concept of education, on a form of education directly and consciously oriented to work and vocation: "The first task on the road to education is for the individual to recognise his work, and to exercise and enhance insight, will and strength in and through that work. Vocational education stands at the gateway to education as a human being" (Kerschensteiner 1904: 94).

In debate with his opponents and with the many admirers of his school reforms in Munich, who were basically attracted by his introduction of workshops, Kerschensteiner formulated the notion of the 'activity school' as a comprehensive principle of schooling more generally. In contrast with the customary understanding of education, he prioritised limitation over against many-sidedness and diversity. In his view, it is service for a cause, grounded on honesty and thoroughness, which also stirs and nourishes the powers of self-education, thus furthering the education of character (Kerschensteiner 1929: 278 ff.).

But Kerschensteiner's views not only conflicted with the Herbartian conception of pedagogy, with its tradition of the syllabus, its independent psychology and contrasting pedagogical aims, which were also manifested in a different idea of what the education of character meant. Even some proponents of the activity school were opposed to orienting this school type toward the aims of civic education. At the conference of the League for School Reform in 1911, Kerschensteiner confronted Hugo Gaudig, likewise a prominent figure in school reform. Gaudig considered the reforming value inherent in Kerschensteiner's conception of the *Arbeitsschule* to be quite minimal. Instead of civic education, he called for the education of personality. In his view, informed citizenship could only be one goal among others, and it was improper to expand or generalise this dimension (Gaudig 1982: 157–160). Kerschensteiner replied that Gaudig's views on the nature of the activity school were quite compatible with his own, though Gaudig himself disputed this "with all the considerable rhetorical means at his disposal" (Kerschensteiner 1982a: 135). Kerschensteiner, as Gaudig saw it, was too exclusively oriented toward vocational life as a point of departure, and failed to give all spheres of life their proper due. In Gaudig's view, to prioritise manual work with a majority of manual vocations in society was somewhat senseless, since it was unfortunately a fact that with the given progressive mechanisation, manual activities required less and less thorough training: "Just ask our industrial workers what they demand of school. Certainly not manual education but schooling of the intellect, with which they can acquire the power and enjoyment of education" (Gaudig 1982: 158). Even with respect to advancing the principle of visual aids in the classroom, Gaudig only assigned manual work a limited function, since the knowledge gained here was meagre and much that was involved exceeded the pupil's capacity to describe it.

After all these objections, one might conclude that Gaudig was against the activity school. But that was not the case; he merely specified his own conception of the *Arbeitsschule*. Education encompassed all of the human being, including the physical dimension. Every individual could realise and represent the intentions of the intellect creatively in and by activity. Motor abilities also suggested that the school should include manual activities. Technical work as knowledge through visual comprehension (*anschauendes Erkennen*) also assisted pupils to learn how to think in images. But school did not become an activity school just by placing more emphasis on manual elements.

This was a necessary step, but not sufficient per se. In order to really create an activity school, the self-activated work of the pupils had to become the activity determining the character of the school.

On the one hand, Gaudig thus questioned Kerschensteiner's political and vocation-oriented premises, while he was more consistent in his methodological approach to the concept of work. In Gaudig's view, the essence of the activity school is the self-active pupil; a community of work only arises on the basis of such pupils. Work is a formal principle, but as such it also determines content (Gaudig 1982: 159) and the structure of the syllabus, i.e. the plans for working with pupils and material. For Gaudig, the *Arbeitsschule* is based on acting subjects. In the matrix of independent action, influences are generated which have an impact on the pupil as an evolving person. In sum, through self-active work the individual develops his or her 'personality'. In contrast, Gaudig argued that Kerschensteiner made the state into an ethical entity, subordinating education to this state. Gaudig claimed that the education of the personality was his paramount concern, and he subsumed the purpose of the state under this more encompassing canopy of the broader purpose of human existence. In addition, Gaudig claimed that Kerschensteiner mistakenly mixed the material principle with the formal principle of work (Gaudig 1982: 162).

These and later criticisms much troubled Kerschensteiner. With the notion of the activity school as a formal principle and its disengagement from a comprehensive social agenda, whether social-political or idealistic, work became attractive as a didactic-methodological principle. Gaudig and later Otto Scheibner linked the education of character with self-activity of the pupils at school, and clearly distinguished this primary principle of activity from too pronounced an emphasis on manual and vocational aspects. In their conceptions, work was far more clearly just a formal principle which required didactic implementation in the classroom (cf. Scheibner 1928).

This was the orientation of the activity school pursued by a number of school reformers. Kerschensteiner's friend Aloys Fischer, who was a professor of education in Munich, also turned against a manual-economic-social vision of the *Arbeitsschule* (Fischer 1924: 425–477). The aim of the activity school should not be to turn out industrial workers or intellectual workers. Rather, all content, aids, methods and activities should serve "in accordance with their degree of appropriateness and fruitfulness, to awaken and school the powers, clarify and strengthen the interests" for the development of personality (Fischer 1924: 456 f.). An activity school conceived along these lines would also provide the foundations for economic and social life. Over the years, Kerschensteiner himself moved more and more away from a manually-centred instruction heavily oriented to school workshops and a concept of work with the primary aim of creating joy in work.[6] Work here is increasingly stripped of its relation to society and its value as vocational qualification and instead interpreted as a central element in the process of education.

5.5 Work and education

Even if Kerschensteiner today is far better known and remembered than his adversaries at the time, the criticism of Gaudig and Fischer is not less convincing for that reason, particularly when it comes to content and its strict conception, namely to what extent work in the school is a method or a material principle.

After all, one of the reasons why Kerschensteiner ultimately was induced to write his work of the concept of the *Arbeitsschule* was based on the dispute with Gaudig, precisely in a bid to avoid further "misunderstandings". In all new publications his statements were constantly modified in accordance with the most recent state of the discussion and his own knowledge. Manual work did indeed occupy a prominent place in his work. Even if he was concerned to stress that instruction on manual work should be a proper subject engaging technically well-trained teachers, already in the first editions of his book on the *Arbeitsschule* the central characteristic was not manual activity as such but the conjunct intellectual work as a contribution to the formation of character. Not until the chapter on "concept of work" intro-

---

6   On the role of joy in work in the discussion in Germany, cf. Campbell (1989).

duced in 1923 is the non-manual aspect of work given a clearer emphasis, when he equates an ode by Horace and the building of a nesting box for starlings. Technical-manual or intellectual skills alone were not the hallmark of an educated personality. If a person is indifferent and unfeeling toward cultural assets, such skills are of little use. What Kerschensteiner lauds is an activity school that contributes to education and contrasts with the philistine, the ideologist, all pedantry and zelotism. Such a school is the antipode of the universal dilettante, the opposite of all mindless assiduousness (Kerschensteiner 1982: 54).

Whether work is manual or intellectual, it should induce a person to become objective. The value and relevance of the subject matter should be realised as much as possible:

> Work in a pedagogical sense should act so that the aims of action trigger an objective reaction, a reaction to objectively valid or timeless values – a truth value, a moral value, a beauty value, a salvation value – in short, a value of the order of the soul and psyche. (Kerschensteiner 1982: 56)

The reason why he had advocated manual labour so strongly was because it was of great pedagogical value, since it showed clear results and thus made self-reflection necessary. With these comments, we have come to the threshold of Kerschensteiner's late world of thought that left its stamp on his final phase of activity, far removed from direct educational policy.

Kerschensteiner saw himself necessitated to make his pedagogical demands even more precise, to 'retranslate' them as it were from an ethical-political slogan or a formula for educational policy into a broader pedagogical conception. In this work of redefinition, the originally dominant conception of civic education receded to a secondary level, while the formal concept of work was given greater emphasis, while at the same time being further 'dematerialised'. Work was now integrated centrally into a comprehensive view of education and seen as a contribution to the formation and development of character. Education of the individual was considered to be achieved through relevance and objectivity (*Sachlichkeit*) grounded on manual or intellectual work. This also eliminated the question of the extent to which school should promote general education or vocational education. Vocational education emerges not as the goal of the school but as a means, an instrument of the *process* of education.

In 1917, Kerschensteiner published his work *Das Grundaxiom des Bildungsprozesses und seine Folgerungen für die Schulorganisation* ("The Fundamental Axiom of the Process of Education and its Consequences for School Organisation"). There he states that "the core of the concept I have termed '*Arbeitsschule*' [...] lies in the recognition of the principle that all education is nothing but the revitalisation of the objective spirit of an asset of culture" (Kerschensteiner 1917: 12). By foregrounding the concept of education, drawing on German neo-Kantian thought and the philosophy of Dilthey, work plays an important and increasingly central role as the development and acquisition of a cultural asset, its *"Erarbeitung"*. This is also evident in his later works *Theorie der Bildung* and *Theorie der Bildungsorganisation*.

If we have looked at Kerschensteiner in close connection with Pestalozzi and Dewey (cf. also Chapters 6 and 7) and directly linked with the natural sciences and their representatives, it is also important to mention the influence of the philosopher, sociologist and educator Georg Simmel and of Eduard Spranger, in particular with regard to the psychological and ethical foundations of the understanding of work in relation to education. Kerschensteiner was crucially influenced by Simmel's work *Begriff und Tragödie der Kultur* ("Concept and Tragedy of Culture"), as he wrote in a letter to Spranger (Gonon 1992: 226). Simmel developed his concept of culture in an intellectual confrontation with German classicism, orienting himself principally to Goethe. He emphasised the genius and especially the artist as a model for the process of education. In order to do justice to Simmel's influence on Kerschensteiner, Chapter 9 is dedicated to the philosophical relationship of their relevant concepts.

5.6 Topicality and effects

In contrast to the emphasis given to the concept of education in the Sunday speeches of many school directors and politicians, pedagogical theory tends to find the going rough in attempting to define this very concept in theoretical terms. That was also Kerschensteiner's experience when his voluminous opus on the theory of education did not find the echo he had hoped for, neither among practical educators nor his academic colleagues. The discussion on education is as a whole a more recent debate. It is not a central focus in the pedagogical lexicon of writings on education in the 19th century. Herbart talks about 'educability', and the word *Bildung* appears as an annex in Pestalozzi, in compounds like elementary education, popular education and the like. Yet it was not a central concept in pedagogy. Even Wilhelm von Humboldt as a renowned representative of *Bildung* was actually only secondarily an educator, and in the 19th century was unknown as a theorist of education. Nonetheless, he provided educators with a key term and a schema that was gratefully accepted by Kerschensteiner and Spranger: the juxtaposing of man and the world, and how in this confrontation human beings can and should shape their own being. But similar to the way in which Kerschensteiner dealt with Simmel, this contrast is divested of its tragic or philosophical background dimension and brought into a pedagogical relation.

The topic of *Bildung* has occupied the interest of educators, literary scholars, language teachers and philosophers down to the present. It is noticeable that there is no really good French or English equivalent to the German word, and that it remains difficult to develop precise theories of *Bildung* or even to make such theories operational. There are educators who would therefore like to see this concept eliminated from the discourse, while others emphatically endorse it. Within pedagogy there is a sub-field of the theory of *Bildung*, though it is of course not grounded on Kerschensteiner's theory. Some regard it as superfluous, while others deem it the very pearl or acme of pedagogical reflexion. With respect to their impact and contemporary relevance, the other central concepts in Kerschensteiner's pedagogy suffered a similar fate. At best, we can find certain traces of civic education as a concept in various ideas on political education.

At the beginning of this chapter it was noted that 'work' constitutes the central category in Kerschensteiner's views and can be pursued as a thread running through his entire opus, from the *Betrachtungen zur Theorie des Lehrplans* ("Observations on the Theory of the Curriculum", 1899) to the *Theorie der Bildungsorganisation* ("Theory of the Organisation of Education", 1933). However, in the sense used by Kerschensteiner, it has vanished from the discourse, as has his idea of the education of character. At best, one can find echoes of the discussions between Fischer, Gaudig and Kerschensteiner in modified variants of shop work or handicraft on the one hand, or methodological-didactic settings on the other, usually building on an 'orientation to action', though the concepts tended to follow their own respective notions in the discussion.

In contrast, the pedagogical concept of vocation with its linkage to general and vocational education is more present in contemporary discourse. It is not accidentally that references to the ideas of Kerschensteiner can be found mainly in vocational and economic pedagogy. If in the immediate post-war era references to Kerschensteiner were quite natural, this has changed since the 1960s (Gonon 1997: 3–24). Criticism is reserved in particular for his conservative-integrative concept oriented to profession, as elaborated in the concept of vocation (Stratmann 1992: 331 ff.). In any event, today's curriculum in the vocational school in Switzerland and Germany is clearly stamped by ideas for organisation that had already been proposed by Kerschensteiner.

5.7 Conclusion

Work is the core and Achilles' heel of Kerschensteiner's pedagogy. There is hardly a single one of his writings in which this concept does not appear. But it was and remains strangely multilayered. Frequent use is not necessarily a mark of clarity but can be precisely the opposite. The same holds true for the term 'activity school', which after the turn of the century became the thematic vogue in school discussion. Kerschensteiner, as a pedagogue of work and the *Arbeitsschule*, was on the one hand viewed as a prominent innovator in education as a result of this call. On the other hand, the rather diffuse definition of his reform concerns also gave rise to opposition. Kerschensteiner was probably conscious of this when in 1911 he decided for the first time to publish a work entitled *Begriff der Arbeitsschule*. The activity school, characterised by work within the school, marked out a central difference between Kerschensteiner's thinking and the school tradition under the influence and legacy of the ideas of Herbart, and this in turn awakened hopes for reform.

In this and other conceptual writings, Kerschensteiner attempted to elaborate central points of interest, such as the education of character and civic education, to link them with the concept of work and to develop them over against competing conceptions. Due to numerous objections, 'misunderstandings' and incorrect interpretations of his central concerns, Kerschensteiner felt it necessary to regularly bring his writings up to date. The repeated reprinting and new editions often contained supplements, revisions and new formulations.

It is precisely the work *Begriff der Arbeitsschule* which most clearly manifests Kerschensteiner's attempt to clarify what he had long been propagating in the field of educational policy, namely the need to make work fruitful for pedagogy and state policy and to convince pedagogy – and the school in particular – of the value of work. By means of this book he even hoped to provide work with a scientific foundation. Yet instead of clarification, ever more questions arose. No matter how evident the call for an activity school was in terms of educational policy, it was hard to imagine and implement an attempt to systematically anchor this within a truly comprehensive concept of education. Despite efforts to the contrary, the activity school and work within the school survived solely as metaphors.

6. Kerschensteiner as the 'Pestalozzi of Our Time' – A Pedagogical Hero and His Tragedy

How did the reform pedagogues in Central Europe come to see one of their own as the new Pestalozzi? When Kerschensteiner advanced the conception of the 'activity school' in his address on the topic Die Schule der Zukunft im Geiste Pestalozzis ("The School of the Future in the Spirit of Pestalozzi") in Zurich in 1908, he was not speaking as a well-versed expert on Pestalozzi. Yet that did not diminish his renown as 'the most brilliant living educator'. As the one educator who completed the work of Pestalozzi (Spranger 1966: 23), he became a classic educational figure himself (Spranger 1924: 324). In this chapter I will argue that Kerschensteiner was 'Pestalozzian' in his attitude as a kind of hero of education.

Pestalozzi's impact on posterity can also be grasped by the extent to which later generations of educators refer to him as a primary predecessor, mentor and paragon. For educators such as Niederer, Krüsi, Carl August Zeller or the so-called Prussian Eleven, for example von Türk, a certain spiritual affinity with Pestalozzi was quite evident. Initially, 'Pestalozzianism' as a current in pedagogy and educational theory was loosely associated with educators who felt an inner bond with Pestalozzian thought and agendas. Whoever worked in Burgdorf, Yverdon or Münchenbuchsee, whoever was determined to propagate Pestalozzi's methods or to refer directly to his inspiration in founding schools for the poor and for training teachers of the poor was considered a Pestalozzian, both in the sense of his or her own self-description as well as in the eyes of others.

Throughout the entire 19th century, we can find pedagogues of various stripes and persuasions, such as Fröbel and Diesterweg, who appropriated Pestalozzi's aura and were able to utilise Pestalozzi and his ideas for advancing their own concerns and conceptions. But how did it come about that educators in the reform movement at the end of the 19th century attempted to make use of his aura for furthering their own ends?

6.1 Pestalozzi as Counter-Herbart (the Natorpian turn)

Reform pedagogy entailed a new assessment of Pestalozzi that turned against the dominant Herbartian theories on the school and its function (cf. Oelkers 1989: 36 ff.). They returned to the sources of pedagogical will or, phrased more ethnologically, they sought to imbue the primal words with a purer meaning by "reinterpreting the accepted canon of holy words" (Bourdieu 1985: 44). For postulates such as naturalness, concrete visual observation (*Anschauung*) and self-activity, there were relevant passages in Pestalozzi's works that could be mustered and brought to bear in the disputes and discourse at the time. Precisely the reference to Pestalozzi appeared useful in pushing for a reorganisation of the schools, over against the 'intellectualism' that had induced Robert Rissmann in 1903, for example, to roundly reject Herbartian pedagogy along with individualism and moralism (cf. Rissmann 1911: 24 ff.). Here it was necessary – at least according to prominent proponents of reform pedagogy – to engage in an almost heroic effort to confront the tenacious powers of tradition. And it was one educator in particular who thus deserved the privilege, in the judgment of his peers at the time and later generations of pedagogues, to be closely associated with the great classic figure of Pestalozzi: That educator was Georg Kerschensteiner. The following excerpt from Eduard Spranger's 1948 preface to Georg Kerschensteiner's *Die Seele des Erziehers und das Problem der Lehrerbildung* ("The Soul of the Educator and the Problem of Teacher Education") illustrates this view:

> But the primal power of pedagogical spirit, which is like some force of nature, seldom descends upon the soul of a mere mortal. The intention here is those human beings who have in their deepest emotion and ethos been seised by the task to educate. Individuals for whom everything they touch turns to pedagogical gold. By that yardstick, the only man in the German-speaking countries who can follow Pestalozzi and Fröbel is Georg Kerschensteiner. (Spranger 1949: 8)

In this essay, I will neither evaluate the primal power of pedagogical spirit praised as a primary virtue of Kerschensteiner, nor will I attempt to weigh and assay his 'pedagogical gold' in the scales of scholarly assessment. Rather, I will try to present the power of definition in Spranger's classic characterisation. It not only impressed Kerschensteiner, who was already in his own day regarded as a pedagogical classicist, but has served to consolidate Kerschensteiner's fame down to the present as a 'Pestalozzian' (see, for example, Suchanski 1947, Schorer 1986).

There is indeed some reason to link Kerschensteiner with Pestalozzi. In his 1926 biography, Kerschensteiner mentions Pestalozzi along with Dewey and Goethe as thinkers who had had a significant impact on his own ideas (cf. Kerschensteiner 1926a: 46). Nor is it merely accidental that a portrait of Pestalozzi, hanging across from one of Bismarck (!), occupied a prominent position on display in Kerschensteiner's study (cf. Kerschensteiner 1939: 166 and illustration).

But the close linkage between the Munich educator and the Swiss teacher of the indigent is largely due to an event that occurred on January 12, 1908 in the Church of St. Peter in Zurich. On the occasion of the 162nd anniversary of the birth of Johann Heinrich Pestalozzi, Kerschensteiner was invited by the Zurich school authorities as keynote speaker. As is evident from his correspondence with Fritz Zollinger, originally he did not intend to give the festive lecture the title *Erziehung zur Arbeit* ("Education for Work", cf. Zollinger AKB 50/ 1907). The title of his 'sermon', as Kerschensteiner characterised his remarks, was initially *Die Schule der Zukunft im Geiste Pestalozzis* ("The School of the Future in the Spirit of Pestalozzi"). However, it was then changed to *Die Schule der Zukunft eine Arbeitsschule* ("The School of the Future: An Activity School"; cf. Chapter 5). This attempt by Kerschensteiner to conceptualise the foundation of his idea of the activity school in the work and thought of this 'master' of pedagogical theory and practice marked the first time the 'real Pestalozzi' had been made understandable in Kerschensteiner's time (cf. Wilhelm 1957: 67).

Marie Kerschensteiner, his second spouse, saw this address as the pivotal and most effective event in his career and postulated a kind of 'intellectual elective affinity' in the Goethean sense between Kerschensteiner and Pestalozzi:

> When he looked down from the pulpit onto the dim nave of the church, reverberating with the heavy tones of the organ, he was overcome like never before by the awareness of a great intellectual bond with the great Swiss philanthropist. And he felt moved by the task which fate had placed upon his shoulders: to be the one to make a living reality out of what Pestalozzi had dreamed and desired. (Kerschensteiner 1939: 139)

But what Pestalozzi actually wanted was and remains a bit difficult to ascertain. A comparison with another speaker at the Pestalozzi celebrations in Zurich in 1903 can serve to illustrate this point. The philosophy professor Paul Natorp, who at the time had already established himself as an exacting researcher on Pestalozzi and was in fundamental dispute with the Herbartians, spoke *Über die Grundlagen der Sozialpädagogik Pestalozzis* ("On the Foundations of Pestalozzi's Social Pedagogy", Natorp 1903).

While Kerschensteiner in his opening words and conclusion limited himself to a few passages from *Wie Gertrud ihre Kinder lehrt* ("How Gertrude Teaches her Children"), Natorp proceeded to argue his case based on close reading of this and other texts by Pestalozzi.

Kerschensteiner begins with a spirited apologia for Pestalozzi. Pestalozzi's "longing, restlessly searching for answers" imbued the elementary school with "those foundations of instructional method" which would dominate the school "for all time to come" (Kerschensteiner 1910d: 97). He quotes the 4th and 10th letter to Gessner from *Wie Gertrud ihre Kinder lehrt*. He is concerned here to find the laws for the development of the human intellect in order to explore a general psychological method of instruction. The "absolute foundation stone of all knowledge" lay in *Anschauung*, in direct concrete observation, and this discovery had been Pestalozzi's great accomplishment. In the conclusion, these passages are brought up once more. He points out that it is possible to look confidently forward to a time when direct concrete observation will have become the foundation of all knowledge and when, as noted in a passage in the 6th letter to Gessner, the "basis of all instruction will be derived from the unchanging primal form of human intellectual development" and will have become a vital and living reality (ibid.: 114).

Pestalozzi's thoughts are connected with didactic and methodological conceptions for the school, and apparently only secondarily are they contrasted with the ideas of the Herbartian Ziller. In contrast to so-called 'scientific pedagogues' – as the Herbartians stylised themselves – who were only prepared to permit a passive form of *Anschauung*, Kerschensteiner stresses 'active' hands-on *Anschauung* as it is facilitated by workshops, laboratories, school kitchens and school gardens (ibid.: 107).

The activity school qua school is not explicitly grounded on Pestalozzi here. Neither was this the case at any later time, although the later writings on the industrial school and on the Neuhof years (1769-1798) might have suggested such a linkage and approach. In Kerschensteiner's Zurich address, it is rather Pestalozzi's role as methodologist that is foregrounded.

Natorp's address in Zurich in 1903 is also directed against the Herbartians, though without their explicit mention. Kerschensteiner did not subject Pestalozzi's concept of *Anschauung* to a more probing analysis; he believed that by transforming 'book schools' into 'activity schools' he was actually doing proper justice to the demand for such an analysis. In contrast, Natorp examined the concept of *Anschauung*, using passages from what he called the 'main works', namely *Wie Gertrud ihre Kinder lehrt*, and from the *Nachforschungen* ("Investigations"), the *Abendstunde* ("Eventide"), the Paris memo and the letter from Stans, passages from *Lienhard und Gertrud* and other lesser known writings by the master educator. Natorp avoided limiting his purview to didactics and the school, and established two closely associated basic lines of thought based on Pestalozzi's work: On the one hand, the idea of elementary education, and on the other the idea of the education of the lower classes. Elementary education and his theories on social life were bound together in a kind of social pedagogy, as he noted in a rather self-willed manner (Natorp 1903: 31). The element of *Anschauung* was then placed within a Kantian epistemological context. He stated that by *Anschauung*, Pestalozzi meant "shaping from within" (ibid.: 33), but this required propinquity, 'nearness', a foundation in "real existing relations". Morality as a work of and on the self was grounded in society, which in turn in its primary form encompassed education in the bosom of the family (ibid.: 37).

According to Natorp, Pestalozzi probably took the concept of *Anschauung* from Kant and his followers. In his publication *Pestalozzi*, Natorp argued that through the concept of *Anschauung* Pestalozzi made ideas become action and reality; *Anschauung* was thus something like *"hinschauende Gestaltung"*, a kind of creation through observation (Natorp 1912: 63).

Despite the often one-sided emphasis on industrial work, which made learning sometimes appear as secondary even though industrial work helped to create moral social relations, Pestalozzi emphasised that every external aspect of work was subordinate to its inner essence, the internal purpose to educate human beings and to lift their souls (Natorp 1903: 38). But the real site for immediate and direct work was the home. Normally, the parents were the sole educators of humankind – and "so it should be", Natorp added, because according to Pestalozzi, education for domestic wisdom could not be supplanted by any kind of scientific guidance (ibid.: 42).

My presentation of Natorp's struggle for an adequate interpretation of Pestalozzi is intended to show that there are in fact two opposed readings of Pestalozzi and his thoughts here. Natorp's admonition at the beginning of his address that one could not do justice to Pestalozzi by praising him while at the same time remaining silent about his research on what is truth simply because of unfamiliarity with this topic (Natorp 1903: 27) might seem to be directed specifically against Kerschensteiner. Natorp's relative distance to questions pertaining to the school is not accidental. Even in his later publications on Pestalozzi, Herbart and Kant, the realm of the school is largely left out. Precisely in this scepticism vis-à-vis education through school instruction lies a key aspect of his critique of Herbartianism. "Community educates. That seems to me to be a decisive insight that can be derived from Pestalozzi as regards the question of the formation of the will", Natorp writes in *Herbart, Pestalozzi und die heutigen Aufgaben der Erziehungslehre* ("Herbart, Pestalozzi and Today's Tasks in Pedagogy") (Natorp 1922: 65). Furthermore, he concludes this treatise by noting:

If action is the 'principle of character', as Herbart says so aptly, then it should be clear that instruction, which offers far too little opportunity for actual action, thus cannot be the actual school for character. The school instructs, and life educates; this will ultimately stay true. (Natorp 1922: 72)

In contrast, Kerschensteiner associates Pestalozzi's *Anschauung* closely with his Munich model of the school. As he states in Zurich, the school should not allow the germs of active character already present in the child to atrophy (Kerschensteiner 1910d: 102). The activity school and *Anschauung* are short-circuited with the shaping and education of character, and this shaping is the prime task of school. In addition, Kerschensteiner posits an agreement between Pestalozzi's methods and the more recent findings in child psychology when he writes that 'affectionate research' is dedicating itself to the soul of the child. He implicitly suggests that contemporary research is picking up where Pestalozzi left off. In contrast with Natorp's scepticism toward instruction that seeks to educate, Kerschensteiner's criticism of Herbartianism is directed to its methodological and didactic arrangement, which in his view is erroneous because it rests on an incorrect foundation. Yet he does not question the ultimate aim of this kind of instruction.

The comparison of the two papers should have demonstrated that when it came to Pestalozzi, Kerschensteiner did not have a very impressive command of the primary sources. His accomplishment was rather to have made Pestalozzi a fruitful source of ideas for the discourse on schooling by resorting to his work in a less focused, more impulsive way. Like Natorp, he also used this classic thinker as a foil against Herbartianism. This is already quite evident in his *Theorie des Lehrplans* ("Theory of the Curriculum", 1899). Again he refers to what he regards as the incorrect construction of the curriculum in Ziller's pedagogy, which is too little responsive to Pestalozzi's call for a natural mode of instruction. For example, traditional instruction in the natural sciences, as elaborated in the appendix to the second edition of *Theorie des Lehrplans*, dealt almost exclusively "with the description of the external structure of the body and perhaps with some sketch of the living habits of the animal" (Kerschensteiner 1901b: 18). In contrast, Kerschensteiner states that three things must be carefully considered: observation of the living animal, close inspection of the taxidermic model and sketching of the characteristic features (ibid.: 19). In and through such a context of direct concrete observation, instruction fosters objectivity and a more direct participation in the life of the creatures observed and studied (ibid.: 25 f.). According to Kerschensteiner, the favourable consequences for the pupil's character are not the result of artificial arrangements of the material, but they are rather attained by moving down the path of science (ibid.: 28). At this juncture, Kerschensteiner's original concept of *Anschauung* is heavily oriented to the scientific observation of nature. Only much later does it move into the terrain of conceptions reminiscent of Kant.

At two points, *Theorie des Lehrplans* contains very vague references to Natorp's publications on Pestalozzi. This first pedagogical polemic by Kerschensteiner shows that in his struggle against the Herbartians he based his argument on Natorp's earlier work, though he avoided adopting his view, which was indeed at a distant remove from the school. His book on curriculum theory appeared the same year that Natorp was vehemently criticised by Rein, Willmann and other Herbartians (cf. Jegelka 1992: 286). This prompted Natorp to issue his thundering critical polemic *Kant oder Herbart?* He declared that even the mobilisation of the best fighting forces in the Herbartian school to encircle him as an enemy and force him to surrender would not dissuade him from continuing to contend a key point, namely that the main segment of the formation and education of character did not come to pass within the walls of the school (Natorp 1922a: 147, 187).

The lack of assurance among the Herbartians is reflected in the fact that they were forced to deal directly with Natorp in their publications on Pestalozzi after 1900. Thus, Wiget's attempt to defend Herbartianism deals with Pestalozzi. Wiget acknowledges that the school cannot do everything but thus must depend on cooperation with and assistance from the family. But following Pestalozzi, the school has to strengthen the motives for work, learning with the head and hand. In his view, the most important such attempt in this direction was Ziller's idea of concentration (Wiget 1914: 203 f.).

For a long time, Kerschensteiner deemed that there was no need for him to enter this intensive debate that was provoked in part by Natorp's interpretation of Pestalozzi, since he had sufficiently demonstrated his opposition to Herbartianism (cf. also Saupe 1927: 63). Indeed, he felt he could look on with composure as the debates raged about the sundry 'fine points' of interpreting Pestalozzi.

It is rather striking that Kerschensteiner's knowledge about Pestalozzi seemed markedly sparse for quite a long time. Down to his address in Zurich, he used only very few references, and always the same ones, mainly from *Wie Gertrud ihre Kinder lehrt*. Nicklis, who combed through Kerschensteiner's papers looking for material on his relation to Pestalozzi, thinks that Kerschensteiner began to be more interested in Pestalozzi about 1907 (Nicklis 1962: 259). This dating seems very early if we examine his publications with an eye to references to Pestalozzi. There is explicit reference to *Lienhard und Gertrud* and especially to *Wie Gertrud ihre Kinder lehrt*. There are also occasional positive citations from the *Abendstunde eines Einsiedlers* ("Eventide of a Hermit") and the *Schwanengesang*, though without any serious dealing with the content of these works. He furthermore appears to have some knowledge of Pestalozzi's biography. In his correspondence with Spranger, there are a number of references to Schäfer's biography of Pestalozzi, which Kerschensteiner found compelling, since in contrast to other descriptions, it vividly presented the "path of suffering" of this "incandescent human being" (Kerschensteiner/Spranger 1966: 66).

Taking the thematic disputes in his unpublished manuscripts as an indication of a new, more intensive interest in Pestalozzi, we can note that in 1914 Kerschensteiner deals anew with Natorp and his interpretation of Pestalozzi. On this occasion it was probably a more intensive probing look, and, as the title suggests, tempered by a certain degree of scepticism (cf. Kerschensteiner 1914). All his longer works contain some reference to Pestalozzi. In a kind of eclecticism, he cites Pestalozzi among various other authors to legitimise his own itinerary of thought, though he rarely indicates his sources precisely.

After his early retirement as the superintendent of the Munich schools, Kerschensteiner was apparently more willing to look in greater depth at Pestalozzi's opus, probably due to his position as a university teacher. Nonetheless, the references to Pestalozzi remain rather pale. In the chapter on methods in his famous *Begriff der Arbeitsschule* ("The Concept of the Activity School"), little is improved in this regard. The school is criticised because in his view the "old demand by Pestalozzi for the self-activity of the child" resembles far more the self-activity of a machine than that of "a soul that shapes itself in a distinctive fashion" (Kerschensteiner 1930: 116 f.). In another place we come upon the following rather casual formulation: "Yes, I would wager that, though without finding these words explicitly in his writings, Pestalozzi was totally convinced that vocational education is the gateway to human education" (ibid.: 167). Even in his more voluminous theory of education, his references tend to be secondary non-essential additions, such as the mention of Pestalozzi's famous trinity of head, heart and hand (Kerschensteiner 1928: 413). One indication of more intensive involvement with Pestalozzi's thought is contained in the revised editions to his earlier works and his final writings, where the references to Pestalozzi have increased in number and become more varied.

A glance at the unedited list of manuscripts shows that after 1926, there are a number of texts that directly refer to Pestalozzi. Along with a lecture tour in Munich, Hamburg and Zurich, he wrote several papers relating to Pestalozzi (cf. Walder 1992: 260, 265 f.). The only published work that mentions Pestalozzi in the title is *Die Prinzipien der Pädagogik Pestalozzis*, published in the year of Kerschensteiner's death in the series *Pestalozzi-Studien* (Kerschensteiner 1932). This essay marks the very peak of Kerschensteiner's engagement with Pestalozzi. After Kerschensteiner went through an extensive turn in philosophy in his thinking on educational theory, with the compass pointing to Kantian thought, shortly before his university teaching career began, there was nothing to stop him from adopting many aspects of Natorp's positive assessment of Pestalozzi. There are references to Pestalozzi already in the introduction, and the principles of Natorp's 1908 book on Pestalozzi have been largely borrowed and incorporated. The Pestalozzian concepts of '*Anschauung*' and 'method' are no longer considered didactic principles, a common and customary 'placing before the senses', but rather epistemological key points, immanent synthetic intellectual acts for the unity of a 'pure' *Anschauung* (cf. Kerschensteiner 1932: 1 f.). Though he would seem to be disputing a commonly held view in the 19th century, he is in fact polemicising against his own earlier view. Pedagogy is on solid ground as long as it follows the compass of Kant's critical idealism, but it struggles primarily for the practical shaping of the principles of activity, totality and sociality (ibid.: 2). Pestalozzi and his principles, presumably springing from the natural character of the process of education (individuality and humanity in the framework of vocational education are also mentioned), assist Kerschensteiner in justifying the reform activity school, rural educational centres, his own theories of vocational and general education, the orientation to the child and the educational typology bound up with Spranger's theory of '*Lebensformen*'.

This brief overview shows that it would be a mistake to regard Kerschensteiner as a well-versed expert on Pestalozzi, except perhaps in his final period. Nicklis' analysis, which explores the pedagogical principles of the two educators, also comes to the rather sympathetic conclusion that in Kerschensteiner's case it is possible to speak of a thematically limited and 'practical' Pestalozzianism. But with regard to his anthropological premises, Kerschensteiner shows an "unqualified non-Pestalozzianism" (Nicklis 1962: 284 f.). Wehle also correctly notes that Kerschensteiner's closeness to Pestalozzi was not based on an intensive study of the sources but, as he argues, on a kind of pedagogical congeniality between the two educators (cf. Wehle 1966a: 195).

6.2 Pestalozzi *redivivus* in the German Länder – Spranger's approach to Kerschensteiner

So far we have examined Kerschensteiner's familiarity with Pestalozzi, comparing it with the knowledge of another, comparatively well-versed interpreter. In what follows, we will turn from Natorp's Pestalozzianism to Spranger's interpretation of and interest in Pestalozzi in broader connection with Kerschensteiner. Spranger's view of Pestalozzi proved far more powerful and influential since it extended beyond the ivory towers of the scholars. Spranger's interpretation of

Pestalozzi begins with a stylisation of the pedagogical biography. The image was transposed to Spranger's friend or, as Wehle formulates it, "it was reserved to Eduard Spranger to interpret Kerschensteiner's life work and personal attitude as an *imitatio* of Pestalozzi" (Wehle 1982a: 197). In order to attain classical and timeless beauty which "triumphs over the suffering inherent in life", there is need for a hero whose wilful manifestation is not contaminated or compromised by his earthly mortal destruction (cf. Nietzsche 1988: 108). There was hardly a figure more suitable than Pestalozzi for such heavy stylisation. In 1912, at the age of 29 and as a recently appointed professor in Leipzig, Spranger wrote to the 58-year-old Georg Kerschensteiner:

> In the Philosophical-Pedagogical Department of the university, whose direction I have been appointed to take over in October, I will this winter deal with the topic 'Pestalozzi, Fröbel, Kerschensteiner' in the sense of tracing a direct line from the beginning of the activity school to its implementation. We will also look at other modern authors, but will consider the 'organisers' more important, and I personally regard you in the sense of your address in Zurich as the educator who brings Pestalozzi's work to completion. (Kerschensteiner/Spranger 1966: 23)

Already Natorp shows a tendency toward idealising Pestalozzi as a hero in the context of reform pedagogy. In his essay *Pestalozzi unser Führer* ("Pestalozzi as Our Leader") published in 1905 in the journal *Der Säemann*, he lauds the 'boldness' of youth: Whoever had youth in his veins, even if his hair had turned grey, was opposed to Herbart, and even more so to the school named after him, because that school would destroy youth for the young, "sending them in the course of a shortened life span through all eight stages of culture" and thereby turning them into old people. "But with joyous enthusiasm would those young people trust in a leader in whose heart indestructible youth was pulsating" (Natorp 1922b: 92).

This image of Pestalozzi as a leader of youth proved little persuasive, even though it was considered a desirable quality for a living educator to be a leader of the young. In any event, at the age of 70, Kerschensteiner was presented with a festschrift whose very title conferred upon him the mantle of the leadership of youth: *Jugendführer und Jugendprobleme* (Fischer/Spranger 1924).

This festschrift is astounding when it comes to the relation between Kerschensteiner and Pestalozzi. There is hardly any reference to Pestalozzi, but Muthesius cites Goethe, and Litt refers to Hegel. Foregrounded is Kerschensteiner's strong emphasis on strength of will and heroism (Martinak 1924: 70) and his many years at the helm of the movement for the activity school (Rehm 1924: 99). In the introduction, Kerschensteiner is heroically portrayed in a manner reminiscent of a leader in the sense of Carlyle – as a man who embodies ideas that are characteristic of 'great men with a mission' (cf. Carlyle n.d.: 1).

Though the volume points to Kerschensteiner's 'pedagogical Eros', it refers here to his efforts of behalf of educational theory. Kerschensteiner is lauded as the 'pedagogical exponent of the past decades'. He assures an insecure and young 'world people' the position of a great power in the realm of education, where the Germans will be educated into becoming a "politically self-confident people dedicated to hard work" (Fischer/Spranger 1924: IV f.). It is not Pestalozzi who is held up as a paradigm in this volume of commemoration, but rather the image of Bismarck as an educator, the other great model for Kerschensteiner, whose portrait also hung on his study wall.

In his comments, Spranger warns of an excessive youth cult and holds up the ideal of classicism, without which there is no genuine education (cf. Spranger 1924: 332). Yet precisely in this initiative we can see his huge effort to recast Kerschensteiner as a 'true and genuine' Pestalozzian figure.

The image of Kerschensteiner as the man who brought to completion the work of Pestalozzi pointed beyond the rather short-lived and 'stylish' needs of the youth movement (ibid.: 307). However, it was exposed to dangers emanating from Kerschensteiner himself, as is evident from his correspondence with Spranger in 1915:

> For years I have been following your writings and inward movement, more deeply than anyone else. I have no doubt that you possess the genuine inheritance of Pestalozzi. For precisely that reason, I would be pleased if you could distance yourself more clearly from the pragmatist Dewey. (Kerschensteiner/Spranger 1966: 30)

Features incongruent with the image of a classic Pestalozzian figure of a German disposition could only prove damaging. In Spranger's view,

Kerschensteiner stood far above Dewey with his "utilitarianism of the kitchen and practical trades" (ibid.: 37) and his purely technical and economist thinking. Still, Kerschensteiner had praised Dewey in his Zurich address. Spranger states that the German idea of the state and of science was too rich for "those on the other side of the Atlantic to ever understand" (ibid.: 30). In the same letter Spranger also makes clear what he believes Kerschensteiner's Pestalozzianism to consist of:

> Your biography confirms what I have long known: In your case, too, the fulcrum is the love of youth, that warm power of education and shaping that was deeper in Pestalozzi too than all the methods he invented later on. My pedagogical program springs from this Eros, and I look forward to the happy hour when our paths will cross. And so my hopes rest upon you, and aside from Stern, Groos, Matthias and Gaudig, I see only pedagogical workmen hammering all about, and unfortunately there are also names among them that you mention. (Kerschensteiner/Spranger 1966: 31)

The revitalised figure of Pestalozzi had to be purified of its contaminating slag. Kerschensteiner had succeeded in putting Spranger's mind to rest regarding Dewey, but in contrast to other sources from the Anglo-American world, he was unable to break with him totally. Right down to the end, Kerschensteiner's distinctive reception of Dewey remained an important point of reference in his writings. In contrast, his references to Kant and Goethe were much less problematic. In a number of places, Kerschensteiner paid homage to them, especially to Goethe. But neither Kant nor Goethe was suitable for a biographical incorporation, for the love of youth or pedagogical Eros. Consequently, Kerschensteiner ended his *Die Seele des Erziehers* ("The Soul of the Educator") with a sentence which was probably also a call and appeal to himself: "The salvation of the elementary school does not lie in Kant or Goethe, but in Pestalozzi!" (Kerschensteiner 1949: 155).

However, Theodor Wilhelm tries to make plausible a surprising variant of intellectual affinity with pedagogical predecessors. In Kerschensteiner's limitation to school pedagogy, in his stress on 'interest' as the actual driving force of the human being, in the concern that the interconnectedness of a topic not be torn asunder for the sake of an inappropriate principle, in his emphasis on instruction as education of character, Wilhelm sees a close internal linkage with the original pedagogy of Herbart. In both thinkers, strength of will was important for the building of character, discipline was essentially self-discipline, and action and activity marked the climate in which character flourished. That is why the pedagogy of both these thinkers had a distinct masculine cast (Wilhelm 1957: 68). He thus concludes:

> In looking back at the era of reform pedagogy, it is more accurate to see Kerschensteiner historically as the person who, *by dislodging Herbartian didactics from the driving seat, actually preserved the true spirit of Herbart, helping it to outlive the era of reform.* (Wilhelm 1957: 67)

Kerschensteiner's book *Die Seele des Erziehers*, based on a lecture published in 1921 and dedicated to Spranger, explicitly addressed the community of German teachers. In this work, the ideal teacher and educator is seen as a "person with Pestalozzi in his heart" (Kerschensteiner 1949: 13). Its intention was to counter demands from the academy for raising the level of teacher training, because exclusive concern for intellectual training would hinder the "social patterning of life", on which the internal calling of teachers and educators was based (ibid.: 155). A profound pedagogical insight could only be reached by "the heart, by love, passion, and pedagogical Eros", and not by knowledge devoid of passion (ibid.: 42). The figure of Pestalozzi was considered representative of this internal calling. Moreover, Kerschensteiner claimed these qualities not only for Pestalozzi, but also for himself. They both were to serve future generations of teachers as an educative paradigm. Pestalozzi's biography was suited to forging a congruency with one's own path while also emphasising the desired virtues of an educator who had answered the 'calling'. The active type of the early Kerschensteiner recedes via Pestalozzi's stylisation into the background, and the socially oriented educator comes to the fore, animated by a pure love for his fellow man, and even imbued with a certain religious touch. There is less talk now about insight into the nature of the state, practical experience, the gift of keen observation, masculinity and the like, as Theodor Wilhelm notes rather regretfully in his book on Kerschensteiner with the telling subtitle *Vermächtnis und Verhängnis* ("Legacy and Fate") (cf. Wilhelm 1957: 170).

All objections notwithstanding, Pestalozzi was stylised into the most perfect educator of modern times, and his herald became his veritable prophet. On the 100th anniversary of Pestalozzi's death in 1927, Kerschensteiner took advantage of a further opportunity to pay homage to the grand master at his grave in the church in Birr, Switzerland:

> We thus can confess: What rendered Pestalozzi great beyond all times and places is not merely consummate love and the unceasing goodness with which he outshines all the pedagogues we know. It is not merely the Christ-like dedication to the work of salvation of all the poor and disinherited which sprang from this inward constitution of the soul. (Kerschensteiner 1927: 2)

The same thoughts are almost literally repeated at the end of Kerschensteiner's contribution to *Pestalozzi-Studien*. Along with love and dedication, he mentions 'perfect selflessness' and 'unutterable humility and modesty'. As a further specific feature, reference is made to the fact that his eternally probing and never satisfied spirit assisted him in "discovering the great principles of all education". May "the spirit of Pestalozzi live in all those who serve in the holy office of education" (Kerschensteiner 1932: 13 f.).

Judging from Kerschensteiner and Spranger's correspondence, they were probably quite satisfied that the discussion on teacher training had been 'Pestalozzianised'. Thus, in a letter of 1930, Spranger writes the following remarks to his friend Kerschensteiner:

> Just think how your ideas are alive everywhere, how you stand at the very peak of an entire pedagogical era which will not soon come to a close. Think how all, really all people of good intention cherish you (while Pestalozzi did not experience that). (Kerschensteiner/Spranger 1966: 305)

This positive summing up seems straightforward and unclouded. Yet we must still look at another question, namely this: Where can we locate the specific tragedy of this hero? If we follow Spranger and use the criterion of the classical tragedy for education, does this mean that we should follow Oedipus of Sophocles, seeing Kerschensteiner in the role of a hero who pushes the father figure (Herbart) aside and marries the mother figure (Pestalozzi), and is initially celebrated as a liberator by the residents of the realm? In this reading, we could see Kerschensteiner's quest for pedagogical truths as the beginning of a tragic destiny.

Or maybe a reading grounded on the philosophy of life in the spirit of Simmel's (Simmel 1983) is more to the point? According to this view, tragedy resides outside the individual, and the hero must prove himself by resolving the tragic conflict of culture in the redemptive vessel of art (cf. Jung 1990: 145).

A more likely paragon could probably be found in Christ as a hero of humility who takes upon himself all the suffering of this world. In this stylisation, Pestalozzi as an educator is also a successor and imitator of Christ – and this is also how he saw himself (cf. Pestalozzi 1943: 48).

Yet there is also a personal component of tragedy in Kerschensteiner's efforts. Note, however, that his early pensioning in the autumn of 1919 is less important in this regard. In fact, although his early pensioning was due to the extreme political turbulence of the time in Munich – turbulence that also spilled over into the schools and their administration and had led to a certain weariness in Kerschensteiner's activity as school superintendent (cf. Walder 1992: 19 ff.) – it was these very conditions which induced him to arrange his honorary professorship at the right moment at the University of Munich (ibid.: 40 ff.). However, the tragic aspect stems from a different source. It must have been painful for the much celebrated educator that his most ambitious work, *Theorie der Bildung*, which had been intended to crown his career, ended in failure. The response of his fellow professors and educational authorities, such as Litt, Spranger, Flitner, Nohl, and Petersen, was telling: none reacted to the book; it was treated with silent reserve (cf. Walder 1992: 209). When some review of his book appeared, it was extremely critical, such as that by Reichwein, who commented that Kerschensteiner's concept of education had at best certain 'aesthetic' qualities. In his view, the book led to a 'krisis' in the literal Greek sense, a decision between science and the living human being (Reichwein 1979: 126 f.). Even younger up-and-coming educators, such as Fritz Blättner, found little that was useful in Kerschensteiner's late theoretical endeavours. According to Blättner, Kerschensteiner had given "thousands of readers and disciples" (!) a 'pedagogy', a complex of ideas for guiding teachers and education – "but he did not give us a 'science of education'" (Blättner 1979: 172).

This critical review in the periodical *Erziehung* in 1930 found a vulnerable spot in Kerschensteiner. Angered, he contacted the co-editor Hermann Nohl in order to discover which of the co-editors had approved the publication of this decidedly 'bad' article. Nohl, on his part, could only cautiously indicate his enthusiastic approval of the critique and its author (cf. Walder 1992: 222).

On a similar note, Spranger had probably more time and will to find the right words in his 1949 preface to *Seele des Erziehers* than when Kerschensteiner was still alive. In his homage for the late efforts in educational theory of the man who had brought the work of Pestalozzi to 'completion', he noted:

> When such a person starts to think about the mystery of his own nature, in order to illuminate for others the steep path to such a towering height, it is not readily certain that he will find a simple formula for this, because that requires a philosophical psychology that has been carefully thought through. It was not until late in his life that Kerschensteiner worked his way into philosophy. [...] But his most original and distinctive element does not lie there. [...] It is necessary to transform the carefully delineated definitions [...] back into life, of which they are but a pale reflection. Not until then does one begin to extract the veins of gold which this stone contains. (Spranger 1949: 9)

Thus, it were Kerschensteiner's late theoretical ambitions that proved to be his personal tragedy. In this regard, he comes close to the hero of Sophocles who refuses to recognise limits and who stubbornly adheres to a decision he has made, even at the cost of self-destruction (cf. Knox 1964: 5 f.).

6.3 The faded heroes

In retrospect, the transposition of Pestalozzi into the 20th century and his revitalising in the person of Kerschensteiner has to be deemed a basic success. It was successful especially since at least down to the end of the 1960s, it possessed a certain appeal for educational theorists, teacher trainers and teachers, for whom such a paradigm was intended and designed. Röhrs names – though probably not with this intention – the decisive criterion for this success: He observes that an analysis of Kerschensteiner's work and achievement "repeatedly must lead back to the personality of this exemplary pedagogue" (Röhrs 1989: 13). He furthermore adds that like the achievements of all great popular educators, Kerschensteiner's work has become the common inheritance of the educational world, a body of thought and action whose validity and importance is not affected or diminished by any polemic (ibid.: 3).

Röhrs disagrees with the objection voiced by some contemporary and later pedagogues, namely that Kerschensteiner's philosophical turn weakened his earlier clarity and verve for reform. It was Pestalozzi who most forcefully pointed the way for Kerschensteiner into the realm of philosophy: "Likewise as a thinker, Kerschensteiner was by nature a Pestalozzian" (ibid.: 9).

As this chapter has shown, Pestalozzianism in reform pedagogy is not necessarily dependent on a highly comprehensive familiarity with Pestalozzi's universe of thought and his writings. Had that been the case, there would have been far more suitable candidates than Kerschensteiner. The suggestive image of Pestalozzi as educator and exemplary figure could not develop its persuasive power without the process of biographical stylisation, a process furthered by Pestalozzi himself and his followers already in the 19th century. Dedication, love, passion, pedagogical Eros and humility are the hallmarks of this gifted hero and educational icon. A certain modicum of interpretative boldness was needed to transpose this school reformer and bureaucrat into this mythical world.

In order for Kerschensteiner to be perceived as a Pestalozzian figure, his writings on civics and war under the impression of Wilhelmine patriotism had to be played down. As a result of this 'Pestalozzianising' of Kerschensteiner, it also proved successful, as in the case of the master himself, to remove and distance his pedagogical writings from the person and his impact. What heroes say or write is overshadowed by their heroic acts.

What is the function of such a process of 'Pestalozzianising' an educator? It can be described as a devalourising of scientific analysis and discussion, in the sense that instead of indulging in 'unbounded' academic scholarship and abstraction, pedagogues should act in accordance with their role models, because what ultimately counts for 'true' educators are not theory and critical discourse, but something quite different. The fact that such a stylisation was largely cultivated by university professors leaves an ambivalent impression, especially if we contrast these endeavours with Max Weber's sober view of sociology as a scientific discipline.

Today, however, the age of pedagogical titans appears a thing of the past, and even the few heroes left are leaving the stage. Yet the longing for idyll and paragons is still with us, even though a Pestalozzi of our times, even a postmodern one, is as yet not visible on any horizon. One might therefore be all the more ready to look on the heroic epics of the past with a modicum of favour. Their power of illumination imbues the craft of education with dignity. Be that as it may: The adventure termed 'school' has become too quotidian, too routinised. Its tasks are hardly spectacular, and the semantics of reform proved successful enough to be co-opted and integrated into existing pedagogical discourse. There is little latitude here for a Pestalozzi-like figure to emerge from the ranks of school administrators or teachers. Moreover, while education as a science today may well produce Pestalozzi researchers, it will hardly produce Pestalozzian heroes, however some may regret it.

Part 2

*Kerschensteiner in Relation to
Dewey, Weber and Simmel*

7. School Reform and Pragmatism: John Dewey's Ambiguous Impact on Modernisation in Germany

In German-speaking countries, John Dewey has come to be consid-ered a school reformer, an advocate of the project method and the propagator of a cognitivist psychology of learning. His ideas on socio-political reform, however, were ignored, partly intentionally, partly due to a lack of sufficient familiarity with them. His major pedagogical work, Democracy and Education, received little atten-tion. In what follows, this selective view of Dewey is discussed mainly on the basis of internal pedagogical theoretical positions.

This chapter presents three aspects of Dewey that are characteristic of the way in which he is usually perceived. The first aspect concerns the historical picture of Dewey as a pragmatist and as the international representative of reformed pedagogical methods and school reform; the second aspect relates to a more restricted version of Dewey, namely as the advocate of the project as a teaching method; and the third aspect concerns his emergence as a psychologist of learning.

John Dewey first became known as the exponent of a child-centred reformed method of education. Even more recent presenta-tions see his student-centeredness at the teaching level as an essential feature of Dewey's contribution to education, as is illustrated by the following analysis of articles in the *Enzyklopädie Erziehungswissen-schaften* ("Encyclopaedia of Educational Sciences") published in the eighties.

Even the historical view at the beginning of the twentieth century largely glosses over the political aspects of Dewey's thoughts on edu-cation. Consequently, it is not his main pedagogical work, *Democracy and Education*, which is in the foreground, but rather *The School and Society*, *The Child and the Curriculum* and *How we think*. These latter works represent only a limited and rather early part of Dewey's thoughts on education and tend to focus strongly on school reform. The fact that Dewey formulated a supra-individual theory of learning which transcends the school horizon by comprising aspects of both science and social life, remained peculiarly unnoticed. The way in which he put matters into a political context – a typical feature throughout his entire work – has had very little impact on how he has been perceived by educators in German-speaking countries. 'Democracy and Education' has thus simply become 'Education' in school teaching.

7.1 Dewey as school reformer – Kerschensteiner's view

In St. Peter's Church on January 12, 1908, when Georg Kerschensteiner sang the praises to the *Arbeitschule* (Activity School) as the school of the future, he cited Johann Heinrich Pestalozzi as a chief witness of his efforts. To be more precise, he referred to a "properly understood Pestalozzi", not the Herbartians' Pestalozzi, who they claimed to be the representative of the *Selbsttätigkeit* (autonomy) school and who thus sought to combine this principle with the *Erziehungsschule* (Education School). Rather than the so-called 'book school', Kerschensteiner emphasised the "active Pestalozzi", who advocated productivity rather than passive reception in school teaching. Consequently, he claimed that a school that teaches "not through words and books, but rather through practical experience" (Kerschensteiner 1910d: 98) was the type of school that was best suited to the mentality as well as to the social drives of a child. He went on to claim that this very reorganisation of the school was also intended by the best educators in the New World, including John Dewey, who in *The School and Society* rightly complained that the school, "with its rows of ugly desks" and all its furnishings was outfitted solely "for listening".

With reference to the Munich school reform, Kerschensteiner added a fiery plea for the "new Activity School" (ibid.: 104), which he said was characterised by manual work. Pestalozzi, the school as the

116

establishment for active work, and, in a thundering conclusion, again John Dewey, formed the pillars of Kerschensteiner's plea for school reform when he prophesised that the establishment of the activity school would represent the most drastic reorganisation of education in the future. John Dewey was again referred to and cited in German translation in order to introduce this "Copernican revolution", as Kerschensteiner reflected Dewey empathically in the words he used: "In this case the child becomes the sun about which the appliances of education revolve, he is the centre about which they are organised" (Dewey 1907: 51).

It is not by accident that Pestalozzi and Dewey were linked together in Kerschensteiner's speech, and this happened again in later writings. Furthermore, in Kerschensteiner's last work, his theory of educational organisation, appreciation is expressed for the way in which John Dewey during the past thirty years had insisted on the need to make schools more orientated to life and on the need to change them from "mere teaching institutions to educational institutions" (Kerschensteiner 1933: 230). Dewey's contribution to education is thus appreciated from a school reform perspective.

Besides Kerschensteiner's perception of a theoretical agreement with Dewey, a reading of the US pedagogue apparently also serves to encourage him at a time of hectic school reforms in Munich, as Georg Kerschensteiner writes in a self-presentation. Dewey – whom he met during a tour of America in 1910 – is thus seen as confirming him in his school reform activities. The purity and clarity of Dewey's pedagogical thoughts strengthened Kerschensteiner's will to take action. The reference to Dewey as a school reformer is supplemented by highlighting his psychological contributions to teaching as they are represented in his book *How we think*. Nevertheless, Kerschensteiner mainly emphasised Dewey's proposals with regard to organisation and pointed out that Dewey actually tested his ideas in practice at his experimental school in Chicago. Kerschensteiner was probably aware that these references covered only part of Dewey's work, since he stated at the same time that during the first twelve to fifteen years in office he had had no time to deepen his pedagogical ideas (Kerschensteiner 1982a: 135 ff.). However, Kerschensteiner's views on Dewey did not change substantially even in later years when he had more leisure to devote himself to working on pedagogical theory. Such a restricted view of Dewey as a mere school reformer is surprising if one considers Dewey's comprehensive writings on logic, ethics, psychology, politics and philosophy. Even school reform itself is clearly incorporated in a comprehensive view of educational philosophy.

The suspicion that Kerschensteiner did not know enough about the context in which Dewey set his school reform can easily be refuted. A footnote to the Dewey references from *School and Society* in the printed version of the Zurich speech on the activity school weakens any potential political readings. Kerschensteiner states that Dewey's *School and Society*, which was already available in a German translation at the time (Dewey 1905), is to be warmly recommended to "schoolmen", but that its basic idea of making the school an "embryonic community life" is difficult to implement (Kerschensteiner 1910d: 259 ff.). The political context, which Kerschensteiner himself emphasised strongly in his early writings like *Die staatsbürgerliche Erziehung der deutschen Jugend* (The civic education of German youth) (Kerschensteiner 1966), and which was indeed the actual motive force behind school reform, was by no means foreign to him. Yet, it seems that he found it hard to accept these political interconnections in John Dewey's case, and so he banished any reference to them to a footnote.

In view of the references throughout Georg Kerschensteiner's works, it is obvious that he was also quite aware of others of Dewey's writings. Dewey appears in many passages in close connection with Pestalozzi in order to legitimise activities and work in education. At the same time, however – as was already the case in the Zurich speech – he is depicted as an anti-Herbartianist, as is also documented in *Theorie der Bildung*, Kerschensteiner's most ambitious work. There is merely one passage in *Theorie der Bildung* which refers to Dewey's major work: explicit reference to it is made by Kerschensteiner in order to make a general comment to the effect that the potential for reforming society which is offered by the school was still far from being fully ascertained (Kerschensteiner 1926: 264).

Child-centeredness, activity school and anti-Herbartianism are the three features which make Pestalozzi and Dewey attractive for this Munich school reformer. Yet, in his entire works Kerschensteiner

118

hardly ever mentions the political dimension of Dewey's works. In another context it becomes clear why Kerschensteiner took little or no notice of Dewey's views on the social renewal through education. It was apparently too profane for him, since he wrote that visitors from Anglo-Saxon countries, steeped as they were in Pragmatism and Utilitarianism, were impressed primarily by the workshops and manual work performed in his reformed Munich schools. Their eyes were fixed on the "skilled, useful workers, not on the human beings who had been educated by sound work". For him, work was only a means, but never the end of education (Kerschensteiner 1982a: 134 ff.). While Dewey's social relevance is not mentioned in this connection, another aspect alongside politically incongruent perspectives which suggest disregard for the democracy postulate still becomes clear. A considerable amount of goal orientation is imputed to pragmatism, as in the American approach, which means that the hoped for usefulness (for the common good) determines pedagogical goals. According to Kerschensteiner it is a misunderstanding to see the formation of useful craftsmen as the goal of the Munich school reform – a misunderstanding that is easily imputed to the Activity school. The fact that work is primarily intended as a tool serving the education of people tends to be ignored.

This alleged defect hardly becomes clearer in the correspondence between the young Eduard Spranger – a *grand seigneur* of German pedagogy to the present day – who had by then just become a professor, and the Munich school reformer. In a letter dated March 22, 1915, Spranger reports on his lectures in Leipzig. He claims that the pedagogy of Pestalozzi, Kerschensteiner and Dewey, unlike that of the Herbartians, takes its starting point in a "life totality" (*Lebensto-talität*), and that this is all that the first two have in common with Dewey. He considers Kerschensteiner's approach to be "far above" the other's "kitchen and handicraft utilitarianism". The aims of the German spirit reach far beyond "economic Utilitarianism" (Spranger 1966a: 37).

However, it seems that Spranger was not so certain how far Kerschensteiner had been "infected" with American pragmatism. That same month he wrote to the "*hochverehrter Studienrat*" ("highly honoured schoolmaster") that he would be pleased to see Kerschensteiner

– who was "Pestalozzi's true heir" – "distance himself even further from the pragmatist Dewey", since the German idea of the state and science was richer than "anyone over there understands" (ibid.: 30). Kerschensteiner was able to put his later pedagogical comrade-in-arms and good friend at ease:

> You need not be afraid that Dewey and his pragmatism could get a hold on me. [...] Of others, we understand only in as much as they speak the language of our own soul. Although three or four years ago I read William James' "Pragmatism" attentively, the book had no effect on me. But to Dewey I owe a great deal of clarity in almost everything which *I myself* wanted and instinctively strove for. I do not consider myself an assiduous student, I learn only what comes easily to me. (Kerschensteiner 1966a: 34)

Kerschensteiner's remark demonstrates how selective his perception of pragmatism was. 'Pragmatism', at least the one represented by James and Dewey, was simply not capable of integration and was viewed by him quite independently of school reform. From their correspondence it is obvious how close Dewey's pragmatism had shifted to utilitarianism. According to this understanding, pragmatic views are of a far lower nature in comparison to the richness of German scientific and political ideas. With this evaluation, the democratic context of education also becomes untenable. At the same time, Kerschensteiner indicates that he feels supported by Dewey as a reflective school reformer who initially advocated child-centeredness and teaching through activity and work.

The Leipzig university professor's friendly words hold far more than a piece of advice. At the same time they reveal his approach to deciding between acceptance and rejection, which amounts to a policy regarding which authors are to be considered worthy of being cited. While Switzerland's Pestalozzi, whose political commitment took place in a distant past, is readily accepted, American pragmatism in the form of James and Dewey is rejected outright.

120

7.2 Dewey as the father of teaching through projects: the Petersen Foundation

Though Kerschensteiner's interest for John Dewey had initially centred on his roles as school reforming pedagogue and organiser, since the thirties it had come to be directed to Dewey as a pervasive figure in connection with innovative teaching. In particular, Dewey has become known as the father of teaching through projects.

The publication *Der Projekt-Plan. Grundlegung und Praxis* (The project plan. Principles and practice) lists John Dewey and William Heard Kilpatrick as contributors (Dewey/Kilpatrick 1935). Two articles by Kilpatrick, "Education for a changing culture" and "The project method", are combined with a number of short pieces on pedagogy by John Dewey, such as "The child and the curriculum", "The way out of pedagogical confusion" and "The problem of freedom in schools". This collection of works by John Dewey and his student William Heard Kilpatrick is not a concise presentation of the project approach, but much rather a presentation of two views on progressive education and the project idea. While Kilpatrick connected the project idea to the students' motivation, Dewey focussed on methodological thought and intelligent activity, as well as on constructive doing as the outcome of manual-technical work. In other words, his contributions were not explicitly on the subject of projects, which may be due to the fact that he considered himself primarily bound to the traditional view of the project, and *not* to a progressive didactic teaching concept (Knoll 1992). However, this distinction is not absolute since Kilpatrick clearly refers to John Dewey with regard to the integration of the project method, i.e., to Dewey as the integrator of education in a democratic context. In the introduction to *Der Projekt-Plan. Grundlegung und Praxis*, Kilpatrick claims that modern life is characterised by three "strong tendencies": mental attitude, industrialisation and democracy (Kilpatrick 1935: 14). It is the experimentally confirmed thought and the ethical requirements of democracy which have made the modern world what it is today (ibid.: 22). Furthermore, in this world of accelerating change, young people are no longer prepared to accept authoritative morals. These assumptions affect the new methods of education, including the very ways in which things are taught. Therefore – as is argued with reference to Dewey – a new philosophy of education is required (ibid.: 83 ff.).

There is no doubt that Dewey and Kilpatrick take a political stand in that the project method clearly seems to be related to democracy. This view, however, is boldly reinterpreted in the publisher's epilogue. While Kerschensteiner disregards Dewey's reference to society, Petersen 'Germanises' it as it were. Such an achievement is all the more remarkable because the view expressed in the selected texts suggests a clear concern with educational philosophy and a socio-critical understanding of democracy. Petersen understands – or chooses to understand – the insistence on education and democracy as influenced by Germany: in the USA, "a school system based on the social community (*Volksgemeinschaft*)" had been created, determined by a "truly Germanic (influence)". Therefore, "Democratisation" would not mean democracy in the European sense but "social community" (Petersen 1935: 207). How far Petersen's more than unconventional twist served to give such an approach an opportunistic touch in unstable times (1935!) or to adapt it to a new political context is a question which must be left unanswered. A similar feat with regard to philosophical acceptance was performed by the Göttingen philosopher Eduard Baumgarten in that he put together pragmatism with comradeship and social community thinking (cf. Konrak 1998: 29). Petersen's re-interpretation at least suggests that Kilpatrick's project approach appeared to be detachable from the political contextual background.

The reactions to *Der Projekt-Plan. Grundlegung und Praxis* in German-speaking countries show that the project became an apolitical and school-related tool for didactic innovation with Dewey as its spiritual founder. This interpretation prevails even to the present day. In a more recent introduction to pedagogical problems, John Dewey appears only once, namely as the "philosophical father" of the project method (Gudjons 1997: 105). In Germany, Dewey is simply conceived as the inventor of the project method, an interpretation which is easily proved to be incorrect (Knoll 1991). For example, Hermann Röhrs, a representative of national and international reform pedagogy, presents John Dewey as the 'head' of the progressive education movement, though 'progressive' is not meant in the political sense but rather points to a closeness to the community and in particular to a 'realistic' approach to life. In this context, it is virtually inevitable to refer to the 'project' (Röhrs 1977: 36 ff.).

An impression of this can be obtained simply by looking for references to Dewey in the *Enzyklopädie Erziehungswissenschaft*, the latest major manual and lexicon of education published in eleven volumes in 1984 and re-published unchanged in 1995 (Lenzen 1995). One article presents Dewey as the founder of the project method, where a project is described as comprising the four phases *setting the goal*, *planning*, *performance* and *assessment* (Groth 1995: 313). Furthermore, in connection with 'open teaching', Dewey's project teaching method is mentioned, which emphasises the importance of joint activity (Groddeck 1995: 625). Another author focuses on experience-related teaching in this context (Jank 1995: 595 ff.). Yet another draws attention to the desirable student-orientation in teaching (Einsiedler 1995: 628). According to the *Enzyklopädie*, the project method is applicable to all grades, including kindergarten (Zimmer 1995: 28).

All the references to John Dewey in these articles are very brief and in most cases do not go beyond a mere reference to the publication edited by Petersen. Only a single contribution to the *Enzyklopädie* treats the project idea in more detail and also more adequately: Tymister characterises Dewey's and Kilpatrick's project approach in the light of pragmatism as an intellectual trend. The outcome of this approach is an understanding of human knowledge that is subservient to action. Accordingly, practical activity is considered a pre-requisite for the acquisition of theoretical knowledge, and this equally applies to education (Tymister 1995: 524). With this as the philosophical-pedagogical basis, Kilpatrick takes up and expands the term 'project' for the context of school teaching and learning. Tymister does not conceal that, according to Kilpatrick, this specific form of work or general activity is a basic condition for life in a democracy and, therefore, must also be applied to learning at school. Consequently, the project method of teaching cannot be understood to be redundant; according to Dewey and Kilpatrick, from a present-day point of view the essential elements of a teaching project must include the following: the starting point must be a socially significant problem situation, on the basis of which the learners must develop an activity plan with the advice of the participating teacher. This plan must also be relevant to goals outside the school. Because students act self-reliantly and on their own responsibility, these experiences also have the outcome of changing the school. This becomes visible, amongst other things, by the fact that the traditional school subjects are no longer treated separately and that, despite differences in the competence of teachers and students, a markedly co-operative working relationship is created between them.

In Germany, reform pedagogy adopted this approach and developed it further, both before and after the Second World War. The curriculum discussions after 1960 were influenced by this idea, though Tymister is sceptical in his assessment of the results when he states that a reform of school teaching in its organisation and content was not "achieved on a broad basis", since teacher-centred forms of teaching theoretical-abstract specialised knowledge predominated (ibid.: 525). Thanks to the efforts of individual teachers, such teaching did take place, albeit in isolated cases. It was project-orientated working methods rather than teaching projects that had prevailed as a compromise between traditional teacher-centred frontal teaching and approaches to student-centred teaching and learning that were mainly concerned with motivating the students. The reality of project-orientated teaching is characterised by many compromises. For example, only rarely did several teachers participate in an inter-disciplinary manner at the same time. Moreover, project teaching was mostly directed to school-related goals and thus only rarely had consequences outside the school context. Nevertheless, Tymister makes up the balance to the effect that progress has been made in the direction of more co-determination in classes, resulting in a contribution to making school – as part of society as a whole – more democratic (ibid.: 526).

In his book *Unterrichtsmethoden II: Praxisband* (Teaching methods II: Practical Work), Hilbert Meyer argues similarly when he ascribes the idea of projects and initial experiments to Dewey and Kilpatrick (Meyer 1987: 335). With a view to preserving the original thought which, regrettably, he does not describe in detail, he then goes on to inveigh against an inflation of the notion of 'project', since it is used to mean a great many things and often amounts to no more than playing with words. In this connection, he points out that project work is always political. In an education policy context, the project idea necessitates more autonomy on the part of students and their teachers with regard to guidelines that have traditionally been dealt with by school directors and school boards. The project, "revived in the rest-less, rebellious seventies" (ibid.: 336), is directed towards greater scope of activity for students and towards self-reliance and autonomy. Today, projects, and in particular project weeks, serve to promote the students' motivation. They are a substitute for school reform, which has now become grounded. With this, Meyer hopes that the collected experiences will contribute to an "alternative learning culture" and will thus also help to promote a reform of day-to-day teaching.

Even if the contributions presented above essentially retain the point of view of school teaching and take over Petersen's historical allegations virtually unexamined, at least some reference is made to the discrepancy between the project as a method of teaching and the integration of the project as a method of social change. In this respect, Meyer differs from most other authors who see Dewey not only as the supporter of the project method but even reduce this approach to an element of the methodological teaching and learning repertoire at school.

In Karl Frey's presentation of the project, the preference for a re-stricted understanding of method in teaching – with reference to and criticism of Dewey – becomes quite clear, too. Dewey's approach is rejected as being too 'cognitivist'. According to Frey, experimental scientific methods cannot be applied to all sectors of life and do not necessarily lead to a better understanding of life and democracy. If projects were arranged the way Dewey understands them, people's emotional and interactive dispositions would wither away (Frey 1998: 50 ff.). Here he accuses Dewey's 'project' of setting the wrong priori-ties and of being incomplete.

With most presentations relating to the project approach, it is striking that Dewey plays a part merely as the founder or father of the idea without placing his theory into a wider context or discussing it in greater detail. Dewey appears essentially as an icon and a cue-giver, mainly with the intention of accounting for the reform-pedagogical roots of the concept (Kost 1984). The concept of 'project weeks' or, more radically, the conversion of the entire school into a permanent project closes the circle of Kerschensteiner's comprehensive school reform approach. 'Project' thus simply becomes a slogan of the school reformers against established structures. All the same, the relationship with democracy is not fully ignored in this post-war version and is 'de-Germanised' once more.

Consequently, the project is viewed either exclusively as a methodological teaching tool to boost student motivation or as the start of comprehensive school reforms. In the process, Dewey's aim of achieving a renewal of society was taken up only partially. Dewey as the father of the project method is thus turned into the inventor of a teaching technology or – as a progressive educator – into the representative of a school-teaching utopia beyond the curriculum.

7.3 Dewey as a psychologist of learning: more Herbartian than the Herbartians

Another reading of Dewey's works which was to find acceptance was offered by Georg Kerschensteiner. In this alternative perspective it was not only the aspect of school reform, but primarily the cognitive-psychology of learning directed to teaching that turned Dewey into a pedagogue (Prantl 1925: 287).

The relevant book in this regard is *How we think* (Dewey 1910), which first appeared in 1910 and which Kerschensteiner came to know during his visit to America and brought home as a gift to Germany. Kerschensteiner valued this book highly, which is demonstrated by the fact that he attempted to translate it. He never published it, however. In his writings, this work appears in several places, for example, in a reference in the chapter *"Das Wesen der geistigen Zucht"* ("The nature of mental discipline") of his publication *Wesen und Wert des naturwissenschaftlichen Unterrichtes* ("Nature and value of scientific education"), which appeared in 1913. In this publication, he wanted to promote the teaching of science alongside the classical languages to achieve what was perceived as a controversial recognition at the time. In order to achieve this, an analysis of thought and learning processes without reference to a specific subject was welcome to him. Accordingly, Kerschensteiner presented Dewey's five-level process of logical thinking, turning it into a subjective, absolutely non-pragmatic teleology where the purpose of mental Discipline is to form "the logical conscience" (Kerschensteiner 1963: 62). Mental discipline puts us "in the position to penetrate higher and higher spiritual matters and thus experience absolute value more and more deeply [...], the time-less value of truth in all that is known" (ibid.: 72). There is a world of difference between Dewey's epistemology and Kerschensteiner's experience of value. Nevertheless, ignoring this discrepancy, Kerschensteiner went on to combine his plea for the teaching of science with Dewey's approach.

In contrast, the understanding of *How we think* as presented in Kerschensteiner's *Theorie der Bildung* is far more in line with reform pedagogy. Starting from the tradition of the Activity school, logical thinking is not primarily situated in the human spirit but in activity, and this must be fostered by the school (Kerschensteiner 1926: 123). Moreover, Kerschensteiner highlights Dewey's concept of interest which is quite different from Herbart's (ibid.: 259 ff.). Interest – as is argued against Herbart in another passage – is not a contemplative but "a highly active condition" which is expressed in activity as is emphasised in Dewey's work *Interest and Effort in Education* (ibid.: 271). It is in fact criticism of American Herbartianism, from which Dewey formulated his position in *How we think* (cf. Ryan 1995: 144 ff.). For Dewey, the formal steps of the Herbartians were too schematic, hardly plausible in their sequence and much too strongly orientated to the school curriculum. Against the four steps proposed by Ziller, he therefore argued for an "analysis of the complete act of thinking", which consists of five consecutive elements of reflection: one encounters a difficulty (1), and endeavours to define the problem (2); an idea of a possible solution emerges (3), and one then works through the idea rationally (4) in order finally to confirm or reject the idea (5) (Dewey 1951: 75 ff.). This sequence was later adopted by psychologists of learning, though in a modified version: Hans Aebli, for example, shortened Dewey's "characteristic process of thinking" to three steps:

definition of the problem, formation of a hypothesis, and verification (Aebli 1985: 99).

Prange adheres far more closely to Dewey's original concept when he compares the learner's situation with that of a researcher and compares the character of learning to that of an experiment. For Dewey, interest stands at the beginning and knowledge is subsequently assigned to skill (Prange 1986: 106), resulting in a conceptualisation that stands in contrast to the Herbartians' methodological point of view. It is precisely in the transfer of this view to the context of teaching that Prange sees John Dewey's lasting merit, in particular in the establishment of an objective relationship between epistemology and the form of teaching in a new way, as it is expressed in *How we think*. Dewey is therefore explicitly applauded for his "orientation towards practical schooling" (ibid.: 104).

Whereas Kerschensteiner saw Dewey's *How we think* in a sharp contrast to Herbartianism, Hans Aebli is quite prepared to discern similarities between Dewey and a "long overdue Herbart renaissance" (Aebli 1985: 24). With regard to Dewey's *How we think*, Aebli argues against an uninspired understanding of visual instruction when he states that sensual impressions are not a sufficient condition for the formation of imagination (ibid.: 86). Had he known more about Dewey (on this, cf. the criticism of Fuchs 2002), Aebli could also have cited Dewey's later publication *Experience and Education*, where this activist aspect of "progressive education" is explicitly criticised (Dewey 1963: 84).

Klaus Prange does not see Herbart and Dewey as being so far apart either when he says that Dewey, as the "inspirer of reform didactics", turns Herbert's basic idea that general interestedness develops from a wish to know, virtually upside down, and insists that interest (as a determinant of behaviour) is a precondition for learning (as a process of clarification) (Prange 1986: 101 f.). However, in its claim that teaching is educational and that learning requires order, the reform-pedagogical modelling of didactics as presented by Dewey – through Kerschensteiner as one of the "matadors of reform pedagogy" – is in fact related to Herbart. Prange sees in it a form of Herbartianism without Herbart. From such a point of view, Dewey's sequence of steps appears to be a continuation of an opportunity for school didactisation at the meta-cognitive level. Other authors, however, emphasise that Dewey's achievement as presented in *How we think* consists of demonstrating the conclusiveness of learning through the experience of doing, i.e., activity. Appeal to the students' intellectual readiness need not be artificially set in motion; thinking, in its instrumental character, rather has a "natural function" (Wilhelm 1967: 356). It is striking in both Aebli's and Prange's versions that the way in which they see Dewey is essentially derived from Kerschensteiner. At least Aebli perceived Dewey through Kerschensteiner (Fuchs 2002). Class activity – as described in *How we think* – is central here. John Dewey also appears in a similar way in conjunction with Kerschensteiner in the *Enzyklopädie Erziehungswissenschaft* whenever criticism of the Herbartian understanding of 'interest' is highlighted (Helmer 1995: 491).

Yet, while for Kerschensteiner motives of pedagogical reform with the Activity school as a defence against the traditional school in the spirit of Herbart clearly stand to the fore, the later view regarding learning and teaching is much more impartial towards Herbartianism. In fact, Dewey's position can be interpreted equally *for* as well as *against* a strongly activity-orientated form of teaching.

However, in all the various views presented here, learning is individualised and merely related to the school. Activity and 'experience' in Dewey's considerations is not simply individual experience but shared and communicated experience. The process of human learning is not confined to the classroom but is reflected in society and in humanity as a whole. Knowledge is based on participation and socialisation, namely as public communication (cf. Dewey 1948: 210 ff.). The school-orientated view which is based solely on *How we think* ignores the fact that Dewey formulated a general theory of learning along Darwinian lines. Thinking in accordance with scientific standards is not only a goal for future scientists, but a source of effective freedom (Westbrook 1991: 169). In a democratic society every person must become his own scientist, as Dewey already explained in *How we think*. This restricted view also results from the fact that an endpoint is assumed for learning. Kerschensteiner provides a good example of how Dewey's cognitive steps can be effortlessly integrated into a Kantian metaphysical concept. Dewey's view that education as the means for the general institutionalisation of intelligent activity holds the key to a never ending orderly renewal of society, as formulated for example in *The Quest for Certainty*, is simply ignored here (Dewey 1929: 201).

7.4 Dewey and the generation of 1968

The presented images of Dewey – the school reformer, the father of the project method and the teaching psychologist – are not to be understood as the only ways of seeing him. There have also been attempts to see Dewey's approach in another light with regard to pedagogy, or at least to make it productive for specific questions. Some works restrict themselves to correcting the picture of Dewey, as for example Fritz Bohnsack's presentation of Dewey's educational thought (Bohnsack 1976). In addition, there have also been attempts to define the concept of activity beyond the context of the classroom, to conceptualise it for didactics (Ebner 1996) or to formulate it as an epistemological process referring to life (Schmitz 1995: 103 ff.). Some authors explicitly point out the democratic goals of Dewey's pedagogy. The *Enzyklopädie Erziehungswissenschaft* also contains a contribution which, with reference to Dewey and Freinet, puts work and further practical life in a relation to education that is adapted to democratic conditions. Besides Dewey's influence on theory, reference is also made to experiments in model schools (Reich 1995: 386 ff.). Nevertheless, these more open views which discuss pragmatism more comprehensively tended to be and still are the exception also for pedagogy. The mainstream is moving within a narrow range (on this point cf. in particular Oelkers 1993).

The basic attitude described above is captured especially in the fact that social aspects of John Dewey's theory of education, in particular as presented in *Democracy and Education*, are simply ignored. Besides the sceptical attitude to pragmatism, which is traditional in German-speaking countries, and attention to the specific problems restricted by school reform, another element is evident as well, namely a general uncertainty as regards John Dewey's political perspective.

The attitude towards the political John Dewey experienced changes accordingly. While in the fifties John Dewey was considered "the leading representative of American leftist radicalism" (!) (Müller 1952: 106), after 1968 in German-speaking countries, he came under suspicion of being in the service of the Establishment. In the lexicon of pedagogy published in 1952, Dewey's instrumentalism is described as 'enigmatic'. According to Dewey, the "economic power of individuals" ought to be broken and "differences in the distribution of property" abolished. In this way, Dewey's freedom approach veiled the potential danger it contained (ibid.: 106). Wolfgang Brezinka also used John Dewey as an example to demonstrate that pedagogical theories can take on "ideological characteristics" (Brezinka 1978: 25). Then, by the same author, Dewey was accused of "naïve empiricism" (Brezinka 1972: 48). As was the case in the days of pedagogical reform after the turn of the century it is political and philosophical reservations which build up and mobilise defences against a view of education as a means of reforming society.

John Dewey experienced exactly the opposite treatment from the Frankfurt School, whose representatives also had a marked influence on pedagogy after 1968. Herbert Marcuse accused Dewey, as the great proponent of method, of approaching or agreeing with positivism. In connection with the positivism controversy, this view also included a politically devaluing characterisation, i.e., a characterisation stabilising the (technological) claim to rule (cf. Dahms 1994: 194). Others again see in pragmatism in the wake of Georg Lukacs the continuation of the irrational and politically fatal philosophy of life. Especially merciless was the treatment meted out to him by Max Horkheimer when, in his *Kritik der instrumentellen Vernunft* (Critique of instrumental reason), he accused Dewey's linking of scientific and social progress of lack of restraint and understanding of how economic, technical, political and ideological factors affect each other (Horkheimer 1967: 77 f). The instrumental approach belittles reason, as Horkheimer brands this American perspective, which is especially critical towards German philosophy – a judgement that he made without a thorough examination of pragmatism (Dahms 1994: 225). From left to right, John Dewey's instrumentalism and idea of social progress was held to be naïve, irrational, or contrary to reason, but then again also technocratic and too credulous of science. Despite a changed political and cultural context, even after 1968 Dewey failed to shake off the stigma of being an instrumentalist and utilitarian indifferent to social emancipation. He was thus on the 'wrong' side in the positivism controversy, which defined the position of German theory in the humanities.

The quite arbitrarily sought distance which was established by protagonists who had themselves grown up in a humanistic tradition was seldom questioned. Even critical pedagogues therefore saw John Dewey initially as the antithesis of the Critical Theory and closely connected with positivism, or even functionalism. Only few German authors, like Theodor Wilhelm, decided to make a more benevolent interpretation. In his essay *"Pragmatische Pädagogik"*, written in 1975, Wilhelm sees in the "coordination of the teaching style of the school and non-school institutions in a democracy" a principle of social reform and at the same time a modern communication of Dewey's point of view (Wilhelm 1975: 198). Of course, at the same time this was to provide a plausible alternative to the humanistic pedagogical tradition on the one hand, and to socialist pedagogy on the other.

If the last comments referred to a more comprehensive philosophical and political discussion, for pedagogy after 1968 we can see a marked preference and orientation towards concrete school reform. In this context, it was quite imaginable that the avoidance of pragmatism could be softened, as is proved by the various borrowings from the project idea. However, there is hardly any indication of an extensive examination of John Dewey's *Democracy and Education* (Dewey 1997) in more recent debates either. This work in particular could have given grounds for subjecting pedagogical theory to critical examination (cf. Oelkers 2000).

In his foreword to the first German edition of *Democracy and Education*, which he translated in 1930, Erich Hylla could not suppress a note concerning his amazement that this fundamental work had not been translated earlier. This applied in particular because many of Dewey's ideas were not new in Germany since, after all, they were introduced by Kerschensteiner – albeit reflected in "quite his own

132

way" (Hylla 1949: 8). Especially because the mutual relationship between the idea of a democratic society and the structure and function of the education system was brought out so sharply, the presentation could be expected to receive special attention in Germany (ibid.: 8). Hylla was mistaken in this, as is indicated by Jürgen Oelkers' foreword to the new 1993 edition (Oelkers 1993).

7.5 Conclusions

If we consider the three views presented here, it is striking to note that Dewey's work was not perceived in its essence. What was and remained dominant was a reform-pedagogical view as substantiated by Kerschensteiner already at the beginning of the century. Activity became work, the right to democracy in school became a working community, pragmatic problem solving and learning from experience became an individual gradation of a cognitive learning sequence. John Dewey as a school reformer, as the father of the project method, and as teaching psychologist are figures connected with the question of reorganising schools without having to include political options in the process. Such a limited view was additionally favoured by the fact that Dewey's political project was perceived as dangerous to the state, doubtful and unrealistic.

This leads one to ask whether Dewey's work can be so easily misunderstood, whether his idea of democracy and the relationship between education and democracy is so unclear, or whether the theory prevailing in German-speaking countries left no alternative interpretation. Here it could certainly be objected that the elucidation of democracy is not very well developed in Dewey's work. Democracy appears as a way of life or as an idea which, however, does not go into much detail as regards institutional conditions and democratic processes. The ideal of a co-operative experimental or communication society was controversial in America itself as well, as the debate with Walter Lippmann and *The Public and its Problems* (Dewey 1927) shows. Nevertheless, on the basis of what has been said above, the answer is quite clear. It was the lack of readiness to recognise the philosophical foundations on which education is based and to examine them impartially which must be made responsible for taking political aspects out of John Dewey's view of education. Thought which refers to science and at the same time wants to overcome dualisms was repugnant to those who sought to avoid technological and economic rationalism. On the other hand, the explicit relationship to democracy was too progressive for the others. *Not* to involve pedagogy in a contrast between the humanities and science, or to offer a "scientific style of thought" for education (Wilhelm 1975: 154) and to go so far as to offer it as the foundation for social reform must have irritated the local protagonists of theoretical discussion.

The approach which took an integrated view of philosophy, education and social reform also met with little sympathy. Dewey's emphasis of the relationship between democracy and education refers also, however not exclusively, to the school but also to the on-going education of the committed citizen (Campbell 1995: 222). The democratic society that Dewey envisaged was a society founded on experience which is based on the model of the impartial researcher (cf. Rust 1996: 233). "Experimental empiricism" (Suhr 1994) understands ideas and activities as elements in a never-ending process which flourish and grow best in a sphere of unlimited opportunity (Neubert 1998: 101). Democracy and science are not only the conditions for an experience which has educational effects, they are not only teachers but also the goal of education. It is exactly this circularity of education, science and democracy that struck German minds as being unusual, especially if education as a process and a goal aims at the same time at education again (cf. Oelkers 2000). What is more, this view did not much suit a pedagogy which saw itself as drawing a line against tradition. This is why Dewey was turned into a child-centred reform pedagogue or, in the final analysis, into an instrumentalist, in order to draw the line between him and humanistic pedagogy, i.e., in the service of the prevailing system.

However, it was John Dewey's aim to extend the scientific method – i.e., learning in the sense of forming hypotheses and testing them experimentally – to all areas of life. Dewey's idea of education is far less strongly bound to an institution than the school reformers

134

would have liked. It is here that a further motive for the lack of under-standing for Dewey's reform project can be seen: Dewey tended to resolve and to dynamise dualisms. The either-or attitude expresses a hidebound style of life as can be found, for example, in the contrast between school and life. Instead, Dewey pleads for learning in and out of school and in democracy because this contributes best "to freeing intelligence for growth, and therefore education should be democratic" (Garrison 1999: 372). Since external authority is repudiated, education must endeavour to provide good habits for a society which requires improvement. What is needed is a critical attitude to facts and value judgements. However, this attitude must not be the privilege of an elite, but should be learned by everyone. Therefore, this is possible only in a democracy since all individuals are to be made capable of continuing their education in this way (Putnam and Putnam 1999: 14).

Disregard for his references to sciences and democracy turned John Dewey into a school pedagogue who discovered that he had a soft heart for children. It is only when pedagogues make the effort of seeing Dewey in a 'non-pedagogical' light that we can expect some-thing new to be learned.

8. Education as Self-guidance – Max Weber's Alternative to Liberal Education

At the beginning of the 20th century, sociology and pedagogy became established as scientific disciplines. In this chapter, the differences between these two disciplines will be exemplified by means of a discussion of two influential representatives, Max Weber and Georg Kerschensteiner, in relation to the topics of education and vocation.

*In his historically and culturally comparative religious studies and his sociology of domination, Weber dealt with the role of vocation and consequently also with educational concerns. Kerschensteiner, on the other hand, based his educational theory on a humanistic-psychological approach in which an individual's vocation (*vocatio*) and social requirements should be brought together.*

Two recurring topics in Robert Musil's outstanding novel *The Man Without Qualities* are the secularisation of the present time and the excess of rationalism and quantification. Furthermore, it is claimed that there are no more human beings in Germany, but only professions (Musil 2003: 200). This terminology could have been borrowed directly from Max Weber's analyses at that time, and as a former student of philosophy and psychology, Musil knew the debates on cultural and social criticism very well indeed. Furthermore, some of the characters in the novel can easily be identified as well-known figures of the time. For example, there is the novel character of a renowned professor of pedagogy who is strikingly redolent of Georg Kerschensteiner (Geissler 1996: 21) and whose conception of education is portrayed with subtle irony (Musil 2003: 949 f.).

At the beginning of the 20th century, the tradition of education and culture came to be questioned since it no longer seemed to be followed in a society increasingly oriented towards work and profession(s). In addition, education and culture seemed no longer directly linked to economic wealth. The words of the Austrian philosopher

Friedrich Jodl at the opening of the centre for national education (*Volksbildungshaus*) of the Vienna association for national education (*Volksbildungsverein*) in 1909 refer to these changing social circumstances. According to Jodl, lack of education could be diagnosed just as often among the members of the so-called intellectual bourgeoisie as in the uneducated classes. He also argued that it was possible to be a researcher and specialist in a certain subarea, yet still be uneducated, or, contrariwise, to know relatively little and still be highly educated (Jodl 1909: 17).

Both pedagogy and sociology were concerned with the question of a broadened understanding of education and with the criticism of a culture-based class conceit. In what follows, Max Weber's sociological approach and Georg Kerschensteiner's pedagogical approach to education and vocation will be contrasted.

8.1 Max Weber and Georg Kerschensteiner

Both Weber as a sociologist and Kerschensteiner as a pedagogue were influential and even prominent in their respective discipline and political field, yet they had little to do with each other. On the whole, they have both had a high international reputation in their disciplines and have been considered classics until today.

Max Weber (1864-1920) was appointed a professor of economics at the University of Heidelberg in 1897. After this appointment, he made a name for himself with his 'Protestantism thesis' and his studies in sociology of religion. He was a co-founder of the German Society for Sociology in 1909. His unfinished work *Economy and Society*, published posthumously in 1922, substantiated the claim of sociology as an independent academic discipline. During the First World War, Weber did not shy away from speaking out on current affairs – with increasing response from the public – and since 1918 he was a dedicated member of the German Democratic Party. In 1919, after a short period of teaching in Vienna, he was appointed to a professorship in Munich. He died in Munich in 1920.

Georg Kerschensteiner (1854-1932) was a teacher of mathematics and physics at various grammar schools in Bavaria before he was appointed as a schools inspector in Munich in 1895. In this position, he implemented reforms on every level of the educational system, and through his travels and lectures he gained international reputation as a reform pedagogue. He was a member of the German Diet from 1912 to 1919 and a long-time member of the German Democratic Party, just like Weber. In 1918 he was appointed a professor of pedagogy at the University of Munich, a position he held until his death. In 1920 he participated at the German *Reichsschulkonferenz* as a prominent speaker. He consolidated his position within the academic discipline of pedagogy with numerous high-circulation publications on a range of topics such as civic education, character building, the activity school, organisation and value of education in natural sciences, and not least as the author of a comprehensive theory of education.

One obvious reason for the comparison of the two scholars can be found in their joint participation at a lecture series at the end of the First World War. According to Kerschensteiner, this series of lectures was organised in 1918 by the general students' committee of the University of Munich. Kerschensteiner's lecture was on "Education as a vocation" (Kerschensteiner 1949: 14), while Weber's two lectures were on "Science as a vocation" and "Politics as a vocation".

Neither of the two scholars left a trace in the respective other's work. Especially Kerschensteiner's lack of consideration of Weber, even in his extensive correspondence with Eduard Spranger, the much adored younger professor of pedagogy with whom no topic seemed too marginal to be discussed, is indeed surprising. Kerschensteiner was interested in the work of many contemporary social scientists, both well known and lesser known ones in Germany, from John Dewey to representatives of psychology, pedagogy and sociology. Like Weber, he was particularly interested in leading figures like Heinrich Rickert and Georg Simmel, with whom he corresponded frequently.

Despite their apparent mutual disregard there are a number of intellectual similarities between Weber and Kerschensteiner. Interpretation and comprehension play a central role for both, and consequently there a parallels in their methodological approaches. Furthermore, they both draw on a naturalistic positivism (cf. Tenbruck 1999: 26 f. on Weber). Like Weber, Kerschensteiner used a culture-based typology to formulate scientific issues (cf. Gerhardt 2001: 483), which he had clearly adopted from his younger colleague Eduard Spranger. In this typology, which Spranger had extensively developed in his *Lebensformen* (cf. Chapter 9), there is a theoretic man next to an economic, aesthetic, social and religious man, as well as a (political) man of power (Spranger 1922). However, it is little surprising that Weber did not refer to pedagogues and was already involved in numerous arguments and discussions with colleagues from his own field of research (ibid.: 893 f.).

Kerschensteiner and Weber did not only have certain scientific points of reference and modernisation concerns in common, but they also shared similar political views. This was manifest in their political commitment as well as in their shared high esteem for Friedrich Naumann, the founder of the German Democratic Party (Radkau 2005: 603; Kerschensteiner 1982a: 137).

8.2 Education and vocation as pedagogical topics: Kerschensteiner and Spranger

The social change at the beginning of the 20th century was accompanied by requests for modernisation by the social elite. These requests extended also to the educational system, and reforms were carried out in the elementary school, in adult education and in particular in vocational education. Georg Kerschensteiner thoroughly reorganised the formerly Herbartian schools of Munich, and he furthermore created a new school type, i.e., the vocational continuation school. This new school followed directly after the period of compulsory schooling and was open to both sexes. It was the introduction of this school type that established Kerschensteiner's reputation as the founder of the vocational school.

The activity school was a further main concern of Kerschen-steiner's. This particular school type was meant to take the latest psychological findings into account and to prepare children and youths for the requirements of the world of work (cf. Chapter 5). In addition, he aimed to establish a new understanding of education in which vocational education was an essential component of cultural education and where manual work and activity became characteristic traits of the educational process (Kerschensteiner 1926).

Pedagogy as a new academic discipline was based on an educational concept that was more open to vocational needs than the neo-humanistic approach of the 19th century had been. Important preparatory work had been done by Eduard Spranger in his book on Humboldt (Spranger 1936), where he aimed to revive the German ideal of education by calling for a connection to German Idealism and classical literature as well as to contemporary psychology and ethics (Spranger 1936: VI). According to Spranger, education was truly the "inner formation of man", and since the spirit of the present had become more realistic, education had to be "imbued by this realistic spirit" (Spranger 1936: 495). However, he substantiated this concept of inner formation only much later in his main work *Lebensformen* by developing a psychology based on the Humanities and outside the mainstream.

Supplemented by ethics, educational theory in the Humanities thus gained a new profile. Kerschensteiner added a political dimension to this new conception by pointing out that the culture of a state did not only depend on every citizen's ability to meet the demands of his or her profession (Kerschensteiner 1912b: 258) but also by everyone's contribution to a homogeneous 'culture state' (ibid.: 295). The ability to make such a contribution had to be acquired through civic education.

The apparent contrast between general and vocational education had been eased already in Kerschensteiner's first pedagogical publications where he characterised vocational education as an integral component in the process of becoming truly human, an argumentation he based on Goethe, who had considered true education to be guaranteed only through practical work and, consequently, vocational education (Kerschensteiner 1910b: 30 ff.). Spranger, too, endorsed the view that the path to higher general education could only lead via vocation (Spranger 1925a: 162). However, even this seemingly unconditional orientation towards vocation cannot hide the fact that pedagogues found it difficult to take the real developments in the world of work into consideration (Stratmann 1999a).

For Kerschensteiner, his contemporary pedagogues and German classicism were not the only points of reference. He was also drawn to Georg Simmel's 'philosophy of life' (*Lebensphilosophie*), in particular as presented in Simmel's publications on Goethe – a publication which was dedicated to Weber's wife Marianne – and Rembrandt (Simmel 1913, 1916). From 1917 onwards, Kerschensteiner's educational theory was based on Spranger's typology-based psychology, Simmel's contrast of life and form (cf. Chapter 9), and Rickert's value theory (Gonon 1992: 240).

8.3 Vocation and education as sociological topics

At the first and second German sociology congress (Frankfurt on the Main in 1910, and Berlin in 1912), vocation and education featured as important topics. At the opening of the second meeting, Max Weber's younger brother Alfred gave a lecture on the sociological concept of culture, in which individualisation was conceived as inner rationalisation and external mechanisation (Weber 1912: 8). At the first congress, Georg Simmel and Ferdinand Tönnies had spoken on the aims of sociology, and Max Weber had argued that the development of associations and societies was affected by objectification and professionalism (*Berufsmenschentum*) (Weber 1911: 56). Werner Sombart gave a lecture on the topic of "technology and culture", in which he discussed the question of how even personal culture is based on technology (Sombart 1911: 66).

At first sight, Weber dealt only little with questions of education and much more with the emergence of what he called 'the professional man' (*Berufsmenschentum*), for example, in his studies in sociology of religion. He claimed that the vocations that had developed in ascetic Protestantism had a much higher methodical potential for rationalisation than all other religions (Weber 1985: 379). In his writings he repeatedly discussed the influence of certain educational attainments on the development of class distinctions (Weber 1998: 195) and, more generally, the averseness of the old-established German educational aristocracy to capitalism and modernisation (Weber 1998a: 224). In historically elaborate analyses he argued that such an educational aristocracy superseded the traditional blood aristocracy in the course of a so-called Pharisaic-gentrified development (Weber 2005: 791). From today's perspective, this explicit connection of educational opportunities and social power relations is a typically sociological approach. Moreover, Weber sometimes seemed inflamed with rage in his political comments, for example in his article on the Prussian electoral law where he gave his opinion on the endeavours to grant privileged treatment at elections to the so-called educated classes, i.e. the holders of educational diplomas. He criticised rather bluntly that "the products of the various examination factories" had politically failed and that the holders of such diplomas constituted the least qualified social stratum in Germany. The lack of political judgement, in particular with regard to the war among teachers in academia, had assumed alarming proportions, and the knowledge acquired at universities did not in the least qualify for political judgement. In his view, the alleged supremacy of the educated elite was nothing more than a ridiculous preconception because every businessman, every employee and every worker, in short: every 'modern' participant in the economic market was better able to judge the political realities of the day than the academic diploma holders (Weber 1984: 230 ff.).

Apart from this characteristically sociological approach with its firm political stand – which was continued in Pierre Bourdieu's studies on the sociology of education and his notion of 'habitus' – Weber took up a critical stance on the traditional German concept of education. It is to this aspect of Weber's work we now turn.

8.4 Weber's understanding of education between professionalism and life reform

Some of Weber's writings emphasise the influence of education on the formation of a capitalistic attitude (cf. Lenhart 1998: 3 ff.). Moreover, Ringer finds a clearly identifiable understanding of education in Weber's intellectual biography, namely an understanding that stands in contrast to the classical Humboltian ideal of the educated man. For Weber, the orientation to antiquity, cultivation and self-perfection is of little importance compared to professional training and intellectual integrity (Ringer 2004: 225 ff.).

Further points of interest in Weber's work are his studies in sociology of religion, for example regarding Confucianism and Taoism in China. According to Zymek, the Chinese education for civil servants showed obvious parallels to the Prussian model. The development of charisma, the training in specialised skills and knowledge and the cultivation of a conduct of life based on social standing are conceived of as transferable to other contexts, and even as universally valid (Zymek 2000: 141). The description of the Confucian gentleman and his virtue based on universalism, i.e., self-perfection, reads like a criticism of the traditional Prussian-German educational ideal. According to Weber, the idea of being a gentleman as an end in itself rather than a tool was inconsistent with the ideal of usefulness and the socially oriented platonic ideal, and was furthermore completely incompatible with the concept of vocation of ascetic Protestantism (Weber 1988d: 449). Such a conduct of life resulted in a society unable to understand modern economic professionalism and the spirit of capitalism (Weber 1988d: 534). Flitner argues that Weber had rather emphasised the importance of the youth's self-education for "sober moral respectability through self-government in collectives" (Flitner 2001: 280). This reform-pedagogic trait was no coincidence. Since the turn of the century, reform pedagogy had been part of an all-embracing movement that could be felt in all social spheres. This movement constituted a sort of romantic revolt against urbanisation and industrialisation. Within this movement, life reform was a kind of programme that was

144

primarily followed by the younger generation. It included 'natural education', hiking in the countryside, collective experiences, nudism, a balanced diet and artistic creation, as well as school reform and the creation of one's own lifestyle, including one's own philosophy of life. These ideas were put into action in various locations and meeting places, for example, on the Monte Verità in Ascona, Switzerland. Weber had always been attracted to the Monte Verità movement, although without giving preference to the corresponding alternative conduct of life (Rossi 1988: 210 f.). Weber's ambivalent relation to educational traditions is also to be seen in connection with the need to establish a balance between professionalism and life reform (Myers 2002: 196). In what follows, Weber's later-years views on vocation and education will be presented, i.e. from the perspective of his sociology of domination. Weber's sociology of religion and his sociology of domination are usually treated separately from each other, yet from a government theoretical perspective the two approaches lend themselves to a combination (cf. Foucault 1991: 87 ff.). There are indeed no insurmountable differences between an individual conduct of life based on asceticism and vocation – as set forth in his Protestantism thesis –, Weber's types of legitimate domination, and the in-between concept of self-government as described in his work *Economy and Society* (cf. Boldt 2001). Quite to the contrary, these represent all different facets of the art of governing: self-government, economic government and social government (cf. Szakolczai 1998: 263 ff.). The linking element between the sociology of domination and the sociology of religion is charisma (Radkau 2005: 600), because charisma is all about individual and social mutability based on both rationalisation as well as enchantment (cf. Hanke 2001: 46).

8.5 Weber's and Kerschensteiner's lectures on the topic of 'vocation' in Munich

The titles of the three lectures – "Education as a vocation" (Kerschensteiner), "Science as a vocation" and "Politics as a vocation" (Weber)

– might have led students to believe that they would be informed about the job opportunities opened up by their subjects of study. However, anyone attending the lectures with this expectation was surely disappointed. Both Weber and Kerschensteiner were rather bad occupational counsellors and addressed the issues of future job prospects and labour-market conditions only marginally. They even advised against, rather than recommended, the vocations they presented. Both speakers used academic professions as the bases of their comments and analyses.

All three lectures with their recapitulation of scientific and political views can be considered to have created a sense of identity for the involved disciplines. In "Science as a vocation" and "Politics as a vocation", Weber recapitulated fundamental turning points in his own theoretical development and outlined his methodological procedure, his sociology of domination and his stance on modernity and politics. Given the big response with which his lectures met it seems justified to speak of them as of two gems with ever new facets.

While the immediate reaction to the lectures was characterised by a disappointment of audience expectations, the long-term effect was very favourable. The later professor of philosophy Karl Löwith – still a student at the time of the lectures – was so impressed by the lecture "Science as a vocation" that in his biography he described its effect as staggering, even as a revelation. In his view, Weber had not taken any cheap short-cuts but had instead torn down "the mist of desirability"; he had not so much talked of the rather too fashionable notion of 'character building' but had demonstrated to have 'education and character' himself – a comment that was as admiring of Weber as it was critical of other pedagogues of the time (Löwith 1989: 16 f.). He considered the second lecture, "Politics as a vocation", to lack verve in comparison (ibid.: 17).

Kerschensteiner's lecture in the same series, entitled "Education as a vocation", was later revised and – as Kerschensteiner put it – improved and was published in 1921 under the title *Die Seele des Erziehers und das Problem der Lehrerbildung* ("The educator's soul and the problem of teacher training"). The ideas put forth in this publication came to be considered an effective basis for teacher training. They represent the pedagogical thinking of the later-year Kerschen-

146

steiner, who had moved away from his positivistic and pragmatic beginnings (Wilhelm 1957). Little is known of the immediate effect of the lecture, but Kerschensteiner's granddaughter and biographer claims that this work was "the most beautiful reflection of his own soul", and that he had pictured "the essence of all pedagogic action" with the methodology of Spranger and the objectives formulated by Weber (Fernau-Kerschensteiner 1954: 123).

In the following passages, the central ideas in Kerschensteiner's and Weber's lectures will be compared. For the sake of argument I will not adhere to the chronology of the lectures but will instead start with Weber's "Politics as a vocation", followed by an analysis of the figure of the teacher and educator as presented in Kerschensteiner's *The educator's soul and the problem of teacher training*, and, finally, Weber's lecture "Science as a vocation".

8.6 Politics as a vocation

Weber wrote this lecture at a time when he was publicly involved with politics and supported the idea of a strong, but democratically legitimated political leader figure (Mommsen 1975: 440). Beyond all political topicalities of the day he wanted to emphasise the importance of political activity in every individual's conduct of life by portraying it as self-dependent, responsible leadership activity (Weber 1988: 505). He limited this activity to political associations and the state and, with reference to Trotzki, he defined the state as the entity that possesses the monopoly on legitimate violence. This includes, however, that the state may delegate this monopoly to selected actors within the state. In this connection he also mentioned the three pure types of legitimate domination and their bearers as outlined in his *Sociology of domination*: (1) the traditional domination of the patriarch and the patrimonial ruler, (2) charismatic domination based on extraordinary conferment, as in the case of heroes, warlords, prophets and demagogues, and finally (3) legal domination, that is, factual 'competence' based on legal articles and rationally created rules, exercised by the modern civic servants (ibid.: 507). The modern state is thus characterised as a domain that is based on obedience and whose legitimacy of the monopoly of violence also places the material resources in the hands of the leaders.

According to Weber, the diversity of political phenomena includes both additional and full time activities. He repeatedly pointed out that politics developed into a business in which it was necessary to distinguish between political and topic-related activities and which furthermore necessitated explicit training in the struggle for political power. The political system as a sphere of interests of political parties had bred a number of professions, not only the civil servant but also the advocate and the journalist. The latter two both argue publicly and use words to fight for their interests. In contrast to these two professions, the trained civic servant had to act in a responsible, disciplined and impartial way.

In Weber's sociology of domination and in his political comments, questions of leadership are much more central than the politician's professional development. In the lecture at hand he also dealt with the question of what qualities should be taken as the basis for the election of political leaders, and he mainly stressed the qualities of will and of speech.

As has been the case with other thinkers too, Weber used the USA as a point of reference for the profile of politics as a vocation (cf. Offe 2004). He pointed out that the figure of the 'boss' had appeared in the USA, characterised as a politically capitalistic entrepreneur with hardly any political principles, who was catching votes and – if successful – could hand out formidable sinecures. In contrast, professional politicians in Germany had much less responsibility and power, since theirs was a parliamentary and guild-based political system. It can be read as an indication of hope when he added that perhaps a reorganisation was taking place, one that favoured a plebiscite machinery and a corresponding leadership role. For Weber, the conditions for politics as a vocation are summed up in the alternative between a machine-like leadership democracy on the one hand, and leader-less democracy with professional politicians without vocation, which would amount to a "reign of the coterie", on the other (ibid.:

148

544). He therefore concluded that the only political professions available were journalism and party-based officialdom.

Weber then continued with a focus on the ethical dimensions and qualities necessary for political activity. He named three essential qualities: passion, responsibility and a sense of proportion. Passion was needed for a true commitment to politics, yet passion had to be paired with responsibility. Enough distance to people and political matters, i.e. a sense of proportion, made the difference between the true politician and the agitated political debutant. This remark can easily be read as an allusion to the 'revolutionary' events in Munich. Conceitedness was considered a trade disease, and egomania instead of objectivity a sin against the "holy ghost of politics as a vocation". No matter whether a politician was committed to progress or tradition, faith was always of the essence, and the ethos of politics had to be directed to the matter at hand. Political activity as understood by Weber did not only mean to act according to ethos, but also with a sense of responsibility, meaning that politicians had to answer for the predictable results of their actions. Consequently, the problem of politics was that in order to reach positive ends, questionable means and undesired consequences sometimes had to be accepted. Weber called all those "political infants" who did not accept this problem as a matter of fact, and he even went so far as to explicitly name the catholic pedagogue and pacifist Friedrich W. Foerster in this connection (ibid.: 554). Weber claimed that no one who wanted to be a professional politician could escape such ethical paradoxes, and yet the politicians who acted only according to ethos could not cope with the consequences of their actions and would lapse into philistinism or escapism. In order to reach the politically possible, one had to dare the impossible; however, this was not given to just anyone but required the abilities of a leader, even of a hero.

8.7 Professional politicians without a profession – Weber's paradox of the non-learnable vocation

Weber did not only describe paradoxes, but his own account of education and vocation was paradoxical itself. To start with, from the perspective of his sociology of domination, politics is a matter of leadership. From among a group of people aspiring leadership, a charismatic leader should eventually arise. Ultimately, the determining factor for politics as a vocation is an unexplained concept of charisma, and to be a politician is consequently a calling rather than a profession. Nevertheless, Weber sees a great danger in dilettantism and irresponsibility, culminating in a 'carnivalisation' of politics. Dilettantism is not primarily the result of a lack of expertise but a question of an ethical attitude and of social action. According to Weber, intellectuals and men of letters are particularly prone to dilettantism because they tend to give too little thought to the results of their actions.

A professionalisation – in a contemporary understanding of the term – of politics was therefore deemed necessary for the sake of leadership and a realistic anticipation of the results of political actions. The capitalisation and operationalisation of politics, in short: political entrepreneurship, was seen as no hindrance to such a professionalisation, but rather as an advantage. Weber claimed that a professionalisation of politics was best achieved if well-meaning men of letters, scholars and scientists kept out of politics – though he clearly made an exception for himself. Journalists and advocates, however, were to be judged differently, and better yet would be a charismatic entrepreneur who would 'arise', as it were, and assume leadership over the administration officers.

Paradoxically, a politician's quality is thus primarily a calling and does not depend on professional education, yet Weber still demanded that politicians needed to be taught specific attitudes. In particular, political action should orient itself towards the expected consequences. According to Weber, pure Kantian ethicists had no business in politics. The humanistic culture and traditional educational ideals were inapt for the paradox requirements of politics. Violence, fighting, war and special interest groups who put up with dishonesty in order to reach their aims are things which can hardly be learned at school or on educational journeys. What is needed is self-education of specific qualities, always in relation to the ever-changing external circumstances; we will come back to these qualities later on.

8.8 Education as a vocation

Kerschensteiner starts his explanations on education as a vocation with a reference to personalities who have had a great impact on the education of the German people, in particular Fichte, Goethe and Bismarck. As exemplary figures they have influenced many of their fellow countrymen, in the sense of enabling them to rise to a higher self (Kerschensteiner 1949: 23). And yet, Kerschensteiner considers 'real' educators to be individuals like Pestalozzi, whose unique and practically oriented dispositions are determined by pedagogical motives. However, since even Pestalozzi had certain shortcomings in his role as practical educator, and since there are different facets of education, the nature of pedagogical action cannot be determined through a consideration of Pestalozzi and Pestalozzi-like figures alone.

Regarding pedagogical motives Kerschensteiner mentions the realisation of values in oneself and others, with altruism as the decisive criterion. He therefore excludes the training of craftsmen and civil servants as well as the scientific work of educational philosophers and experimental pedagogues from his analysis of pedagogical action.

According to Kerschensteiner, an educator needs to perceive the possibilities of those entrusted to him for a realisation of values in them to be possible. The educator matches a social type of man because he does not campaign for himself or for some abstract cause, but all his activities are geared to other people, i.e., to the pupils. As someone rooted in a social life form, the educator needs to perceive whether his pupils' potential and abilities lie in handicraft or in intellectual work. Kerschensteiner then distinguishes between different types of man: a theoretic, religious, social and an economic man, and furthermore a man of imagination as well as a man of power. This typology clearly refers to Spranger's psychology based on the Humanities, which in turn had developed out of the tradition of Dilthey. Kerschensteiner holds Spranger's psychology in high esteem – particularly because it relates to various cultural systems – and claims that the path to "pure humanity" leads via fields of activity "to which we have an inner calling" (ibid.: 35).

Pedagogues are of the social type of man; this becomes clear from Kerschensteiner's treatment of his pedagogical hero Pestalozzi and his love for mankind. Pestalozzi stands out as an educator not due to pedagogical knowledge and scholarliness but due to humbleness and pedagogical love. Based on this understanding of pedagogical quality, it is easy for Kerschensteiner to polemicise against those who think that anyone could work as a teacher if they merely studied pedagogy, psychology and teaching methods. He argues that there is no infallible method, and even his great example Pestalozzi had failed in the attempt to mechanise education and pedagogy in this manner.

Kerschensteiner then goes on to compare the educator to the man of imagination, since the latter too is a creator who loves his (intellectual) work. By perceiving children as the future bearers of his values, i.e. the values of humanity, the creative educator loves his children, the more so as he shapes a substance that is in fact his own. Similar to the religious type of man, an educator is concerned with other peoples' souls, but in contrast to priests or religion education teachers he does not merely aim for religious values, and in contrast to physicians and nurses he does not primarily attend to physical health care. Furthermore, the educator also differs from the teacher in adult education, because the latter is not concerned with the development of his pupils' personalities. The educator, however, has to tune in to the unique personality of each and every of his pupils. By doing this, he also renders a service to society as a whole, because the fostering of ethical and moral development in individuals results in the same development in society. Consequently, the educator is seen as a basic social type with the innate ability to influence immature individuals in such a way as to enable them to become bearers of timeless values in accordance with their respective dispositions. Moreover, the educator finds satisfaction in the performance of this very activity (ibid.: 54).

After this discussion of the educator's role from a humanistic perspective based on a psychological-ethical typology, Kerschensteiner proceeds to a more concrete analysis. He asks what qualities an educator needs to possess, and suggests the following indispensable qualities for educational activity – i.e. character building – to be successful: empathy, power of observation, diagnostic capability, willpower and excitability of the mind. Quasi as a bonus he mentions a sense of humour and the pursuit of perfection (ibid:. 88).

Kerschensteiner relates these considerations to the question whether a school teacher could be an educator. He argues that the conditions of the time require a teacher not only to impart knowledge but to act as an educator. It is important in this respect to distinguish between the attitude towards the content to be imparted on the one hand, and the personal attitude vis-à-vis the pupils on the other. In contrast to opinions voiced in the pedagogical literature, Kerschensteiner claims that the elementary teacher differs both from the scientist and from the artist: while the scientist is oriented towards the objective gain of knowledge and the artist is concerned with subjective creation, the elementary teacher's basic attitude has to be "his love for the pupil as the future bearer of values". This love for the pupil as a primary requisite is linked to a love for the educational task itself, but not to an academic research interest. In other words, being a teacher requires an inner calling. A teacher's love and dedication is rewarded simply by its effect on the pupils' spiritual and emotional development.

A further, more hands-on and rational requirement is added to these demands on teachers, namely classroom management. This means that apart from knowledge transfer, teachers always also have to keep an eye on the immediate effect of their actions in the classroom (ibid:. 103). In addition, Kerschensteiner names the ability to experience values as a third special requirement of teachers. These three requirements need to be added to the above mentioned qualities which an educator needs to possess.

At the end of his lecture, Kerschensteiner examines the consequences of his analysis for teacher training. He succinctly states that there is no pedagogical educational institution that bases the formation of teachers and educators on such a social spirit. In the existing institutions for teacher training, a new spirit uniting social, religious and national values therefore needs to be established. For the sake of moral and ethical development, the fostering of these values has to be understood as an important mission (ibid:. 126 f.). To back up his argumentation he refers not only to appropriate examples in England and in the USA, but also to Sombart and the Social Democrats.

In agreement with Spranger and his averseness to the so-called 'encyclopaedianism', Kerschensteiner asserts that teacher training is not to be geared towards an uncomprehending piling up of knowledge and skills, but towards intellectual education and the ability to experience values. Like Spranger, he considers these requirements for the time being to be best met in a pedagogic academy because the universities focus too much on specialisation and technology. As long as the spirit of teachers and learners at universities did not change, they could not be considered the most adequate institutions for the education and training of elementary teachers, since the ultimate achievement of the social life form in the ideal of the teacher and educator could be found in Pestalozzi, and not in Kant or Goethe (ibid.: 155).

8.9 The educator as a gifted shaper of souls – Kerschensteiner's paradox of the non-learnable vocation

It is indeed a rather vague purpose statement to say that the altruistic ambition of education is "to develop values in pupils". This purpose is to be seen in the context of a Kantian-Platonic concept in which a higher self is tied to an ideal state and national guidelines. From a contemporary perspective such an ideology appears truly wrongheaded, but this is not our focus of attention here (cf. Chapter 6). A pedagogue is a social type of man with the basic motive of pedagogical love and the intention to shape the personalities of those entrusted to him. Furthermore, whoever aims to shape the pupils' personalities needs to perceive their potential. Apart from giving love to the pupils, a pedagogue needs an inner calling that enables him to manage the class and to enable them to experience values. One such value that Kerschensteiner attached much importance to is objectivity.

Kerschensteiner furthermore stressed the importance of the pedagogue's task by pointing out that through the ethical and moral development of individuals, the same development happened in society as a whole. He therefore demanded that the pedagogues' activities were not restricted to the immediate tasks in the classroom, but that they acted as educators of individuals as well as of the nation. As a consequence, a reform of the educational institutions was necessary in order for the nation's educators to be trained in the social spirit.

It is exactly this ability to educate which cannot be learned but is considered a gift. In addition, Kerschensteiner claimed that only the social type of man could be an educator with a true calling. The educator is thus portrayed as a modern minister and shaper of souls. Kerschensteiner's account, too, is therefore paradoxical, since he based education as a vocation on a single specific talent and a non-learnable ethical attitude, i.e. altruism, yet at the same time he required educators to be pedagogically trained.

8.10 Science as a vocation

Both Weber's lecture on politics as a vocation and Kerschensteiner's lecture on the teacher as an educator are based on a concept of vocation that is much more related to a calling than to a trainable profession. In the lecture "Science as a vocation", Weber mentioned a number of additional factors, resulting in a more concrete concept of vocation and education. In this lecture he again used the USA as a point of reference to show the peculiarities of the German system and to identify possible directions for future development. The first part of his explanations was dedicated to a description of the social and institutional conditions of science as a vocation. In Germany, a scientific career starts with a private lectureship, while the first post in the USA is an assistantship. He argued that in Germany it was rather risky to start an academic career without the necessary funds; in the USA, in contrast, there was a bureaucratic system that paid young men a salary – although a moderate one – from the very beginning. Unlike in Germany, however, if an assistant's performance did not meet his employer's expectations, he could be dismissed. For German universities he observed the dilemma of having to decide whether only a limited number of private lecturers should be promoted to professor, i.e. just enough to supply the necessary teaching staff, or whether the criterion for this promotion should be the lecturers' aptitude.

Weber made the point that the German universities developed towards the American system – just like everyday life which also underwent an Americanisation. Large medical and natural science institutes had become state-capitalistic enterprises with conditions of work like in capitalistic companies. An example would be the dependency on the director of the institute, or the big gap between full professors and the rest of the institute's faculty. On the other hand, he thought that there were unquestionable technical advantages, like in all enterprises that were capitalistic and bureaucratic at the same time (Weber 1988c: 585).

Weber had experienced the influence of pure chance on his own academic career. This influence of chance on the recruitment process could be seen in the fact that there were many who did not get a position reflecting their aptitude. Weber considered the dominance of chance over competence to be due to the laws that govern the (human) interaction between institutions like ministries and faculties. Since the recruitment process was based on collective decision-making, he thought it even surprising that the number of appropriate fillings of university jobs was still reasonably high.

One reason for the importance of chance lies in the two-sidedness of the vocation, that is, the quality of being a highly qualified scholar and a teacher at the same time. Very often, brilliant scholars are horribly bad teachers. While the number of students attending a lecture is a quantitative, easily graspable criterion, it is much more difficult to assess the quality of a good scholar. To make an uneducated but receptive mind understand scientific problems and to guide someone to independent thinking are the pedagogically most difficult tasks, and they cannot be determined by student numbers. Here, Weber referred

156

to art and talent as necessary qualities, and he clearly distinguished those from scientific qualities.

Weber characterised scientific education as a matter of the intellectual aristocracy: in combination with chance and the fact that mediocrity was often given preference over high quality, candidates were tested so rigorously that few of them endured an academic career without suffering damages (ibid.: 588).

In the second part of his lecture he turned to the "inner calling to science". As a first point he mentioned efficient performance, which could only be achieved through strict specialisation. What were needed were utmost concentration and a great passion for even the tiniest aspects. In addition, he claimed that intuition was of the essence, because scientific results could not be forced. Therefore, not only passion but also ideas were necessary, and these prospered only as the result of hard work. Admittedly, even amateurs might have good ideas every once in a while, and often they provided brilliant solutions to scientific problems, but they lacked the security of scientific methodology.

Weber compared the scholar to the tradesman, to the modern entrepreneur and also to the artist: obsession and intuition played an important role for all of them, in particular when it came to creating. Only with complete and utter dedication it was possible to make a mark in the arts or in science, and there was no room for a voguish personality cult (ibid.: 591). The scholar differed from the artist insofar as scientific work followed the logic of progress, corresponding to a process of intellectualisation that had gone on for thousands of years. While a true and perfectly executed work of art could never be surpassed and could therefore never become obsolete, it was the very purpose of scientific work that its results could be outperformed. According to Weber, science as a vocation does not provide any answers to the search for meaning in life and the search for god. Scientific knowledge is useful for a description of the physical world and for technical advances, but it cannot answer questions of meaning.

As Weber argued, intellectual integrity meant to distinguish between the establishment of mathematical and logical facts on the one hand and the assessment of the value of culture on the other. Prophets and demagogues were to be precluded from speaking in lecture halls because the true understanding of the facts required the reservation of judgement (ibid.: 602). The scientist also had to teach his students the ability to accept inconvenient facts. Weber claimed that modern people found it difficult to cope with everyday life under conflicting ethical conditions, and this weakness led to an addiction to pleasure and adventure.

In closing, Weber addressed the educational system in the USA again. He stated that the American youth learned much less than the German youth, and that despite the great number of exams they had to take they could not be considered 'exam people' in the same sense as their German counterparts who saw their diplomas as the entry tickets to the realm of sinecures. In the USA there was much less respect for tradition and office, but only for an individual's very own achievement. American teachers sold their knowledge and methods for money, and being paid for this job was their only motivation. They would never think of counselling their pupils on such topics as *Weltanschauung* (view of life) or the proper conduct of life, and similarly, their pupils would never think of asking them for advice on such topics.

Weber then demanded that professors in Germany, too, should refrain from taking on a leadership role in political matters and with regard to advice on their pupils' conduct of life. Academic teachers and scholars did not stand out due to leadership qualities and it was therefore questionable for them to act up as leaders in the lecture hall. Weber regarded rationalisation and intellectualisation as the fate of his time and he claimed that this development led to disenchantment with the world. Religious devotion required a sacrifice of the intellect, yet the virtue of the lecture hall rested on intellectual integrity (ibid.: 613).

8.11 Science as a modern vocational paradigm

According to Weber, the scientist is to be categorised between the tradesman, the entrepreneur and the artist. The demands on the scientist are consequently of a hybrid nature, yet this seems to be character-

158

istic of modern professional activities quite generally. From this perspective, science is a modern profession, maybe even the vanguard of future professions – though this interpretation goes beyond Weber's explanations. Weber mentions efficient performance and the importance of good ideas as the positive characteristics of the professional scientist, and the same is again true for most modern professions. Weber claims that there is one heroic quality of science as a vocation, namely the complete dedication to the subject matter and a narrow specialisation, and he consequently argues for the paradoxical combination of objectivity and passion. This characteristic of professional work can be found in other modern professions too. In this respect, the development perspectives presented by Weber apply to more than just science as a vocation.

8.12 Vocational education between calling and bureaucracy

All three lectures contain demands on the respective vocations that are difficult to meet due to their complexity. All told, Weber and Kerschensteiner argue against dilettantism and stress the aspect of vocation as a calling. In addition, they also stress the importance of subject-specific requirements, even though this point is less prominent than the comments on the more general attitude towards work and politics. Ethical requirements are a more central concern; for Kerschensteiner, these requirements have to be met at an early stage in life, while for Weber they can be met over the course of one's biography.

For Kerschensteiner, talent, vocation and social environment have to be brought in line. For Weber, the vocations in question are not accessed via a pre-defined career path, and vocations are not really jobs that require training but much rather positions one achieves as a result of a multiplicity of factors. The loose connection of education and training with vocation implies a stronger emphasis on the more general conduct of life. In view of a regime of chance and bureaucracy it is necessary to manage one's own (working) life. There are only few professional opportunities that rely solely on selective learning and training.

None of the three lectures answered concrete questions such as the following: How can lack of talent be compensated? Is it really that hard to learn politics? What course of action should students take who are attracted to scientific work? In sum, the three lectures did not pick out practical problems of vocational choice or even career tips as their central themes, but they rather provided a zeitgeist analysis.

Weber's explanations reveal an ambivalence of modern developments. Bureaucratisation has become a fact and it is neither purely negative nor to be welcomed without reservation. Vocations are largely specified by guidelines created by scientists and politicians, who should therefore act like entrepreneurs. Chance decisions and rationalisation create their own laws, and there has to be an answer to these laws. The foundation of Weber's educational concept is training in a specific professional field and specialisation. In addition, the need for ideas, entrepreneurship and leadership play important roles.

8.13 Charisma and conduct of life: education between passion and self-limitation

In the years following the three lectures discussed here, there were only few explicit references to Weber in the pedagogical literature. However, it would be wrong to conclude that Weber was not taken notice of. The contributions to the Festschrift for Kerschensteiner's 70th birthday (Fischer/Spranger 1924a) prove that Weber's "Politics as a vocation" was indeed noticed by the leading pedagogical figures of the time, and that they furthermore shared his longing for a charismatic leader. The title of this Festschrift mentions a 'youth leader', obviously referring to Kerschensteiner. With "all the uncertainties of a young people of the world", Kerschensteiner was depicted as having

160

become the "pedagogical exponent of the decades" by developing the idea of educating the German people to become a politically self-confident nation of workers. He was considered to have initiated the rebuilding of the German national self-conception and of an intellect-based cultural work (Fischer/Spranger 1924a: IV f.).

These comments show the ambivalence with which the modernisation of Germany and the political stabilisation after the First World War was perceived. In his lectures, Weber ascribed a decisive role to leadership. His demands on strong leadership did not arise from a general cultural criticism, but were motivated by the difficult political situation at the end of the First World War. The students, too, shared Weber's yearning for strong leadership. Weber had introduced this issue in his vocation lectures by the back door. For him, lack of leadership was an ill in itself, and the notion of leadership plays a central role in his sociology of domination in *Economy and Society*, where domination and its legitimacy are mainly described from the perspective of leadership. The idea was to transform local, collaborative action into rational and well-regulated societal action (Weber 1985: 569 f.). Rational leadership is the leadership of an impersonal, systematic order and of a legislation that functions "like a technically rational machine" (Weber 1985: 469). Since Wilhelmian Germany had not gone through a process of mechanisation and since instrumental reason had hardly developed in the German population – two elements of rationalisation that Weber deemed essential – he focussed on parliamentarism but also on the "recourse on charismatic elements" (cf. Breuer 1991: 213 ff.). Not only societies but individuals, too, need guidance and leadership, or else their lives drift like leaves in the wind. Leadership in the sense of self-guidance is thus a prerequisite for a conscious conduct of life and for everyone to forge his or her own destiny (Weber 1988c: 507 f.). For Weber, conduct of life was deliberately not a psychological or pedagogical notion, but followed the logic of rationalisation.

Weber argued, very metaphorically, that he and his contemporaries lived in a time of polytheism and that these various gods struggled with each other. In such a time as this, everyone who strives to become a personality requires skills which Weber subsumed under the notion of charisma: courage, passion, dedication and the belief in the higher cause of one's endeavours. These are the characteristics that connect the civilised man to leaders and heroes (Weber 1988: 560). Weber pointed out personal responsibility, understood as the ability to give account to oneself, as a concept that is complementary to charisma (cf. Bienfait 1999: 140 f.). Since modern society is marked by ambivalences, there can be no unambiguous decisions; instead, compromises have become the norm (cf. Goldman 2005: 63). Moreover, bureaucracy and the factory stand in the way of a fulfilled conduct of life based on vocation (cf. Müller 2003: 290), because if the specific kind of self-limitation that is required by the vocation is not carried out, this amounts to emptying vocation of its last significant meaning (Weber 1988b: 494).

In this sense, Weber and Kerschensteiner have different concepts of vocation. While the pedagogue Kerschensteiner sees vocation as an element that links directly to education, the sociologist Weber is mainly concerned with change, restructuring, social restriction and rationalisation, all of which are manifest in vocations and require everyone to make decisions and compromises with regard to one's conduct of life. It has to remain undecided whether Weber's notion of education and vocation is more matter-of-fact and less mythologically charged than that of Kerschensteiner and other pedagogues (cf. Grottker 1990: 388 f.). At least Kerschensteiner's idea that the soul should create a harmonious unity not only within itself but also with the state is alien to such a sociological approach. According to Weber, civilised mankind is neither created through the legitimation of experience nor by turning one's life into a work of art, but by being objective without passion and not eluding the world of work and bureaucracy (Weber 1988c: 591).

8.14 Conclusion: education as self-management

Leadership was a central notion for Weber, and he distinguished between at least two different concepts of leadership. On the one hand, he referred to leadership in a societal context, and in this meaning the notion formed part of his sociology of domination. On the other hand, he used the term to refer to the conduct of life (*Lebensführung*), which he understood to be subjectively shaped by professional work. These two meanings of 'leadership' are not unrelated, even though Weber hardly ever made explicit reference to their interrelation.

Rational action requires a critical distance to the naturalistic-romantic ideal of personality held by the pedagogic tradition (Weber 1988a: 132). Kerschensteiner's and Spranger's efforts to fashion the educational concept in a more realistic way and closer to the professions went only half way insofar as the concept was still geared to inwardness. Rationalisation applied not only to society but also to the individuals' conduct of life, as Weber argued with an overarching postulate in his studies in sociology of religion.

In contrast to pedagogy and psychology, Weber forwent a psychological-ethical theory of talent or references to a philosophy of life (*Lebensphilosophie*). Neither the contrast of life and form nor the struggle of the individual against society was his central concern. According to Weber, the modern individual must strive to achieve a particular balance: on the one hand, he or she must develop the ability to systematise and rationalise his or her conduct of life, independent of a prospect of salvation, yet on the other hand, the ability to transform oneself and one's surroundings depends in particular on the dissociation from tradition and rationality (cf. also Myers 2004a: 284). Therefore, a conscious conduct of life crucially rests on the ability to bear paradoxes (Schluchter 1988: 82). Furthermore, conduct of life means the leadership over oneself. Education as self-management is thus the cultivation of the self beyond rationalisation and routinisation.

9. Georg Simmel's Discourse of Life and Form as a Blueprint for Georg Kerschensteiner's Theory of Education

In this chapter I aim to show how Kerschensteiner developed his later-year pedagogical theory out of the concept of the Arbeitsschule (activity school; cf. Chapter 5) and his earlier educational reform concepts. In this endeavour, he drew on a number of philosophical currents of his time, such as pragmatism, neo-Kantianism, and in particular cultural criticism and philosophy of life (Lebensphilosophie). This approach thus marked his departure from the upcoming empirical sciences psychology and sociology. As will be shown, Kerschensteiner's theory of education developed on the basis of Georg Simmel's philosophy of life.

In contrast to most promoters of the activity school and supporters of the journal *Die Arbeitsschule*, who regarded 'work' primarily in its connection with lesson planning and the configuration of teaching in the classroom, Kerschensteiner attempted to develop the concept of 'work' on a more philosophical grounding in order to enhance the legitimacy of his concerns. Such lines of argument were also what motivated him at a later point to formulate his theory of education. In this endeavour, Kerschensteiner examined the prevailing philosophical currents of his time. Initially, his arguments on the question of work were influenced by Paul Natorp's neo-Kantian interpretation of Pestalozzi and his social pedagogy (Natorp 1904). Kerschensteiner was later also heavily influenced by the philosophy of Eduard Spranger. In contrast to his often emphasised connections with Spranger and his relation to John Dewey's pragmatism, the secondary literature on Kerschensteiner contains only few references to the influence of the philosophy of life (*Lebensphilosophie*),[7] especially cur-

---

7   On Simmel's philosophy of life, cf. Habermas 1996.

rents shaped by the ideas of Georg Simmel. However, we know from his autobiographical sketch that Kerschensteiner looked into Simmel's thinking when he developed his theory of education (Kerschensteiner 1926a: 80). Simmel, a widely known intellectual and cultural critic in Germany and co-founder of sociology, developed his *Lebensphiloso-phie* in a kind of intellectual debate referring to German classicism. His writing about Goethe emphasises the close link between experience and creativity as exemplified in Goethe's personality. The great classical author is lauded as a paragon of German culture, as its greatest 'hero' (cf. Simmel 1888, 1906, 1913).

9.1 Goethe's 'full personality' and cultural criticism

Simmel was by no means the only admirer of Goethe. The famous poet and intellectual Friedrich Gundolf too sees in Goethe's artistic power to shape a theme a necessary turning point in his biographical trajectory. It transformed "all his talents given him as rare materials by Nature into culture and vibrant living education" and "vitality in productivity" (Gundolf 1918: 3). In Goethe's *Wanderjahre*, individuals are taught to become "useful members of a community ordered in accordance with the recognised laws of Nature and humanity" (ibid.: 717):

> Their value is bestowed upon them solely by society. That value is determined by special gifts and talents, present from birth, instilled by education, and developed only for the sake of the community. Society gives them their activity, their action – because only through action do they serve – and provides their vocation. Vocation, i.e. the relation to the community, becomes the hub, the core, and around it is ordered all their being, thinking, action – and indeed the fact of the person, after it has been recognised as a predisposition and chosen as a duty, along with concomitant renunciation of any separate independent existence as a human person outside society. The person renounces that separate existence, consciously and willingly, in favour of the circle into which he or she is placed. (Gundolf 1918: 723)

Referring to Goethe, Simmel for his part describes the urge to create art, similar to the orientation in his study on Rembrandt, based on an earlier critical review of Langbehn's *Rembrandt als Erzieher*. He stresses in particular the ability of the genius and artist to create "a unity of life and form", which does not seem achievable solely through the medium of mere thought (Simmel 1916: 70). Goethe's notion of immediate experience, the artistic world view, is presented also the antipode to Kant's analytical interest in truth (Simmel 1906). Simmel's confrontation with his own former Kantian approach led to an engaged interest in Goethe and an apologia for artistic productivity. He stresses the personality of the creative individual (the artist), whose activity imbues life with form. The process of creation is conceived as a "counter-design" over against the "condition of alienation" (Jung 1990: 145). For Simmel, art embodies the dynamic reconciliation of life and form.

Dealing with Goethe in the context of *Lebensphilosophie* also left its stamp on the pedagogical discussion, leading via an interpretation of Goethe's "pedagogical province" in *Wilhelm Meister* as an activity school ("Arbeitsschule") on to the general problem of education as an enterprise of cultivation.[8] The reductionist view that art is exclusively an expression of life had its price, specifically with regard to society and education, as becomes clear from Kerschensteiner's analysis and reception of Simmel's *Lebensphilosophie*. In a study written in 1914 but never published entitled *Kulturproblem und Persönlichkeit* ("The Cultural Problem and Personality"), we find an attempt by Kerschensteiner to bring his previous ideas on civic education and the activity school into harmony with Simmel's thinking as set out in his essay *Der Begriff und die Tragödie der Kultur* ("The Concept and Tragedy of Culture", Simmel 1911 [1983]).

Initially, Kerschensteiner's criticism refers to art – and probably to the German *Werkbund* at the time – in noting the "chaos of a wild individualism" and a "disgusting element of wildness permeating the

8   However, it should be recalled that the apparently all too hasty readiness to generate philosophical theory and elements of *Weltanschauung* from reading Goethe was also seen as something negative. For example, in the introduction to his critical book on Goethe's *Faust*, Rickert warns about this very danger (Rickert 1932: 13).

architecture in our German cities". Instead of "culture for culture's sake", it has now been made subservient to a generally "acceptable purpose" (AKM 359 – [Kerschensteiner 1914 a]: 32 f.):

> In artistic handicrafts too there are organisations that compel the creative fantasy of a large number of artists to willingly agree to serve common ideas. From internal necessity, not external compulsion, whole branches of industry have re-oriented their sights and have begun to introduce production regulated in accordance with certain norms in place of an unrestrained application of design in their products. (ibid.: 33)

An "ever stronger uniformity and organisation of the current cultural chaos" could be achieved precisely by education for shaping a "full personality" (ibid.: 34). This "full personality" cannot be dispensed in sovereign fashion by the state and does not permit persons able to pursue a profession to remain unemployed (ibid.: 43).

Full personalities like Goethe embraced supra-individual aims in keeping with their intellectual individuality, which is why personality is "individual predisposition brought to full active development by means of elements of culture" (ibid.: 46). Agreeing with Simmel the culture of personality is made dependent on a condition: "the contents taken over from the realm of the supra-personal appear, as if through a predetermined harmony, to develop in the soul only what already exists as its most individual drive and internal pre-determination of its subjective perfection" (Simmel 1983: 185). For his part, Kerschensteiner states that personality – Simmel speaks here of 'culture' – arises "when the subjective soul and the objective intellectual product (be it art, custom, science, religion, law, technology, etc.) come together" (Simmel 1983: 186, and AKM 359 – [Kerschensteiner 1914 a]: 47). It should be noted that Kerschensteiner does not ask what the nature of the cultural artefacts is, such as what specific religion it is grounded on. Rather, full personalities are to pursue a unitary aim (ibid.: 66).

Human beings become personalities by actively striving for their highest self-value, their *Eigenwert*; in this process they become strong integrated individuals. Kerschensteiner bases his perspective in reform pedagogy on this notion, a view which later spurred him to develop a more comprehensive theory of education.

For a person who demands culture of personality, the postulate is not a 'well-rounded' symmetry of education but a distinctive peculiarity of education. Goethe, who, like all strong personalities, doubtlessly placed great value on the freedom of personal design of one's life and the impact and realisation of a person's autonomous life designs, characterised this very clearly in his notion of the pedagogical province [...]. By presenting the pupil with the cultural goods appropriate for him, allowing him to grow and prosper by manifold work in their field, we will educate personalities, furthering in this way at the same time the total complex of culture. (ibid.: 49)

Here and in the conclusions of his treatise, Kerschensteiner formulates as a goal "the future possible cultural unity". Over against a culture devoid of purpose, the productive activity of the personality is to be mobilised (ibid.: 60). The entire project must be organised moving in the direction of the state, based on culture and the rule of law. Such a cultural consciousness also contains a world view, the belief in the value of reason and the divine world order revealed within it. A state based on reason and personality would then not be antipodal any longer, and such a culture would overcome "the anarchy of the current cultural processes". Civic education is an "act of culture" through which all citizens are educated for "shared work in the realisation of the state based on culture and the rule of law" (ibid.: 72, 63). Cultural goods must not be passed on as a dead legacy to the next generation, but rather transmitted as tools. Thus, commonality of culture was not a matter of cognition and knowledge but of intention and will (ibid.: 68).

Kerschensteiner picks up on Simmel's concept of culture, but without sharing his pessimistic final conclusion. Only occasionally is there a flash of pessimistic doubt, for example in his memoirs *20 Jahre im Schulaufsichtsamt* ("20 Years as a School Supervisor"). There he states his fundamental pedagogical 'credo': Only through action can moral character develop. And that is the final goal of all education and schooling (cf. AKM 177 – [Kerschensteiner 1914]: 52 f.). Yet he also asks the following questions: Can education prevent some countries from attacking peaceful nations? Or: May Simmel actually be right in concluding that all culture bears the seed of destruction within itself from the very beginning (ibid.: 53 f.)?

This basic mood, characteristic of cultural criticism (cf. Schnä-delbach 1983: 172 ff.), is the other side of the coin of Simmel's *Le-bensphilosophie* and little suitable for any application in pedagogy. Nonetheless, Simmel's perspective appears in almost every publicati-on by Kerschensteiner since his *Deutsche Erziehung im Krieg und Frieden* (Kerschensteiner 1916). At the same time, in his *Das Grund-axiom des Bildungsprozesses* ("The Fundamental Axiom of the Pro-cess of Education"), Kerschensteiner brings Spranger's categories from the main work *Lebensformen* (Spranger 1922) into theoretical harmony with his own anthropological-psychological categories. Drawing on Simmel's conceptions of culture and personality, he later also develops his much more extensive theory of education. More-over, in his correspondence with Spranger we can find a significant statement of influence: "[...] it was you and Georg Simmel's concept and tragedy of culture which helped me to fundamentally extend and develop my own thoughts on education" (Kerschensteiner 1966b: 307).

9.2 Life and "the tragedy of culture"

Georg Simmel's essay on the concept and tragedy of culture, pub-lished in 1911 in the collection of essays *Philosophische Kultur*, is considered by some as "one of the absolutely fundamental texts of German *Lebensphilosophie*" (Monar 1988: 557) and part of a dis-course in the humanities that should not be underestimated, especially in education and philosophy. For Schnädelbach, the reason why phi-losophy of life is hardly noted as a philosophical current during that time is due to its restructuring and 'further development' by existen-tialism (Schnädelbach 1983: 172 f.). Along with the cult of life and creativity as manifested in German classicism and especially in the opus of Goethe, 'life' as a term is used in cultural criticism mainly as a slogan against convention, institution, alienation and routine. After the turn of the century, Simmel viewed the concept of life even as *the* centre and basic motif in a world view in which "reality and values –

metaphysical and psychological, moral and artistic – have their point of departure and meet" (Simmel 1987: 153).

This romanticising view of life was developed already in the 19th century in Hegelianism and in Schelling, as well as in Simmel's *Schopenhauer and Nietzsche* (Simmel 1991). Over against what was ossified, isolated, abstract and mechanical, he contrasted the organic, the visible, the community, in short: 'vital life'.[9]

A large number of publications deal with this problem, such as Bergson's concept of '*élan vital*', formulated in his work *L'évolution créatrice*. It became the key for the evolution of life, re-evaluating intuition over against the intellect. Artistry and life are understood as a "creation of self by self" (Bergson 1911: 7).[10] *Der Sinn und Wert des Lebens* ("The Sense and Value of Life") is a corresponding publication by Rudolf Eucken that wishes to see the cultural and political preeminence of Germany in the claim to unite soul and work, to place soul within creation, and to imbue work with an inner soul. In this way, the problem of life and work are interconnected (Eucken 1921: 154 f.). Ferdinand Tönnies' famous classical sociological book *Gemeinschaft und Gesellschaft* likewise deals with the organic/mechanical dichotomy (Tönnies 2001: 1 ff.), and also Sigmund Freud in his *Das Unbehagen in der Kultur* elaborates a sharp contrast between cultural development and original human existence, a contrast from which discontent springs (Freud 1993).

Again another protagonist of the discourse on life and form is the young, pre-Marxist Georg Lukacs. In his view, the question of culture is the "question about the possibility of life free of alienation" (Markus 1977: 103). In his essay volume *Die Seele und die Formen*, this

---

9   Contemporary critical theory also suggests such dichotomies, as Habermas' distinction between system and life world (*Lebenswelt*) shows (Habermas 1981).

10 Inter alia, craft manufacture is viewed in a positive light: "A manufactured thing delineates exactly the form of the work of manufacturing it. I mean that the manufacturer finds in his product exactly what he has put into it. If he is going to make a machine, he cuts out its pieces one by one and then puts them together: The machine, when made, will show both the pieces and their assemblage. The whole of the result represents the whole of the work; and to each part of the work corresponds a part of the result" (Bergson 1911: 92).

famous pupil of Simmel's notes that form is the highest arbiter of life, "being able to give shape and form is something ethical, and a value judgment is intrinsic to every shaped configuration" (Lukacs 1971: 248). The truly epic lies in the affirmation of the process of life through experience, as he states in his 1920 published *Theory of the Novel* (Lukacs 1965: 131).The alienation as an offspring of the life-form contrast opened the door for his Marxist analysis of society in his later years.[11]

Other well-known cultural critics such as Ludwig Klages' work argue likewise (Klages 1932). Oswald Spengler's *Der Untergang des Abendlandes* (Spengler 1923) was also especially popular. The emphasis on life stamped the discussion and life had advanced to an important concept after the turn of the century. But frequently it slipped into a metaphysics of the irrational, at times combining obscurities with reactionary elements (Schnädelbach 1983: 174, 190), as when Spengler in his *Der Mensch und die Technik – Beitrag zu einer Philosophie des Lebens* ("Man and Technology – A Contribution to a Philosophy of Life") characterises man as a predator who by his very own creations – and therein lies the tragedy – has placed himself behind bars (Spengler 1933: 25 ff.).

9.3 Pedagogy and the discourse of life

Pedagogy is also permeated by this 'vocabulary of life', for example among other reform pedagogues like Herman Nohl. In his *Die Philosophie der Gegenwart und ihr Einfluss auf das Bildungsideal* ("Contemporary Philosophy and its Influence on the Ideal of Education"), Theodor Litt, a well known pedagogue and philosopher, notes that initially the pedagogical reformers were more inclined towards posi-

---

11 That is why Dilthey and Simmel come under sharp attack by the elder Lukacs. He argues that Simmel's *Lebensphilosophie* was an expression of the basic mood in the imperial era before World War I; it reproduced a good conscience, a kind of cosy *Weltanschauung* (Lukacs 1984: 358).

tivism or – as he makes more precise elsewhere – psychologism than Kantian logicism (Litt 1925: 29). Dominance was not given to the experiential science of an experimental pedagogy. Rather, people opened up to "moods and ideas" that were "at home under the spell of this *Lebensphilosophie*" (ibid.: 35). Litt also speaks of 'life pedagogy', a discourse for which an extremely copious use of the word 'creative' was symptomatic and which tended toward pedagogical expressionism. The work or activity school movement was on the one hand based on science and psychology, while on the other it was opposed to a "division between the disciplines, seeing a totality of body and soul as the most meaningful experience" (ibid.: 39 f.).

It is quite popular to talk about the 'misery' of classroom instruction, where the school concentrates on processing finished objects, cut off from life, and where the 'vital and living unity' is not central to the classroom experience. Such statements were able to count on a certain consensus. Examples of these images are the "false patina" of knowledge transmitted by the traditional school, which is then later trashed by the exigencies of practical life (Kerschensteiner 1910b: 25), the "all-warming sun of productive creation", which facilitates a viable content in one's life (Kerschensteiner 1910c: 66). Herman Nohl pleads on behalf of life when he propagates the pedagogical connection with the following words: "Thus, as educators we stand ever anew with our general insights before the individual and the living moment in its totality. And here, too, what is ultimately decisive is this 'touching the soul with soul, the power of life with the power of life'" (Nohl 1976: 46).

9.4 Contemporary criticism on *Lebensphilosophie*

Yet this insistence on 'life' was not shared by all. Theodor Litt noted how powerful the pull of *Lebensphilosophie* was when he identified tendencies toward philosophy of life thinking even among neo-Kantians such as Natorp, Cassirer and others, who originally were inclined toward strictly idealistic principles. Litt complains that "the structural fundamental motif of spiritual reality is the contrast between life and idea, the peculiar tension between flowing movement and the world beyond of lasting meanings" (Litt 1925: 53). But he does not try to see this antagonism as a permanent gap which cannot ever be surmounted.

The neo-Kantian Heinrich Rickert termed the *Philosophie des Lebens* a "fashionable current", as stated in the subtitle of a publication from 1920. By glorifying intuition and *Anschauung* (outlook, world view) at the cost of scientific formation of conceptions and philosophical system-building, a 'philosophy of life' approach would eventually lead to the end of philosophy:

> Moods of life can also be expressed with slogans of multiple meaning. Indeed, precisely in the dark unity of the feelings of life that they generate lies a substantial proportion of their attraction and their extra-scientific value. [...] The most general tendency of life centres on what is immediate, direct, what is vivid and intuitive more generally, in contrast to every "destructive" concept. Their concept of life can thus be termed the concept of the absence of the conceptual. (Rickert 1920: 35)

Rickert does not consider *Lebensphilosophie* totally irrelevant, and even attributes literary qualities to the rhetoric of its exponents, seeing positive aspects in this philosophy as a critique of previous philosophical currents. Nonetheless, he polemicises against this 'fashion' in strong terms, warning about the irrational elements lurking within this current (Rickert 1920: 184 ff.).

Rickert deals more mildly with these aspects in his criticism of his former friend Simmel, acknowledging that Simmel was the one who had seen the problematic nature of *Lebensphilosophie* most clearly when he proceeded to theorise from the contrast between life and form. Life depends on forms, but life over the longer haul does not tolerate anything fixed, non-fluid. For that reason, a philosopher of life should have no interest in entities that persist for long periods of time. He has to try to reconcile form with content, what is rigid with what is movable, the solid with the fluid, and the boundary with what is unbounded, and to do so in such a manner "that ultimately life is what retains primacy" (ibid.: 64).

Indeed, Simmel calls this conflict between life and form "the

174

tragedy of culture", since life is forced to struggle constantly against its own products, which have taken on solidity and which no longer flow along with life's incessant streaming. It is in his view a "struggle of life for its own Being. Where it expresses itself, it wishes only to express itself and nothing else, and it thus breaks through every form" (Simmel 1987: 158). Precisely in shedding previous forms, life is 'creative', but life "wishes to achieve something it cannot attain: It wishes to determine itself and appear over and beyond all forms, in the nakedness of its own immediacy – but knowing, wanting and shaping as determined by life can only substitute one form by another. It can never supplant form in general by life itself, as that which is beyond form" (ibid.: 158, 172).

As problematic as the stylisation of life and the 'tragic' distinction between life and form in terms of philosophy may be, they nonetheless allowed Simmel to develop a 'modern' perspective in his analysis of society, and he later built on this perspective to become a classic figure in the discipline. He postulates that sociology has the task of investigating the reciprocal effects, kinds and forms of sociation arising from the spatial and temporal ordering of human existence (Simmel 1908: 7). A key notion here is differentiation. Subjectivity is viewed in connection with increasing degrees of sociation, related to the compression and intensification of social relations. An individual is a member of a variety of social groups; individuality is placed in reciprocal relation with social differentiation (Simmel 1989: 174).

Simmel sees life as a stream or river whose "drops are the beings. That stream does not go on through them. Rather, their existence lies totally and solely within the flowing of that stream" (Simmel 1987a: 205).

Subjectivity and the way it is constituted are connected with social experience. They are then neither unitary nor indivisible. According to such an understanding, education must necessarily be conceived as a process of self-differentiation that is never-ending and cannot be concluded (Biesenbach 1988:151).

In his *Philosophie des Geldes* ("The Philosophy of Money"), Simmel develops a concept of culture that describes the culture of objects as a human culture, "so that we only educate ourselves by forming and shaping things". This concept highlights the discrepancy between objective and subjective culture:

> The work of countless generations is precipitated as spirit turned into object in language and custom, political constitutions and religious doctrine. Everyone takes from this as much as he can or wants. But no individual can exhaust its riches. [...] Just as the content and meaning of a book as such is in an indifferent relation to whether its circle of readers is big or small, understanding or lacking in any such understanding, every other cultural product stands before a cultural circle; and though it is ready to be grasped by any and all, there is only sporadic acceptance of that readiness. (Simmel 1989a: 622)

By reinserting this concept of culture in *Philosophische Kultur*, Simmel describes cultivation as an acceptance of supra-personal elements of content which, in secret harmony, only unfold in the soul what the psyche already contains and is pressing for its subjective realisation and completion. Art and custom, science and objects formed in accordance with some purpose, religion and law, technology and social norms, are all stations the subject must pass through in order to acquire his "culture":

> The paradox of culture is that subjective life, which we feel in its continuous flow and which presses from our innermost being outward for its fulfilment [*Vollendung*] – this fulfilment, viewed from the idea of culture, cannot be attained by itself but only via such forms that have now become so alien to it, crystallised to a self-sufficient seclusion. (Simmel 1983: 186)

In these selected remarks, we can see that Simmel stresses those elements that Kerschensteiner was able to make use of for his theory of education. Work emerges as the mediator par excellence between life pressing for inward fulfilment and perfection on the one hand, and external form, so necessary for cultivation, on the other; in other words, work as the mediator between subjective psyche and objective intellectual product. But Simmel does not develop this cultural-critical dichotomy any further in anthropological concepts or psychological basic assumptions. Kerschensteiner thinks that he can read a whole theory of education into a pithy quote from Simmel that he repeatedly cites: "Culture is the way of the psyche to itself, from a unity closed in itself on through unfolded multiplicity to an unfolded and developed unity" (Simmel 1983: 185).

176

9.5 Kerschensteiner's approach: work as a means to overcome the contrast between life and form

Kerschensteiner translates this process of cultivation as a theory of education, though without taking over Simmel's conclusions pointing to a tragedy (which he lets stand as an antinomy that can be resolved through religion or the philosophy of culture) (Kerschensteiner 1928: 57). Yet the tragic element does not readily lend itself to pedagogical application. Therefore, the contrast between life and form is conceived in pedagogical terms solely as a *tension*. Through work, in the sense of German classicism and Goethe as Kerschensteiner interpreted him, education, the school and society can be 'vitalised'. The apologia for productive work and creativity makes it possible to surmount this gap.

Education, as he states in his *Grundaxiom* (1917), is the forming of the psyche by means of the objective culture surrounding the person, the "individualising vitalisation and reinvigoration of this objective culture", or also the "forming and moulding of individuality to the highest most perfected human type accessible to it" (Kerschensteiner 1917: 29). Pedagogy is thus faced with the task of integrating the cultural circles and cultural goods found through this abstraction in a cultural unity once more. The theory of education must summarise and contain the forming of the unitary psyche by means of the typical forms of behaviour. It must seek the principles that make it possible to develop the structure of the psyche into an integrated personality (ibid.: 29).

Kerschensteiner links Simmel's theory of culture with psychological types which, inspired by Eduard Spranger, he first developed in his essay *Deutsche Schulerziehung im Krieg und Frieden* ("German Education in War and Peace") in the study *Weg zum Pflichtbewusstsein* ("Pathways to an Awareness of Duty"), published during World War I (Kerschensteiner 1916). In the *Grundaxiom*, these categories are further refined and also accommodated with Spranger's types, and then form the basis of his theory of education along with Simmel's conception of culture over a number of years, down to the posthumous publication of his *Theorie der Bildungsorganisation* (1933).

In his *Grundaxiom des Bildungsprozesses*, dedicated to the "immortal memory" of Goethe (Kerschensteiner 1917: 3), the process of education is subdivided into object, means and purpose. Already in the foreword, the pupil's education is made dependent on whether the psychological state of the individual to be taught corresponds to the intellectually formed energy of the cultural good or asset. As Kerschensteiner states, "the entire process of education is nothing else but a reinvigoration of the objectified spirit in ever new individuals" (ibid.: 7), and therefore, the intellectual structure of the cultural asset must be adequate for individuality. Referring to Dilthey, he sees this reinvigoration of the objective spirit as something the activity school can guarantee. He assumes here a necessary harmony between psyche and object. The contradiction between life and form is interpreted as an individual problem of education requiring pedagogical intervention:

> A person whose psychological constitution is not inclined to theory cannot be tempted by the theoretical assets with their truth-values. A person incapable of a truly religious experience will not be captivated by religious objects and goods. Only a person who contains within himself a longing for greatness of the soul, even if unconscious and slumbering within, will be seized by the ideal of the greatness that a human being can achieve. (Kerschensteiner 1916: 41)

This analysis sheds light on Kerschensteiner's critique of schooling and his turn towards the theory of education. The task of the educator and teacher now consists in exploring the individual pupils' psyche and in organizing education in a larger frame in keeping with the corresponding cultural goods and assets. In Kerschensteiner's view, the dominant cultural asset and corresponding structure of psyche for the elementary school is *practical manual behaviour*.

A sense of value is required if the duties that follow from this task are to be understood as obligations. Such a sense of value is only active in the spheres of work which are suitable for our (human) nature. In Kerschensteiner's view, all forms of psychological behaviour derive from our 'psychic nature'. One can experience individual values via these forms of psychological or mental behaviour, which vary among human beings and which any plan for education must take into proper account (ibid.: 41 f.). Kerschensteiner initially distinguishes between active and contemplative behaviour, and he associates the latter with theoretical and aesthetic behaviour. The former, active behaviour, is equated with practical behaviour, which is further divided into anti-socially practical (i.e., egoistic), socially practical and asocially practical behaviour. These sub-categories are also grasped by the concepts of egoism, altruism and impersonalism (i.e., material to be taught for the sake of the material, or perfection for the sake of perfection, such as in all 'genuine' scientific research, where truth is sought for the sake of truth). Beyond what can be experienced, Kerschensteiner posits a sixth form of psychological behaviour, termed religious behaviour. He notes that Spranger also distinguishes six basic forms for designing and shaping life: the theoretical man, the economic man, the social man, the man of power, of fantasy and of religion. Every area of culture demands certain duties of us, and referring to Carlyle, Kerschensteiner notes that the principal duty is the one a person feels most inclined toward.

Kerschensteiner further legitimates the activity school with this cultural-pedagogical and ideal-typical, psychologising analysis. Educational institutions are to promote practical asocial (i.e., impersonal) behaviour by manual labour, while collective practical work at an early age furthers practical social behaviour and attitude. In the edition of 1916 he even stresses a "patriotic attitude toward the fatherland" which can arise and develop in practical service to a society (ibid.: 60).

Through our actions we discover where our strengths lie. This is why education for duty means that the child should learn in what direction its psychological behaviour leads him. By his activity, the child experiences the values of the goods that are adequate for him:

> Some children find the way to truth, honesty, industriousness, endurance and perseverance, thoroughness, carefulness, dedication to work, self-appraisal, self-control and finally self-respect in a theoretical field, some in an aesthetic one, but most in some practical field of endeavour. (Kerschensteiner 1916: 58)

9.6 Spranger and Simmel as central points of reference for Kerschensteiner's theory of education

In his work *Lebensformen*, Spranger set out to describe a humanistic psychology, to be distinguished from experimental psychology, which later became a key orientation for Kerschensteiner's theory of education, along with Simmel's analysis of culture. Psychological topology serves or is associated with ethical ends. The central problem is that a desired experience of values does not follow objective criteria but rather is a subjective achievement, because an individual does not experience everything as valuable that is generally considered valuable (Spranger 1922: 15).

The individual is surrounded by objective spirit. In this formulation grounded on the philosophy of culture, Spranger follows Wilhelm Dilthey, his teacher and founder of the *Geisteswissenschaften*. For Spranger, the spirit is 'objective' not only in the sense of what is external to the ego, but also in the sense of what is "genuine and valid" (Spranger 1922: 16). The individual finds himself confronted with a "normative spirit". Accordingly, the individual psyche is a meaningful complex of directions in value that can be described not only psychologically but also in terms of the ethics of culture:

> The empirical ego finds itself already embedded in super-individual intellectual-spiritual structures of value which have disconnected from the experiencing ego. In them, the constructive lawfulness of value already has to a certain degree created a super-individual meaning extending beyond the individual ego. (Spranger 1922: 17)

The creation of meaning or its experience is an accomplishment of intellect that allows the individual psyche to reach out to the super-individual spirit. According to Spranger, there is not only a tension between individual psyche and spirit, but between historical and eternal laws (ibid.: 20). Kerschensteiner largely follows Spranger's thinking here, considering culture as a problem of individual acquirement of artefacts in accordance with psychological types.

180

Simmel's contrast between life and form is reinterpreted as a problem of pedagogy in the sense that access to values is foregrounded as a decisive question. While Simmel's approach, grounded on cultural criticism, sociology and *Lebensphilosophie*, focuses on contingency in the interplay with social dynamics and reciprocal influences, Spranger and Kerschensteiner look for an opening into eternal values. In that regard, Simmel is far more sceptical, as when he notes in his lectures on Kant that "our feelings and ideas about value have no principle relation to the real order of things in the world whatsoever, but rather solely a contingent or accidental relation" (Simmel 1905: 123). The individual cannot always look for the moral legitimation of his actions in a general law (ibid.: 106). Simmel notes that this is where Kant's ethical exaggeration lies, in that it falls prey to "a far too extended notion of the concept of morals beyond the sphere of values" (ibid.: 112).

Kerschensteiner does not only set out a boundary marker against such relativism. He also regards a sociological perspective, as emerges from his confrontation with Durkheim's *Education et Sociologie*, as an insufficient basis for a foundation for morality. He raises Kantian demands over against a view of education as a 'social fact', which must be described and empirically observed as a process of socialisation of youth, because from what exists you cannot derive what should be. In contrast, in Durkheim's view morality springs from social purpose (Durkheim 1989: 51 ff.), whose common feature lies in recognising and respecting "*de la raison, de la science, des idées et des sentiments, qui sont à la base de la morale démocratique*" (Durkheim 1989: 62).

Kerschensteiner, however, would like to educate the community into a moral collective personality, which depends on the strength of the individual members (AKM 40 – [Kerschensteiner n. d.]: 6). Valid values are needed for that, for whose proof he cites Spranger's *Lebensformen* and Rickert's *Allgemeine Grundlegung der Philosophie* (1921), which in his view have provided an unassailable foundation. Values such as truth and justice implicate an order of what should be:

Whoever has really experienced these values also experienced the call of obligation for their prioritised realisation over any other values [...] For each individual, the experience of objective value means most especially the realisation of that value in one's own personality. "To be human" means to be the agent of values considered to be objective, i.e., to have a structure of the psyche in which such objective values determine inner and external action. The actual moral personality, i.e. the personality under the rule of values considered to be objective, thus becomes our highest inner good. [...] Value demands recognition by my will, and demands of my will its realisation. That is the moral autonomy of a will which in this way commands itself [...]. (AKM 40 – [Kerschensteiner n. d.]: 9)

In any event, this is how Kerschensteiner would like the difficult-to-interpret formulation of culture as the "the way of the psyche to itself, from a unity closed in itself on through unfolded multiplicity to an unfolded and developed unity" (Simmel 1983: 185; cf. above) to be interpreted. In his comprehensive work *Theorie der Bildung* he states:

Now we also understand the definition Georg Simmel gave for the concept of education in his essay "Der Begriff und die Tragödie der Kultur". [...] Closed unity is the unity of animal being with all its individual possibilities for development, its value system oriented to the preservation of physical life and a primitive set of meanings. Developed multiplicity is the multiplicity of sensual and intellectual experiences of value which comes about when individual functions of consciousness are activated in a cultural environment filled by sensual and intellectual goods. But the unfolded unity lies in an organisation, beyond contradiction, of the consciousness of value and all the material circumstances or facts which we have incorporated into our consciousness as meaningful content. (Kerschensteiner 1926: 13)

Kerschensteiner tries to take over Simmel's image of the acquirement of culture through goods by individualising this in terms of the theory of education, while obligating it ethically to a level of value. In contrast, life seen as a "constantly flowing current" in Simmel's thinking (Simmel 1918: 17) is characterised as a "removal of constraints". Forms are retained only to be "broken in a continuous process" (ibid.: 27).

Simmel and Spranger also serve Kerschensteiner as an educational-theoretical basis for his previous ideas on the activity school. Traditional transmission of knowledge in the classroom is rejected as insufficient since it only takes into account the psychic-mental profile (*Seelenrelief*) of a small circle. Only if cultural goods are actively acquired is there something beyond the merely mechanical transmission of knowledge. Character is only shaped if access to the agents and vessels of value so decisive for the character – including goods as well as 'personalities' – is rendered possible. Kerschensteiner proceeds from an a priori: "Individuality as acquired at birth bears within its core an individual law which includes that individuality within a specific relation to the world of objective spirit" (Kerschensteiner 1959: 37).

In Kerschensteiner's final version of the *Grundaxiom*, he explicitly extends the concept of work. In the contrast between life and form, he ascribes additional value to activity and an active contemplative behaviour. Understanding a mathematical formula, for example, is dependent on a "contemplative acquirement," which is the "*actual* activity of all true learning, and thus the characteristic hallmark of the activity school" (ibid.: 42, emphasis added). The actual essence of the child, however, consists in activity, in the sense of personal expression through material facts and circumstances. Yet it is precisely the elementary school which fails to recognise this essential productive and reproductive activity of the child (ibid.: 47). Thus, he considers genuine pedagogical behaviour to be actively altruistic or, as in the case of civic behaviour, actively social (ibid.: 56).

In the theory of education, it is the experiences of value that make education possible in the first place. The bridge between the object of culture and the subject to be educated and cultivated, or between form and life, is not made possible by abstract knowing but by concrete work, as an agent and trigger of culture. It creates access to the values which objectified spirit counterposes to subjective spirit in an ethical, intellectual, social, aesthetic, religious or technical form. The prerequisite and aim (barely attainable in full perfection) for this experience is 'objectivity' (*Sachlichkeit*) as a virtue freed from egoism and partial thought. Such 'work' reconciles the contrast between life and form in the experience of non-personal values. It must find entry into the activity school or the system of educational organisation.

Kerschensteiner is mindful, along with Spranger's categories and Simmel's understanding of culture, of the theory of value associated with Rickert's neo-Kantian thinking. The experience called forth by one's own work is oriented to values which in their absolute validity make education possible in the first place. With this notion of "values that can be experienced concretely", his thinking differs from Cornelius' conception of education, which is oriented to the knowledge of values, and from Simmel's antinomy of cultural development and the tragic dynamics it contains (ibid.: 54 ff.). For his part, Kerschensteiner defines education 'axiologically', i.e. the central vantage is precisely the 'experiencing' of the spiritual, of values which the cultural goods contain: "Education is an individually organised sense of value awakened by the cultural goods, of individual breadth and depth" (Kerschensteiner 1926: 17).

But this structure of values can only be experienced if the individual person can find his or her field of work. The person who can create congruence between his or her natural gifts, inclinations and field of activity in society, i.e. in a vocation, can achieve "centrality of the soul". It is necessary to grasp the meaning and multiple value relations of things and persons in the circle of active life and activity (ibid.: 22 f.). Getting accustomed to meaning corresponds to an insightful habit and differs from mechanical habit (form-oriented habit), mere technique and technological ability, virtuosity and routine. This soulful custom corresponds to the "essence of the true artist" (ibid.: 30 f.). Along with axiological and psychological conditioning factors, education is also defined by a teleological side, because only in and through vocational education is the prerequisite given for an education of values.

For Kerschensteiner, "vocational education" is education "which qualifies the pupil for the field of work to which he feels inwardly called" (ibid.: 39). Thus, creating congruence between psychic-mental structure and the object involves not only the school but the society in a broader sense. To harmonise vocation and calling ('*vocatio*') is the problem to be solved by educational organisation. Kerschensteiner rejects Spranger's objection that vocation and a sense of calling are frequently far from congruent (ibid.: 190 ff.). Through his 'calling', a pupil is tied to a community of value. Kerschensteiner calls this the sociological side of education, as a sub-concept of the teleological sphere. Vocational education should not be seen in a technical sense of training for work, but it neither focuses on the mere social being (ibid.: 47).

184

The effect of education depends on the experience of value, but this is only possible by laborious acquirement (ibid.: 59). Special emphasis is placed on experience because Kerschensteiner, as he concedes, cannot precisely delimit the realm of values and their validity. As a consequence, it is the 'feeling, sympathetic consciousness' (*das fühlende Bewusstsein*) (ibid.: 62) that plays the essential role for the theory of education, since values, "and most especially moral values, are only experienced in action" (ibid.: 65).

Kerschensteiner's critics at his time already harboured serious doubts about his views on the 'experience of value'. Should the 'objective immanent meaning' of the cultural goods be experienced? And was there only one such meaning, and only determinable by an achievement of thought? The very selection of cultural objects for education demands a translation by the institution and its teachers into the framework of the school, despite autonomous activity by the pupils. The same educational goods have various densities of meaning. Accordingly, morality and intellectual-spiritual structure can differ enormously. No school can be constructed, Kerschensteiner argues, in accordance with the various and diverse types of individuality.

9.7 The Simmel-Kerschensteiner controversy

Georg Simmel and even Eduard Spranger were highly sceptical about Kerschensteiner's theory of education (Kerschensteiner 1959: 85 ff.). They both criticised the too narrow nexus posited between individual gifts and predisposition and the adequate objective spirit supposedly necessary for the experience of value. Kerschensteiner quotes Simmel's objections sent in a letter to him in the last revised version of his *Grundaxiom*, as well as in the posthumous work *Theorie der Bildungsorganisation*:

People see even in individuality the final telos: the super-individual, even counter-individual is one of the elements in and through which individuality develops – by means of respect and opposition, by self-preservation against its onslaught and by simple actual recognition, by determining one's own essential boundaries, and by gaining strength to digest the indigestible. (Quoted in Kerschensteiner 1933: 39)

With this statement it becomes clear that Simmel's understanding of education, unlike what Kerschensteiner's interpretation suggests, is mediated not by harmony but by difference. Education as confrontation and as a process of differentiation can be considered a process of self-differentiation. In the final revised version of *Grundaxiom*, the following passage is quoted from the same letter by Simmel to Kerschensteiner: "You are trying to attain individualisation by means of differentiating the teaching material. [...] I look for individualisation more on the side of the subject, and the function, rather than in terms of objective content of material and curriculum" (quoted in Kerschensteiner 1959: 86).[12]

In contrast with Kerschensteiner, Simmel stresses individuality in the social function. One main problem of the school is to transmit a certain fund of knowledge and ability which a pupil must acquire as something objective, and which is indifferent to his or her individuality (Simmel AKB 1917: 1).[13]

Simmel's pedagogical concepts can also be derived in part from his collection of lectures *Schulpädagogik*, published posthumously in 1922, directed to the "vital creative teacher" (Simmel 1922: 10). These lectures appear to be quite 'traditional' in contrast to reform criticism of the schools, since they stress activity by the teacher. As

12 But Kerschensteiner does not quote him exactly, as a comparison of Simmel's original letter with the printed passage indicates. Kerschensteiner quotes Simmel's position as follows: "I look for individualization more on the side of the subject, as in function" (ibid.: 86). But in Simmel's letter he clearly writes: "I would see the means for individualising more on the side of the subject, and the function" (Simmel 1917: 2). His exclusion of the word "means" creates a substantial shift in the meaning of Simmel's objection: "I look for individualization" vs. "I look for the means of individualization" makes for a decisive change in the variant.

13 Simmel writes that Kerschensteiner should not misunderstand his statements as asceticism or anti-individualism, and Kerschensteiner did not. He read the letter more as agreement with his theory of education than the contradiction stressed here might suggest (Kerschensteiner 1959: 87).

such, they give a similar impression like Simmel's letter to Kerschensteiner, where he states that "the future teacher should only be provided with the pedagogical attitude relevant for his practice" and that
therefore he "should keep his distance from any word *de lege ferenda*"
(Simmel 1917: 1). Dominant in Simmel's *Schulpädagogik* is his perspective grounded on *Lebensphilosophie*, though it has little in common with his other publications (cf. also Danner 1991: 124 f.) and
does not lead on to postulates of reform pedagogy.[14]

Kerschensteiner's activity school, conceived as a reform program
against the 'book school', shifted its critical emphasis over the years
from the introduction of manual activity to facilitating and organising
education in a more encompassing sense of *Bildung*. Work as a contribution to reinvigorating the school was not clearly distinguished
from that broader aim; rather, as method and goal it was at the same
time in keeping with its content. If the pupil acquired the subject material – whether meant for the head or the hand, or manual and mental
at the same time – and if there was an adequate balance between individual life and objectivation, then – according to Kerschensteiner's
theorising – access to agents and vessels of value was possible. What
is decisive is "that all procedure in pedagogy is only meaningful if it
leads to some meaning in life. But the meaning of life means that life
is related to a lasting, unconditional, timeless value" (Kerschensteiner
1926a: 78).

In this reading, *Bildung* aims at understanding or *Verstehen* in a
comprehensive sense; it is the "possibility of the reinvigoration of the
last and deepest meaning of a concentrated and succinct work" (Kerschensteiner 1959: 92). *Bildung* extends beyond merely rational
knowledge: "In education what is important is that the meaning of the
goods, their most profound meaning, is reanimated and made vivid,

---

14 This understanding does not reject all educational tasks of the schools, as Ker-
    schensteiner notes elsewhere in reference to Condorcet (Kerschensteiner 1933:
    164). Rather, it combines knowledge and education in its own way: "Rather, an
    educated person is one whose objective knowledge has entered into the vitality
    of his subjective development and existence, and whose mental energy is filled
    with as broad a range as possible of valuable contents, constantly growing"
    (Simmel 1922: 33). For an American edition of Kerschensteiner's "Industrial
    School" (Kerschensteiner 1912), cf. Kerschensteiner 1913.

transformed into a personal being" (ibid.: 93).

Work as an educative element opens up access to bearers of value. If a balance of subjective soulful reality and objective form was ensured, this would lead to the same totality for all types of individuality (ibid.: 104 f.). The experience of timeless values does not only bring about reconciliation between individual life and objective form. It also provides a basis for the "hope for development of a new unitary culture encompassing the entire folk community" (ibid.: 105). As school becomes more 'enjoyable' and attuned to the psyche as a result of work, it contributes more than just to the education of the individual. This fiction of a unity that can be created by education extends beyond the framework of the school, aiming through a moral transformation of society at higher goals.

Leo Weber is certainly correct in seeing the problem of Kerschensteiner's theory of education in the idea that these conceptions of value should culminate in unity, and that – referring to *Theorie der Bildung* – God is described as a unity of ideas of value.

> In the intellectual development of the individual, which leads from man as a purely instinctual being in dialectical mutual interaction with the objective contents of the surrounding culture to a personality abounding in values, on this path "from a unity closed in itself on through unfolded multiplicity to an unfolded and developed unity", K. sees the movement which leads men from lower levels upward, from narrow vistas to broad perspectives, from a creature driven by instincts to a creature of reason guided by norms, which in the sphere of ethos finds access to something enduring and absolute. (Weber 1936: 77)

There is good reason why in Kerschensteiner's later works references and allusions to religion, as well as direct statements on it, abound. He wanted to apply religion in order to 'resolve' Simmel's classic antagonism between life and form. The dominating religious connection is also evident from his attempt to transform the previous typology into an overarching trinity, thereby building heavily on Spranger: a philosophical, aesthetic and religious foundation for life or base structure, in which the various psychological behaviours could be reinstalled. The reinvigoration of culture leaves the residue of a split in the ego, even in active aesthetic behaviour such as creativity. Only in the realm of religion is the separation of form and content fully overcome

188

and eliminated (Kerschensteiner 1959: 51). Nonetheless, he relativises this statement when he notes elsewhere that one can "arrive at and achieve an internal unity" only "down the path of conducting one's life grounded on philosophical, aesthetic or religious conceptions" (ibid.: 61).

In Kerschensteiner's construction, 'life' as antipode to 'form' turned out to be the longing for unity and fusion, a "pseudonym of God" (Cioran 1990: 113), and did not slip into some sort of anti-metaphysical backwash. The creation of a dimension in the theory of pedagogy which might also evince quite modern features – for example, when individual education is paraphrased as an initiation into cultural traditions – is in a sense cancelled out once again by the over-riding obligation to adhere to a metaphysical lawfulness and validity of values.

Part 3

*Kerschensteiner in Relation to
Systems of Vocational Education and
Vocational Educational Reform*

10. Apprenticeship, Vocational Education and the Rise of the Dual System

It is generally assumed that the German system of vocational education was invented by a pedagogue, or at least that it was the result of deliberate planning. However, this is only partially true, although some elements had indeed been systematically thought through prior to their implementation. For example, it is true that Kerschensteiner's concept of the vocational continuation school formed the basis for the development of the vocational school. In contrast, the Dual System in Germany evolved out of a debate among economists who were associated with the German Verein für Socialpolitik. *In these debates, they referred to theories of Adam Smith and his forerunners. Georg Kerschensteiner and other pedagogues in turn referred to proceedings of the same* Verein für Socialpolitik *as well as to other opinions and analyses in educational policy, including their own.*

The present essay explores how theorists like Mandeville, economists like Smith, Hayek and Bastiat, and later the Verein für Socialpolitik *have dealt with the question of education, and more particularly apprenticeship and vocational education. It will become clear that it was in particular the education of the lower classes and their integration into society at the end of the 19th century which assisted vocational education in its new form to a kind of practical breakthrough.*

10.1 Education and vocational education as a contribution to the uplifting of the lower classes

Appended to Bernard de Mandeville's *Fable of the Bees* in its second expanded edition of 1723 is an essay that takes a clear position on the question of schools for the poor, the so-called charity schools. My focus will be less on Mandeville's intention to present vice and egoism as socially beneficial qualities, which has frequently been discussed in connection with morals, but more on recapitulating his model of vocational qualification.

Mandeville expressed nothing but scorn regarding sympathy, compassion and honourableness as the supposed motives for founding charity schools. In his view, such institutions merely manifested their founders' and directors' vanity and desire for power and mainly served the sentimentality of the upper classes. In addition, and this was the main reason why Mandeville was opposed to them, institutions of this kind provided a dangerous distraction for those from the lower classes with other. The more a shepherd or fieldworker is distracted from his work and everyday activity, the less he is inclined to endure its travail, difficulty and strain with cheerful satisfaction. Mandeville argues that compared to the rigours of work, to attend school is a kind of idleness, and the longer young people lead such a comfortable life, the more unsuitable for regular work they become as adults. Reading, writing and arithmetic are important for those whose vocation requires such skills, "but where People's livelihood has no dependence on these Arts, they are very pernicious to the Poor, who are forc'd to get their Daily Bread by their Daily Labour" (Mandeville 1980: 320), and furthermore:

> A Servant can have no unfeign'd Respect for his Master, as soon as he has Sense enough to find out that he serves a Fool [...] No Creatures submit contentedly to their Equals, and should a Horse know as much as a Man, I should not desire to be his Rider. (ibid.: 321 f.)

Mandeville expressed great scepticism about efforts to raise the general level of education, which also aided and abetted the formation of trade unions for servants. In addition, better qualifications and a reduction of working hours, resulting in higher wage costs, was not economically profitable. This was exemplified by the ruin of English wool export in comparison with foreign competition, which had the advantage of cheaper workers (ibid.: 345).

Another factor to be considered is that due to more education (in reading, writing and arithmetic), the demand to enter more qualified professions also mounts, yet there are already enough potential candidates from wealthy strata. If more children of the poor seek qualified jobs, that will lead to a large surplus of workers in trades and handicrafts. For that reason, society has to take great care about the regulation of the number of apprentices, for it will suffer if there are no longer enough poor people to do the more menial jobs that secure existence (ibid.: 332 f.). Mandeville summed up his argument by stating: "The Welfare and Felicity therefore of every State and Kingdom, require that the Knowledge of the Working Poor should be confin'd within the Verge of their Occupations, and never extended (as to things visible) beyond what relates to their Calling" (ibid.: 320).

A number of Scottish philosophers and scientists expressed opposition to Mandeville's position that viewed society "in its totality as a kind of body" with various "members" which worked for the well-being of the others (ibid.: 418). Adam Ferguson, in his *Essay on the History of Civil Society* (1767), pointed out that the division of the arts and professions promoted industriousness and the readiness for more instruction. This in turn led to progress in the arts and crafts, which gave the more refined nations additional talent for invention, and that led to more knowledge, order and wealth (Ferguson 1988: 341). In his political and economic essays, David Hume also noted that public opinion and the advancement of the arts and sciences were aided by commerce and education, and that in turn was beneficial for freedom and social progress (Hume 1988: 132). His adversary Thomas Reid believed that it was absolutely necessary, in view of the division of labour, to have a proper education and training, and the state should view this as one of its most important concerns (Reid 2007).

Adam Smith rejected Mandeville's view that virtue was uncalled-for in the socio-economic structure of things. Although Smith's *Inquiry into the Nature and Causes of the Wealth of Nations* contains some sceptical comments on the educational system of the day, he nonetheless believed that efforts in education were important for the prosperity and growth of the economy and society. He was specifically concerned about the education of the lower strata or 'common people'. This, in contrast to Mandeville, is reflected in the following quote: "The education of the common people requires, perhaps in a civilised and commercial society, the attention of the public more than of people of some rank and fortune" (Smith 1904b: 269). A more civilised and commercialised society demands not less, but more, education, precisely for the lower social classes. But the education of the 'common people' did not come about on its own, because they had little time for education. As soon as their children were old enough to work they had to work, and under conditions which Smith did not regard as favourable to learning:

> That trade too is generally so simple and uniform as to give little exercise to the understanding, while, at the same time, their labour is both so constant and so severe, that it leaves them little leisure and less inclination to apply to, or even to think of anything else. (Smith 1904b: 269)

A lack of education and habit not only restricted their power of judgement, their statements were seldom heard in public deliberations and given but little attention.

In contrast to the mainstream of the reception of economic theory, which paid scant attention to these statements, the reform of the educational system in the French Enlightenment had a much clearer relation to the argumentation above. The guilds and their system of vocational training was abolished (Smith's view of this will be dealt with later below). Condorcet explicitly cited Smith in formulating his influential theory of public education. The ever deepening and expanding division of labour and mechanisation must not be allowed to stupefy the population; the only remedy against this was "l'instruction publique" (Condorcet 1989: 52).

The connection between division of labour, progress in trade and commerce, personal freedom, emancipation from the low estate of the servant and education is stressed by Hume, Smith and later generations, such as in John Millar's *Observations concerning the Distinction of Ranks in Society* (Millar 1967: 260).

In his lectures, originally called *Lectures on Political Economy*, Dugald Stewart, the first important biographer of Smith, dedicated an entire book to the education of the lower orders. The deficiency of the school system, as reflected in the local 'parish schools' in Scotland, is

196

roundly criticised. Stewart knows that Smith shared his views in this regard. Instead of an excessive stress on Latin, geometry and mechanics should be taught, as well as more literature (Stewart 1994: 327 f.). This was followed by praise for the promulgation of a new general law on education. Widespread education – and Scotland was proof of this as well as Switzerland – led to lower crime rates in the population (ibid.: 332 f.) and was generally good for public morality, as was explicated with reference to France. The spread of a sufficient general elementary education was the best guarantee for morality and order in society. It was also a kind of equalising justice, a proper recompense, if those who preserved others from daily strenuous physical labour were themselves allowed to participate, at least in part, in the "culture of understanding" (ibid.: 341 f.). Because wherever knowledge was expanded, advantages and errors were eliminated, thus furthering happiness and virtue:

> Wherever the lower orders enjoy the benefits of education, they will be found to be comparatively sober and industrious [...] The cultivation of mind, too, which books communicate, naturally inspires that desire and hope of advancement, which, in all the classes of society, is the most steady and powerful motive to economy and industry. (Stewart 1994: 346 f.)

Economic prosperity goes hand in hand with social progress – if there is a well-developed educational system on hand.

10.2 Adam Smith's critique of apprenticeship

The statements quoted so far should be seen more as general comments on educational policy. Only little has been said explicitly about vocational education per se, even though there is a connection here with the education of the lower orders of society. However, Smith's *Inquiry* does contain statements on apprenticeship which are analysed through a prism of economic policy. They are of some interest since they decisively relativise Smith's comments on the system of public education which are often held up by economists as proof of his scepticism. They should not be interpreted to mean that he prioritised private forms of education instead.

The apprenticeship is seen as a means to keep down the number of competitors in several trades, and is thus considered one of the privileges the guilds enjoyed. It is alleged that such special rights which might have facilitated the unhindered exercise of a trade necessarily limit competition in a city. In order to arrange this, apprenticeship with a specially suited master is made a binding requirement. In addition, the number of apprentices a master is allowed to train is commonly specified in guild rules, along with the prescribed duration of the apprenticeship. Restrictions on the number of apprentices and the length of the apprenticeship increase the expense for such training, and thus operate as restrictions.

The cutlery forge in Sheffield stipulated in its guild regulations that a master cutler could have only one apprentice at a time; the weavers in Norwich allowed two, as did hatters throughout England, and an infraction was punished by a fine of five pounds sterling. There was also such a guild spirit among silk weavers in England, as across Europe, manifested in the rule that an apprenticeship should last seven full years.

The law of 1562 made these municipal guild regulations general and raised them to the status of public law by stipulating that no one in England could exercise a vocation or art unless he had completed at least a seven-year term of apprenticeship. In France, the apprenticeship was limited to five years, but then there was a subsequent required five-year period as journeyman, and only after that was it possible to become a master.

Smith's views on guild regulations are unequivocal. He says that they lead to absurd consequences, in that for example a coach maker is not allowed to make wheels but must purchase these from a wheelwright, yet a wheelwright is allowed to build coaches, although he has never served an apprenticeship to a coach maker.

Smith claims that the property which every human being possesses in his labour power is sacred and inviolable. To prevent a poor man whose power (capital) lies in the skill of his hands from using them unhindered is thus a violation of this most sacred of possessions and a transgression against the freedom of the worker and all who are prepared to employ him (Smith 1904a: 123). The worry that such measures served to keep out those deemed unsuitable is in his view hypocritical, outrageous and oppressive.

Moreover, the regulation of a lengthy apprenticeship cannot guarantee that no bad products will enter the market. What is relevant is not whether an artisan spent seven years in an apprenticeship but whether the quality of the product is ensured. Moreover, the institution of a long apprenticeship does not automatically train young people for industriousness and diligence. On the contrary, individuals developed a quite natural antipathy to work if over a long period of time there was no visible utility to their endeavours:

> Long apprenticeships are altogether unnecessary. The arts, which are much superior to common trades, such as those of making clocks and watches, contain no such mystery as to require a long course of instruction. (Smith 1904a: 124)

Once the necessary inventions have been made and the mode of operation is well understood in a given craft, Smith argues that

> to explain to any young man, in the completest manner, how to apply the instruments, and how to construct the machines, cannot well require more than the lessons of a few weeks: perhaps those of a few days might be sufficient. In the common mechanic trades, those of a few days might certainly be sufficient. (Smith 1904a: 124 f.)

After that, manual dexterity is required, and this can only be acquired by practice and experience.

Smith thus calls for doing away with apprenticeship and integrating young people directly as journeymen into the work process. Such training is in any case more effective, less boring and less costly. But it is clear that a master would lose influence and profit because he would have to forego the saving of seven full years of wages for an apprentice. In such an easily learnable profession, competition would increase. This would lead to a drop in the profits in trade, commerce and handicrafts. Similar to other discussions in his *Inquiry*, as is especially clear in his arguments against mercantilism, Smith sees apprenticeship ultimately as an institution which serves to protect producers.

To eliminate apprenticeships would thus benefit consumers. The community as a whole would also be a winner, since products and services would be made cheaper (ibid.: 108).

Only in this juxtaposition does it become clear that despite all his criticism of the school system, Smith did not have an alternative in mind such as removing education from the public sphere and then privatising it through firms or the church, or to delegate it back to the family. This image is confirmed if we look more carefully at what educational institutions Smith criticised in particular. He regarded the public schools as far less inferior than the universities, which did not impart the knowledge they were actually responsible for. Nor did they provide young people with adequate means to acquire knowledge, so that their graduates often left university without any general knowledge whatsoever. Nonetheless, even though the maligned universities did not provide the best preparation for later activities, they were still important:

> The parts of education which are commonly taught in universities, it may, perhaps, be said are not very well taught. But had it not been for those institutions they would not have been commonly taught at all, and both the individual and the public would have suffered a good deal from the want of those important parts of education. (Smith 1904b: 254)

For Smith, it is especially justified for the educational system to be covered, at least partially or even mainly, by general state revenues, since their general utility for the common good was evident (ibid.: 695). Although there were stages of social development where most citizens would, on their own and without intervention by the government, acquire almost all the abilities and virtues required in the state, the mounting division of labour led to a restriction of activities to a small number of work procedures. These restricted and isolated procedures necessarily limit the understanding of most people:

> The man whose whole life is spent in performing a few simple operations, of which the effects too are, perhaps, always the same, or very nearly the same, has no occasion to exert his understanding, or to exercise his invention in finding out expedients for removing difficulties which never occur. He naturally loses, therefore, the habit of such exertion, and generally becomes as stupid and igno-

rant as it is possible for a human creature to become. The torpor of his mind renders him, not only incapable of relishing or bearing a part in any rational conversation, but of conceiving any generous, noble, or tender sentiment, and consequently of forming any just judgment concerning many even of the ordinary duties of private life. (Smith 1904b: 267)

Such a worker acquires his specific occupational competence at the expense of his intellectual and social suitability and military-soldierly fitness. Intelligent conversation, differentiated sentiment and healthy power of judgment would thus disappear, to say nothing of the lack of an ability to judge and weigh alternatives with respect to the important and far-reaching interests of the country.

But in every improved and civilised society this is the state into which the labouring poor, that is, the great body of the people, must necessarily fall, unless government takes some pains to prevent it. (Smith 1904b: 268)

From this springs Smith's unequivocal call for the need for the public in a developed and commercialised society to concern itself more with the education of the common people. The elementary basics, such as reading, writing and arithmetic, could be taught with little expense. Indeed, the state could facilitate a school education for the entire population, encouraging and even obligating children to participate.

While Mandeville was hostile to measures of education, arguing that this endangered the division of labour and its social reproduction in dominant and dominated classes, Smith and the Scottish Enlightenment wished for public education to be mobilised to dynamise social limitations. Education was to compensate the negative consequences for the individual of the division of labour and reduce the resultant social gap between the classes. In Smith's view, vocational education as it had established itself through the apprenticeship system across Europe was perceived in its present form as a hindrance, limiting and blocking mobility, precisely for the working classes as well.

10.3 The role of education and vocational education in Bastiat's and Hayek's theory

The view of Smith stressed here regarding the problem of education, schools, the market and the public – which admittedly plays a more subordinate yet still important role in the total expanse of his opus (cf. Ross 1995) – was not picked up on and developed further in any serious way by later economic theory. On the contrary: the problem of education was limited to the question of the role of the state in education.

In this model, public schooling is to be reinvigorated by more competition, so as to regulate its own agendas in the interest of more freedom and greater efficiency in financing. But Friedrich August von Hayek goes further in his critique. In his extensive writings, the questions of education are clearly subordinate. He looks at the problem basically in terms of whether there should be more or less state intervention, and its negative consequences for freedom. Hayek rejects claims about democratic ends to which schools supposedly contribute as hypocritical. Historically, he argues, it has been more the needs of general conscription and military service that have induced governments to institute compulsory schooling, rather than general suffrage and the right to vote (Hayek 1971: 463). Nonetheless, he seems to avoid calling for abolishment of compulsory education, even though he admits — referring to the reasoning of his friend and influential economist Ludwig von Mieses — that a good argument could be made for leaving some children without any formal education (ibid.: 466). The fact that the liberal educationalist Wilhelm von Humboldt ultimately came out in support of state education, even though he had enjoyed a private education, had lauded its merits and had described public schooling as useless and disadvantageous, is a veritable sin in the eyes of Hayek.

In Hayek's view, a further danger for political stability is that the schools create an intellectual proletariat (ibid.: 470). The similarities to Mandeville's view of the negative effects of education are evident (cf. Bouillon 1991). He sees 'spontaneous' order and evolution as a guarantor of freedom and a way out of (rather than into) servitude, benefiting the market and society. These did not require any third-party rationalistic intervention.

This creed runs like a red thread through Hayek's writings. In contrast, intellectuals who had spent the most time in school tended toward socialist views and an "abuse of reason", as he noted in a publication in 1952 entitled *Counter-Revolution of Science: Studies in the Abuse of Reason.* Here it is positivism and the natural-scientific faith in progress that was entering the schools at the expense of the humanities which Hayek sought to struggle against. In his view, it was the intellectual attitude in natural-scientific thought, devoid of any knowledge of society and values (Hayek 1959: 151), as it appeared prototypically in France for the first time in the Ecole Polytechnique, which led to a mechanisation of the world and a subjugation of freedom. Via positivism, Saint Simonism, the religion of the engineers, the Young Hegelians and Marxism, it had paved the way for totalitarianism in the 20th century.

Hayek refers several times to John Stuart Mill, who was sceptical about intervention by the state. However – and this is carefully overlooked – that same Mill expressly excluded public instruction from his views on governmental non-intervention in his *Foundation of Political Economy* (Mill 1921: 697 ff.), since only the educated could competently judge education. For that reason, it was justified for the state to do more than what the consumers of education could reasonably undertake on their own.

One figure worth highlighting in rounding off the sceptical image and distrust of education, is Frederic Bastiat, a forerunner of Hayek, who as a representative of *'laisser faire'* in the 19th century enjoyed considerable influence in France and Germany. In his 1848 pamphlet written on the occasion of parliamentary debates and entitled *Baccalauréat et Socialisme*, Bastiat dealt with the position already under discussion in France for two decades: the question of the *'liberté de l'enseignement'*. In his view, such a *'Bac'*, which was the foundation of many career trajectories in economy and society, should be abolished. Bastiat saw a danger of excessive overloading of the mind with Latin, alienation from the real world and socialism lurking in classical education, not in the natural sciences and their attitude of mind, as

Hayek had criticised a century later. His attack was initially directed at the legally anchored monopoly enjoyed by the state high schools and universities, which demanded that children had to "fill their head with Latin" from an early age (Bastiat 1858: 15). The path from "Platonism to communism" was short, and ancient classical societies had been based on robbery, not a free market, and had despised work. Rousseau, Robespierre, Saint-Just, but even more 'harmless' thinkers such as Fenelon and Montesquieu, had been led astray by classicism. A chimerical faith in the state had been implanted.

Instead, public education by the state should be abolished as soon as possible, because as long as education was entrusted to the state, that was a reason for the political parties to seek control of it. Instruction by the state was thus instruction by a political party (ibid.: 60). True instruction as could be found in free institutions was the study of the works of God and Nature in the moral and material order of things (ibid.: 69).

10.4 Vocational education as a contribution to the solution of the social question

While the mainstream in economics paid little attention and accorded scant significance to the question of education, a new current developed in Germany, namely the 'historical school of national economy', which grappled with Smith's theses and revised them with respect to the question of vocational education. When in 1875 in Germany the then three-year-old *Verein für Socialpolitik* held a convention to discuss the future of the apprentice system, it was based on 16 expert opinions, one of which will be cited here.

Lujo Brentano, a leading representative of the so-called 'lectern socialists' alongside the older and more conservative Gustav Schmoller, sought to contextualise and thus relativise Smith's arguments against the apprenticeship system in Britain. He called for preserving the apprentice system through reform. What was needed was a clear contractual basis for the relation between apprentice and master and instruction at industrial schools, precisely in the interest of the workers.

Brentano argued that Adam Smith had primarily looked at the decrepit state of small handicraft business at the time (Brentano 1875: 51) and had mainly attacked the law on apprentices, but had apparently not been well-informed about education in the large factories then emerging. Brentano then claimed that under the conditions of large-scale industry, a reformed apprentice system would take on a new significance. Like most writers in the 18th century, Smith had had no eye for the huge differences in human talent. It was important to elevate the great mass of the population, which tended toward an average level of competence, to the highest level possible by means of special institutions for the purpose. If left to fend for themselves, they would go down to ruin. For that reason, special education was needed for the various vocations and trades. Smith's call to fully abolish the apprentice system had actually come to pass in England. Brentano looked at and rejected Smith's predictions based on empirical evidence, and he was himself a specialist on working conditions in Great Britain. The consequence of abolishing the law on apprentices had been a lower qualification of the workers as a whole, and an increasing number of arbitrary decisions on the part of management. Moreover, apprentices had also not fulfilled their obligations. The trade associations had then pressed for a reduction in the number of apprentices in order to counter a surplus of cheap labour. This had been in their interest, since half-trained or unskilled workers who were unemployed later became a burden for their budgets.

It was in the interest of what today is termed 'social partnership' that partners with equal rights representing their interests in separate organisations should operate under clear legal arrangements, and that if disputes arose there was some sort of court or office for arbitration. The same negative consequences were evident later with the Trade Regulations Code of 1869, which consciously eliminated a written apprenticeship contract (ibid.: 64 f.). This was reflected in publications like *Das deutsche Handwerk und die sociale Frage* (Danneberg 1872).

As German and English experience clearly showed, the apprenticeship system should thus not be abolished, but reformed. As one key aspect of such reform the apprentice system as the sole means of instruction was to be supplanted or supplemented by instruction in special industrial schools, where technical subjects such as drafting, geometry, mechanics, physics and chemistry should be taught. It was also important to enhance the versatility of the workers, as factory owners would doubtless agree. In such a combined instructional system, the apprentice "would thus really learn something". Another of Smith's proposals should be heeded: the apprentice should receive a nominal fair wage (ibid.: 68).

It was this perspective, based on regulated and well-grounded vocational education at school and in the firm, coupled with social partnership, which established itself in the field of apprentice training in the German-speaking countries in the 20th century. Ferdinand Steinbeis supplemented these ideas by calling for obligatory attendance at a school for further education (*Fortbildungsschule*). This was contained in one of seven expert opinions prepared for the discussion in the *Verein für Socialpoliltik* in 1879 (Steinbeis 1879).

Contrary to a *laissez-faire* attitude, which was predominant in the leading economic school of "Bastiat advocates" at the time (cf. Brentano 1931), Brentano and the *Verein für Socialpolitik* insisted on a policy of social reform. Intervention by the state would increase the influence of the working class. That was to be achieved primarily by strengthening their rights and implementing their claims as based on these rights. Over against protection for the producers, which was sought in part through import tariffs and further restriction, and a system of guilds still to be created, free trade was also defended. This was to be coupled with an educational system geared to better qualification for the workers and the improvement of product quality.

This conception, which from today's vantage seems astonishingly modern, was formulated in contrast with socialist and extreme paternalistic-nationalistic notions such as espoused by Treitschke. It can be considered a critical further development and elaboration of Adam Smith's views.

10.5 The social question and pedagogy

In pedagogical discourse and in the young fields of sociology and philosophy, the important role attributed to the education of the working class in order to achieve appropriate participation in economic life and society raised a new set of issues towards the end of the 19th century: the 'social question' or the 'question of labour'.

It was in particular the German-speaking countries which sought to achieve economic qualification and social integration of the working classes by means of vocational education, through a combination of instruction in the firm and in special industrial schools. The discussions in the *Gemeinnützige Gesellschaft* (Commonweal Association) in Switzerland emphasised that it was a human, social, patriotic and republican duty to make vocation-oriented further education accessible to the entire nation (Hunziker 1872: 224). Democracy was based on intellectual-moral strength and insight (Christinger 1877: 268).

In his reform efforts on behalf of vocational education, Georg Kerschensteiner also pointed to the close link with the actual conditions of the workers, repeatedly referring to the literature and observations on social developments in Britain. It was Friedrich Engels' book *Zur Lage der arbeitenden Klassen* which prompted von Nostitz, Kerschensteiner's key source, to examine Engels' thesis that the dynamism of capitalism would lead to revolution and social upheaval. Both Nostitz and later on also Kerschensteiner stressed that educational measures for the working class would assist workers to integrate into society. That is why Kerschensteiner advocated pressing ahead with vocational education supplemented by instruction in schools for further education. He also based his ideas on experience in nearby countries, such as in Switzerland. This accumulated experience served to bolster his position. In his famous prize-winning treatise, he stated:

> If our efforts in education are to succeed, then there must in particular be a need for education. But it is an observation nowadays often confirmed that this need is closely intertwined with conditions of work and wages. Even if the work is easy, very long hours and low wages lead to a complete degeneration of the working classes – not only physically, but also intellectually and morally. By contrast, high wages and shorter working hours […] always spur an increase in

the need for education. Brentano was probably the first to call attention to this, and demonstrated that fact in connection with English workers in textiles, machine construction and mining. (Kerschensteiner 1966: 24)

Even if this conception served primarily to assuage the conservative Wilhelmine elites, it is nonetheless important that vocational education not be overlooked and excluded in its vital relation to society. This connection faded in Kerschensteiner's thought and among vocational education theorists in subsequent years. Vocation in the course of time was moralised and reduced to an ethics of class. Social problems were conceptualised as an individual task for instruction in the service of the further education of the human being.

10.6 Conclusion

Vocational pedagogy as a subfield of educational theory building is an heir to the economic discourse of the historical school of national economy in the German-speaking countries. The "idea which did not come so naturally to German pedagogy, namely to see vocation as a basis and vehicle for political education" (Greinert 1990: 401), entered pedagogical discussion via the 'social question'. This also mirrors the confrontation with Adam Smith's views. In any case, this debate contributed to the establishment of vocational education in its present-day form in Austria, Germany and Switzerland. However, people soon lost sight of the question of education for a society based on a division of labour, which had still been a matter of concern for Smith. The division of labour was not broached by pedagogy as a topic in its economic and social dimensions which constituted a specific problem for vocational education. Rather, the concept of vocation was strengthened in pedagogical thought as a question of *personal* calling and choice. The preferred vantage among educational theorists was no longer the question of social participation or exclusion but the so-called "access to higher values" (Kerschensteiner 1926: 79) and a kind of educational personalism.

11. Efficiency and Vocationalism as Structuring Principles of Vocation-oriented Education in the USA

My aim in this chapter is to provide a historical reconstruction of the pedagogical and educational political discussion about education for the industrial sector in the USA. Unlike in Germany, the dual model of vocational education and training characterised by an interlocking of school-based instruction and factory training has never been established on a consistent basis. Education for industry in the USA is provided mainly in vocational schools and tends to be oriented towards the criteria of efficiency and vocationalism.

11.1 Introduction

In the German-speaking countries, international comparative studies of vocational and economic pedagogy usually focus either on England and France (cf. Deissinger 1992; Koch 1998; Greinert 2002) or on perspectives of educational politics in Europe (Münk 2001). Even Japan seems to be of more interest to German-speaking vocational pedagogues than the USA (Georg 1993). This lack of interest may be explained by the fact that the US system of vocational education and training is not considered to be exemplary (cf. Gonon 1998). Unlike in the realm of academia, it is Germany that can offer reform recommendations to the USA for once. This was the case already at the beginning of the 20th century when Georg Kerschensteiner was on a lecture tour in the USA (Kerschensteiner 1911). To this day, knowledge transfer in vocational pedagogy has been from Germany to the USA rather than the other way round (Schütte 2001). Only few German comparative studies saw positive aspects in the US system beside its obvious deficits (cf. Monsheimer 1968).

The presentation of differences generally serves the purpose of pointing out different, possibly new ways of problem perception. In this chapter, a nation-specific discourse will be presented first, based on which the present situation of vocation-oriented education in the USA will be outlined. My main interest here is not in system issues or institutional and socio-historical differentiation, but in the reconstruction of debates in connection with contingent developments that could pragmatically be described as alternative options.

11.2 Efficiency and vocationalism as focal points

In Paul Monroe's encyclopaedia of education at the beginning of the 20th century, education – no matter in what form – is said to be vocational. Thus, the entry for "vocational education" includes the following passage: "In a certain sense all education is vocational in that it aims to prepare one for the most efficient and satisfactory performance of the activities of life" (Monroe 1913: 740).

Even general education – or "liberal education" – is said to be vocational because it too aims at the efficient application of one's acquired knowledge. In his article "Culture and Cultural Values" in the same encyclopaedia, John Dewey challenged the concept of culture put forward by the highly acclaimed Matthew Arnold, a man of letters and school reformer. Dewey criticised Arnold's endeavour to familiarise learners only with the very best a culture had to offer, arguing that this approach was too narrow and one-sided (Dewey 1911: 238). In his view, modern culture also included "manual and industrial activities". Surely it is nothing new to stress that any form of education is related to vocation and that the world of work is part of culture. However, Dewey's argument is relevant in the present context insofar as it has essentially shaped the thematic profile of, and the language use to describe the relationship of education and the world of work to the present day. On the one hand, education is considered to be a question of efficiency, but on the other hand, the need to integrate education into a new context is understood to require its "vocationalisation". To quote from Monroe's encyclopaedia again: "Even in the classical period, when the conception of liberal education was formed, it aimed to produce (!) the liberally educated man or the man efficient in the application of his knowledge" (Monroe 1913: 740). Education is efficient if it is successfully geared to current social and economic developments and if it enables learners to apply the acquired knowledge and skills if required.

11.3 Efficiency as a parallel of academic education and industrial production

The idea of efficient application of academic knowledge draws on an analogy with industrial production, as several pedagogues have postulated. In their publication "Efficiency in Education", Wright and Allen set up the following parallels of the production and educational process (Wright/Allen 1929: 5):

The Manufacturing Process	*The Educational Process*
1. Utilises material	1. Utilises learners
2. Subjects the material to mechanical operations and processes	2. Subjects the learner to educational methods and procedures
3. Changes the characteristics of the material as to form, shape, physical or chemical properties	3. Changes the characteristics of the learner as to attitudes, ideals, and possession of skills
4. Turns out a manufactured product ready for the market	4. Turns out an individual with additional abilities for some form of social adjustment and service

This parallelism of academic education and industrial production can be found even in more recent publications. In their 1992 publication "The Double Helix of Education and the Economy", Sue Berryman and Thomas Bailey distinguish between effective and ineffective learning and argue that traditional workplaces feature a similar structure like ineffective learning:

Characteristics of ineffective learning	*Characteristics of traditional workplaces*
▪ Limited transfer	▪ Narrowly defined jobs and tasks
▪ Learners are passive vessels	▪ Passive order-taking in a hierarchical work organisation
▪ Bond between stimuli and correct response	▪ Emphasis on specific responses to a limited number of problems
▪ Emphasis on getting the right answer	▪ Rather than improving the performance a task has to be done
▪ De-contextualised learning	▪ Focus on specific task independent of its context

In their view, both traditional workplaces as well as outmoded ways of schooling are characterised by a narrow definition of tasks, a limited learning environment and hierarchical structures that force workers and learners into a passive role and that offer little incentive to engage in self-dependent learning and problem solving. It was also said that a main challenge of the 20th century was to "reduce or eliminate waste – waste of time, effort, money and lives" (Leake 1913: 7). Like in industrial production, efficiency in the educational sector too was defined in terms of a reduction of waste of time, effort and money.

11.4 Efficiency as a historical argument of reform pedagogy

As the above excerpts show, efficiency was a topic in early 20th century pedagogy as much as in economy or the then emerging management theory. The philosopher and pedagogue John Dewey relied on Charles W. Eliot in his remarks. Eliot taught in Harvard; in 1906 he published "Education for Efficiency and the New Definition of the Cultivated Man" in which he postulated that education should be directed to the training and development of effective power for work. Indeed, he understood efficiency to mean "effective power for work and service during a healthy and active life" (Eliot 1906: 1). He furthermore expected every woman and every man to strive to become possessed of this form of power. His argument is rooted in a sensualistic, Herbartian tradition, as becomes clear in his claim that during childhood and youth it was necessary to invest in the training of the bodily senses and the care of the body. In addition, children should be trained in a variety of subjects and "in as large a variety of mental processes as possible, and to establish as many useful mental habits as possible" (ibid.). Such an "initiation" enabled youths and adults later on to master new subjects in a short time. He also argued for sentiment as the "real motive power in every human life, and in national life"; therefore it was necessary for education to involve a person's whole character. Only if a person's whole character and activity was determined by some sentiment or passion, it was possible to reach the highest efficiency (Eliot 1906: 27). It follows from this kind of reasoning that education necessarily encompasses not merely a short period of time in childhood and youth, but a person's whole life (Eliot 1906: 1). Continued education in adult years not only provided opportunities for a consolidation of everything learned earlier on but it was also considered to be beneficial for society as a whole.

Efficiency was also a concern of Irving King's, a professor at the State University of Iowa. Explicitly referring to John Dewey and Georg Kerschensteiner, he argued that schools as institutions for character building should cultivate manual work and teamwork, and include a playful element in class. As social centres, schools should serve social progress by incorporating aspects of life from outside the school (King 1913: 266 ff.). His contribution in particular shows that (classical) postulates of reform pedagogy – like manual work and the inclusion of extracurricular aspects – could easily serve as arguments in the efficiency discourse.

11.5 Manual work in elementary school as a contribution to external efficiency

In the claims presented so far we can distinguish between 'internal' and 'external' efficiency. Internal efficiency simply means that some measures are considered more efficient than others because they are better suited to further learning and education. In addition, 'external' references also play a role, in particular to the world of work. Education is efficient if it meets the requirements of professional knowledge and skills. For this reason, E. Davenport calls for adequate consideration of vocational needs at school. Though literature and the arts were undisputedly part of the curriculum, practical matters too should be part of it for the crowd of future workers and their tasks in the industry and the service sector (Davenport 1914: III). In other words, the traditional school system is criticised for its implicit assumption that all children and youths need a short period of general education only, irrespective of their later occupation, and that the populace need no continuing education. The aim of manual work or, as it came to be called later on, 'industrial arts' should be to provide children and youths with an intelligent understanding of industrial production processes and of "the nature of industrial society" (Copa/Bentley 1991: 900). With this reference to external efficiency, understood as adequate provision for the world of work in general schooling and integration of manual work in the curricula, vocation-oriented education appeared on the educational reform agenda (Herbst 1996: 117).

According to Bennett, it was not merely a matter of enriching general education with handiwork, but this integration in general schooling served the purpose of technical education and training. Manual skills could be imparted more effectively in general schools than in the traditional apprenticeships in firms (Bennett 1937: 46). Consequently, Bennett too established a link between manual work and a vocation-oriented educational reform (Bennett 1937: 550). It was widely agreed that efficient education needed to consider the requirements of the world of work. Manual work in the general school system lent itself well as a contribution to vocation-oriented education.

11.6 Vocationalism and vocational schools as contributions to 'social efficiency'

A more comprehensive notion of efficiency was put forward by David Snedden. Before he became a fellow professor of Dewey's at the Teachers College at Columbia University, Snedden was a teacher, a school principal and superintendent. As one of the most prominent progressive educators of his time, he had taken an interest in questions of vocational education since early on, especially elaborating his concept of 'social efficiency'. He expected 'social efficiency' to advance society as a whole "by making its members more vocationally useful and socially responsible" (Snedden 1910: 3). Efficiency was therefore closely tied to social responsibility and focussed on the prospective social position of the youth. Everyone should be trained for their specific role, which included that all pupils had to be confronted with vocation-related knowledge, skills and attitudes. He presented this view of social efficiency as a result of democratic needs; indeed he expected a curriculum based on the concept of social efficiency to enable students to survive and advance in their work and social life. Social efficiency resurfaced as a topic in the life adjustment movement in the 1940s and 1950s (Drost 1967: 100).

The starting point for these considerations can be found in the Herbartian concept of directing all subjects to one centre of interest. It was for this reason that some advocates of social efficiency, like Davenport, pleaded for a comprehensive high school. Snedden, however, wanted to establish separate schools for each profession (Snedden 1910: 129 ff.), because – in contrast to liberal education with its focus on the consumer – vocational education aimed at the education of the producer. According to Snedden there was no discrepancy between efficiency and democracy, but both could be served best by the establishment of a multiplicity of schools providing vocational education. With this perspective, vocation-oriented continuation schools and the German model of vocational education became interesting to North American educational reformers.

11.7 Vocational schools as alternatives and complement to comprehensive high schools

David Snedden was surprised to see John Dewey argue against an education system characterised by a number of different schools types. In contrast to Snedden's vision of a organisation of the educational system in which general and vocational schooling were clearly separated, Dewey adhered to the idea of a single school type with integrated components of vocational education. Snedden's expectation was that if vocational education was integrated into the system of general – or liberal – education, it would soon adapt to the dominant academic tradition (Snedden 1910: 132). Yet Dewey considered such a separation to lead to a restriction of both educational branches. In his view, Snedden's position was too much influenced by the idea of social predestination. However, workers should not adapt to existing structures and submit to an industrial regime but rather 'transform' the system. Snedden replied that Dewey's system hindered access to education for many youths, and that it could therefore hardly be said to add to democracy and efficiency. Only a comprehensive vocationalisation of the education system might enable every single member of society to realise his full potential. Snedden on his part was criticised on the grounds that his goals could be better reached with a model in which apprenticeships in firms are supplemented by school instruction, rather than exclusively with schooling. It may well be that Snedden was not completely averse to the idea of basing vocational education on both firms and schools, like in the German system. Even though some local initiatives were geared to a dual model of vocational education (Cooley 1913), it was eventually the system with

216

comprehensive high schools in which vocational content was integrated into the existing curricula that found its way into the legislation in the 1920s. Thus, a 'hybridisation' of the curriculum was established, resulting in the combination of general and vocational content within a single educational institution (Kliebard 1986: 213 ff.).

11.8 Examination of the German apprenticeship system

The aspect of efficiency was also dominant in the question of whether an apprenticeship system should be introduced in which in-firm training of vocational skills was combined with school instruction. It was said that industrial incompetence was a major problem and a serious cause of economic loss in the USA and that support by the educational system was therefore necessary. Taking additional classes at evening schools was considered important because the division of labour prevalent in manufacturing left employees with little scope for in-firm learning and training. In these discussions, the German system of vocational education was often taken as a point of reference.

Leake assumed that the apprenticeship system might develop in certain subareas in the USA, similar to Europe, where some sectors had seen a revival of in-firm apprenticeship training. However, the higher education standard of German workers was not considered to be a consequence of the national system of vocational education, but a result of the overall highly developed education system (Leake 1913: 182). Therefore, he warned against taking over the German apprenticeship system unseen. Germany in particular could serve as an example for the fact that industrial education was a comprehensive task, and the most important lesson to be learned from Germany was that the industrial workers were better attended to than in other countries (King 1913: 188 ff.).

Though the discussion is outlined here only briefly, it should have become clear that the design and direction of vocational education in the USA was considered to be a matter of efficiency. Two alternatives emerged: vocationalisation of the school system versus an apprenticeship model following the German vocational education system.

11.9 Vocationalism as a constitutive element in school curricula: how vocational education found its way into the schools

In the debate on the form that vocational education should take it was Dewey who eventually won over Snedden (cf. Knoll 1993). Instead of separate vocational schools or a dual model of vocational education like in Germany, an integrated high school was established. In American pedagogical history books, however, Snedden as an advocate of vocationalism has been considered the winner in this debate. While his preferred model with two different school types may not have been realised, the high school curricula have been divided into general education and vocational education content (Kliebard 1999: 146 ff.). According to Kliebard, the basis for the vocationalisation of school curricula in the USA was laid in the 1920s, with efficiency as the main criterion. Since then it has been virtually unthinkable to ignore the argument of work place success in debates on educational reforms (Kliebard 1999: 171 ff.). Much to the regret of many pedagogues and historians of education, external efficiency – understood as a relation to the world of work – has gained too much importance as a yardstick for reforms. At first, the vocational education movement was considered to be effective (Lazerson/Grubb 1974: IX–X), but later on the notion of 'vocationalism' was met with scepticism in the English-speaking world. Vocationalism means that the education system as a whole is constantly to be reminded to orient towards the world of work. This claim was made an imperative in the sense that education had to be oriented towards workplace relevance (Oakshott 1989: 83 ff.). The education system should mainly have a preparatory function for the world of work by training specific skills and conveying a positive attitude to work. The focus was clearly on manual training, which

218

was justified, on the one hand, with the welfare of the child and, on the other hand, with the necessity of acquiring relevant skills for the future working life. This rationale ties in with Kerschensteiner's clever idea of describing his *Arbeitsschule* (activity school) as a school for character building, thereby extending the traditional purpose of the schools to new contents (cf. Gonon 2000). Even though there has been an ambiguous appraisal of the effects of introducing handiworks into the curriculum, this development has nevertheless prepared the ground for further tendencies towards vocationalism in the educational system (Kliebard 1999: 26 ff.).

The drift towards vocationalism was nourished by the argument of the demand for highly qualified workers. This argument was first put forward by employer associations, but the idea of a stronger vocational orientation in the education system instead of the failed introduction of an apprenticeship system modelled after Germany soon caught on with labour unions as well. Apart from the argument of economic benefit, the social question came to play an important role, too: "The redefinition of equality of educational opportunity cleared the way for the triumph of vocationalism in American education" (Lazerson/Grubb 1974: 25 ff.). As many commission reports make clear, since the beginning of the 1920s it was undisputed that the public school system should be vocation-oriented. Vocationalism was made a national priority and even became a topic in Wilson's presidential campaign. In 1917, the demand for vocationalism resulted in the Smith-Hughes Act, also called the Vocational Act. Vocationalism as the vocational orientation of curricula now extended beyond the high schools; it had become a matter of establishing vocational education in the whole school system.

11.10 Spread and ambivalence of vocationalism

The increasing importance of vocationalism between the 1920s and the 1970s is reflected in the legislation, which continually strengthened the financial basis for the corresponding claims. The influence of the vocationalism movement on the US school system is furthermore shown in its general orientation during that time. Schools ought to convey job skills and introduce learners to their future occupational activity. Sometimes even a specialisation and fragmentation of the curriculum for individual pupils was favoured. Thus, the industrial order had reached the school system (Lazerson/Grubb 1974: 50).

Harvey Kantor and David Tyack point out that at the beginning of the 20th century it was a widespread idea among reformers that it was the schools' task to train young people for work (Kantor/Tyack 1982: 1). Schools have undergone many transformations throughout the 20th century and have had to cater to the needs and concerns of many different interest groups. This reorientation is mainly due to the rather dramatic transformation of work between 1880 and 1930, in particular regarding specialisation, management and division of labour. An explicitly vocation-oriented education was seen as the solution for the resulting challenges and problems in the world of work and the labour market (Kantor/Tyack 1982: 43).

Vocationalism was not restricted to the upper secondary level, but this trend was felt even at the level of colleges and universities (Hyland 2001: 178 ff.). In connection with the vocationalism trend, around 1920 the notion of 'adult education' appeared which denoted more than a voluntary approach to self-improvement for its own sake. Rather, it was seen as a matter of social advancement and a deliberate focus on the accomplishment of work-related tasks (Kett 1994: XII ff.).

To many historians of education, the impact of vocationalism was quite surprising. Despite its ambivalent success, the public could be convinced of the usefulness of the vocationalisation idea, in particular with regard to the opening up of opportunities for underprivileged youths (Tyack 2003: 188).

11.11 Efficiency as an argument against vocationalism: Snedden's utopia "1960"

So far, 'efficiency' and 'vocationalism' have been presented as closely related and mutually strengthening concepts with explicit options for educational reforms. However, for Snedden its was actually efficiency as a formal principle which, many years after his controversy with Dewey, made him question the usefulness of vocational schools and the vocationalism tendencies. In 1931 he published an educational utopia which he deliberately presented as a continuation of existing trends: "American High Schools and Vocational Schools in 1960". His utopia describes the visit of a Chinese educational delegation to the USA at the beginning of the 1960s: After the successful advancement of their elementary school, the Republic of China would like to profit from the US experience of reforms on the upper secondary level and of the developments in the higher education sector, in order to take corresponding measures at home. In Snedden's utopia, efficiency and democracy are the highest principles (Snedden 1931: 17). Surprisingly, in his vision all pupils are first of all introduced to the main cultural and political achievements. He argues explicitly against vocational part-time schools (Snedden 1931: 97). Instead, he calls for high schools for all youths up to age 18 based on the argument that the 'quasi vocationalism' of the hitherto existing high schools had failed: "By 1935 it had become evident that the compulsory continuation schools offered practically no useful contributions to genuine vocational education" (Snedden 1931: 108). He considered the pupils to be too young and already too much involved in the world of work, and the field of activity of the schools to be too large for it to be pedagogically effective. Furthermore, he doubted that the teachers were adequately trained. Since traditional apprenticeships had virtually vanished in all professional fields in 1930, the evening schools had largely become dispensable, too. Based on this evaluation, he preferred a general, not vocation-oriented high school, and vocational schools would only be available as schools for adults. The role of education was primarily to offer advice and guidance and to enable learners to enter the vocational schools for adults after the general, pre-vocational phase, because the vocational orientation and desire of youths only develop around age 15. In a first phase up to around age 18, education was therefore a matter of imparting values like competence and responsibility (Snedden 1931: 79).

Because of its lack of efficiency, Snedden had thus turned against the idea of extensive vocationalism and the establishment of part-time vocational schools. The criterion of external efficiency as the relation of the educational system to the world of work had proved too ineffective and had therefore been rejected.

11.12 Conclusion

Even though the US vocational education is not at the centre of to-day's discourse on vocational pedagogy and educational policy, a reconstruction of the respective controversies may offer valuable insights by highlighting the complexity but also the contingency of the struggle over the relation between education and work. Both the semantic and the institutional implementation are country-specific, yet the formal principles can be found in a variety of contexts. The request for 'efficiency' might well come to play an important role in the European and the German vocational education system as well.

Looking at the latest developments of vocational education in the USA (cf. Häfeli 2001) it is surprising how topical Snedden's utopia has become. Historically, the issue of qualification for employment in the industry and service sector was mainly discussed in relation to a vocational orientation of the schools. In reality, however, today's high schools have little relation to vocations, while the community colleges on a higher level in the education system have developed into vocational schools for adults (Grubb 1999). In this respect, today's American high schools with their marginal vocational orientation resemble neither Dewey's nor Snedden's vision. External efficiency in terms of a request for vocational orientation has its difficulties, and this had led Snedden to abandon his original scheme. It may be seen as irony of fate unforeseeable to all involved actors that efficiency has been put forward as an argument *for* general education and against an early orientation towards skills development and practical use.

12. The Development of Vocational Pedagogy in Germany

A so-called Berufs- und Wirtschaftspädagogik *(vocational pedagogy) has taken root in the German-speaking countries, especially in Germany. It proceeds academically from the sphere of teacher training at the universities, is geared to non-academic career profiles and is oriented to instruction at the upper secondary level. This pedagogical subfield deals with questions of vocational education and training and more recently with the challenges of further education, primarily in the industrial and commercial sectors. Its focus is mainly on the need for, and design of reforms, and can be characterised via a prioritised set of particular topics and focal themes. The renewal of vocational pedagogy after the Second World War was facilitated by an acceptance of empirical social and historical research approaches and by a concurrent rejection of rationales and identification figures that had been typical for the development of the German system of vocational education at the beginning of the 20th century. Pedagogical arguments became less important and were at least partially replaced by a more pluralistic and social-scientific discourse. After 1968, the 'classics' of vocational education, including Kerschensteiner, have virtually ceased to play a role in this discourse.*

12.1 The institutional basis and historical-scientific premises of vocational pedagogy

From an international perspective it seems that pedagogues tend to concentrate on the problems of elementary school instruction and general academic education. Accordingly, questions concerning instructional programmes and schemes after compulsory education with respect to basic training and further education for non-academic vocations have generally been of secondary importance to date. The situation is slightly different at the upper secondary level in Germany and Austria, because since the 1960s professorial chairs for vocational pedagogy have been established at the universities. The point of departure for this institutionalisation can be found in the programmes for teachers of commercial subjects which were set up already before 1900. With a small temporal shift with regard to chairs of pedagogy oriented to general education and in response to demands for a more academic commercial training already voiced in the late 19th century (Witte 1889), these programmes were established at the universities. The field that had been called 'economic pedagogy' (*Wirtschaftspädagogik*) since the 1930s was broadened in the course of the 20th century and was additionally strengthened by the university-level training of vocational school teachers. Furthermore, in the early 1960s it was massively expanded at the universities, which has become manifest in the standard appellation for the subfield since that time, i.e., *Berufs- und Wirtschaftspädagogik*. This name expressed a pragmatic compromise between an education for the 'economic' vocations in the realms of business and commerce on the one hand, and industrial teacher training such as is customary for job profiles in the industry and crafts on the other (Pleiss 1986: 102).

With these conditions, springing historically from specific needs of the profession and seeking to combine knowledge from the area of teaching the subjects and more general educational perspectives, a distinctive and independent tradition sprouted and thrived. Depending on the observer's standpoint, it was perceived as either closely related to, or far removed from the discipline of pedagogy. Besides the institutional anchoring that derived from teacher education at the university level, several specific chairs were set up in the subfields of industrial pedagogy, small-firm industrial pedagogy and the pedagogy of work. These chairs had to clarify their position vis-à-vis a 'general' science of education and programmes oriented to occupational training, which generally led to their inclusion within the framework of vocational pedagogy. Common to all these subfields was not only the positioning of the field in relation to related disciplines, but also the treatment of specific problems deriving from the special context.

Writing on the concept of 'Vocational/Economic Pedagogy' at the beginning of the 1980s in the *Enzyklopädie Erziehungswissenschaft*, Karl Wilhelm Stratmann cautioned against carrying the differentiation too far, since the pedagogical questions of vocational training deserved a more comprehensive treatment and the differentiation essentially followed the lines of peculiarities in teaching methods. As a further reason, there was some danger that "the recently restored connection with the educational sciences and their self-image might once again be abandoned, in favour of a one-sided re-articulation with the so-called subject disciplines" (Stratmann 1983: 186 f.).

Along with the vocational pedagogy anchored at the universities and in connection with the thematic treatment of non-academic vocational training it is important also to refer to the governmental and semi-governmental offices and the associations of business owners and trade unions. At regular intervals, the German Federal Ministry for Education and Science publishes reports on vocational training, the Swiss Federal Office for Statistics deals in detail with questions of occupational training, and the Austrian Institute for Research on Education, allied with management circles, undertakes analyses, such as on the costs of apprentice training. The Nuremberg Institute for Research on the Labour Market and Vocation (*Institut für Arbeitsmarkt- und Berufsforschung*, IAB) and the Federal Institute of Vocational Training (*Bundesinstitut für berufliche Bildung*, BIBB) in Berlin and Bonn engage in extensive investigations and maintain their own publication series and journals.

As these explanations demonstrate, non-academic vocational training is thus not an exclusive field within the university-based educational sciences or vocational pedagogy. Although the training of teachers for vocational schools is solidly anchored in the universities in Germany, this has recently been questioned due to the problems in public funding it poses (cf. Bader 1994). In contrast, research on the content area is ramified and extends far beyond the universities. In particular, it needs to be more transparent, as has been noted by the Working Group Vocational Training Research Network (*Arbeitsgemeinschaft Berufsbildungsforschungsnetz*) in a cooperative agreement between the IAB, the BIBB and the Commission on Vocational Education (*Kommission Berufs- und Wirtschaftspädagogik*) of the German

Society for Educational Sciences (*Deutsche Gesellschaft für Erziehungswissenschaft*, DGfE) in 1991 (Diepold/Ziegler 1993: 9).

The 1990 memo of the German Research Agency (*Deutsche Forschungsgmeinschaft*, DFG) does not consider the contribution of university research on vocational training to be especially substantial. It explains this assessment by the fact that, historically speaking, there has been more emphasis on teacher training, and the dominant tradition oriented to the humanistic disciplines tended to be more distant from empirical research, as Achtenhagen and other authors note (DFG 1990: 16 f.). This view is basically accepted by vocational pedagogy, although the authors have been criticised for their marked preference of empirical-analytical research and their tendency to pay only marginal attention to research on further education (Arnold 1992). On the other hand, the institutions outside the university sphere – with the exception of the Max Planck Institute for Educational Research in Berlin (1963), which is not dependent on third-party funding with regard to its choice of research foci – are distinguished by a specific thematic focus. The BIBB examines mainly in-house training with respect to regulations on training codes. Their research in the area of planning and structural analysis is intended as useful input for the ministry and consultations between firm owners and labour (Hilbert et al. 1990). Writing for an American audience, Durden (1996) notes that the BIBB consists of federal officials, state officials, and representatives of employer associations and unions. Its specific responsibilities entail the development of guidelines for worksites and classroom training for apprenticeships in each occupation, in order to guarantee standardisation and to ensure that the skills taught match current technology and employer needs. BIBB guidelines also help guarantee that employers provide their trainees with worthwhile experiences. The BIBB issues guidelines for some 373 job titles, establishes exam requirements for each title, and provides a timetable for training for the classroom portion of the Dual System, which generally takes place in state vocational schools. The German *Länder* follow the BIBB guidelines in the development of the curricula that are part of the apprenticeships. The Nuremberg Institute for Research on the Labour Market and Vocational Training looks at questions of the labour and vocational market in a comprehensive sense, and is not obligated to pursue any specifically pedagogical questions.

The disciplinary anchoring in academic pedagogy regarding questions pertaining to vocational training is not always clear and unequivocal, extending as it does to matters of vocational school instruction and teacher training, especially since neighbouring disciplines in the social sciences also address several aspects of vocational training. Yet since the 1960s other fields in the social sciences have also had an impact on the education sciences, such as industrial sociology, the sociology of knowledge, developmental psychology, educational psychology, labour psychology, organisational psychology, economics and some areas of political science. The expansion of further education in firms and schools eventually led to the inclusion of topics extending beyond the upper secondary level, particularly the topic of vocational further education for adults.

Thus, vocational pedagogy is extraordinarily multifaceted, not only with regard to its subject matter and scientific foci. It has so far been little amenable to a more precise characterisation due to its tradition, which was rooted in a primarily disciplinary orientation geared mainly to the humanistic disciplines and cultural pedagogy. This approach was closely intertwined with German reform pedagogy around the beginning of the 20th century, which viewed the educational value of a vocation within the context of a more comprehensive 'community of values'. In the early 1960s, it became involved in a more or less unacknowledged confrontation and debate regarding a scientific direction more insistent on the need for realism and empiricism.

This insecurity in orientation which entailed its disciplinary, thematic and methodological standpoint as a field was not a new phenomenon in the 1960s, but has a longer history. In 1929, in her book *Die Idee der Berufsbildung* (The Idea of Vocational Training), Erna Barschak commented that it had "by no means been sufficiently clarified whether the problem of vocational training, which also includes the question of the vocational school" should be placed as a discipline "within the social sciences or in education" (Barschak 1929: V). She herself did not explicitly pursue and answer this question. Barschak's historically based study indicates that she leaned more towards the education side. In her view, vocational training and its theory had gone through various phases. There had been an orientation to industrial policy in the 19th century, followed by an era with greater stress on social policy, seeking in particular to integrate the workers in society. Only after that did a more culturally oriented approach emerge, viewing vocational training as part of *Jugendbildung*, the education of youth (ibid.: 123).

Barschak's three-stage model also provides a differentiated perspective for the approach linked to knowledge rather than policy. While industrial policy belongs in economics, a perspective geared to social policy suggests prioritising approaches in the social sciences. Those were indeed applied by the so-called 'lectern socialists' (*Kathedersozialisten*) in their studies on the question of the apprentice (cf. *Verein für Socialpolitik* 1875) (cf. also Chapter 4). Even the educational theorist Georg Kerschensteiner, who according to this scheme might be perceived as belonging to the subsequent, culturally oriented stage, used empirical observation as a method at the beginning of his reform activity, which involved revamping and expanding the schools for further education in Munich, i.e., the later vocational schools. In his little known study *Beobachtungen und Vergleiche über Einrichtungen für gewerbliche Erziehung ausserhalb Bayern* (Observations and Comparisons on Institutions for Industrial Training Outside Bavaria, Kerschensteiner 1901a) he provided a quite detailed picture of vocational training in the other German states. This became the conceptual point of departure for his later famous book *Die staatsbürgerliche Erziehung der deutschen Jugend* (The Civic Education of German Youth, Kerschensteiner 1966), oriented primarily, as the title suggests, to social policy and its legitimation.

According to Barschak, only a follow-up 'cultural' analysis of the problem of vocational training, grounded on a previous successful institutionalisation, can grant access to explicitly pedagogical perspectives. Along with the expansion of the school system and the conjunct questions in education policy, a key task was to clarify the function and educational value of vocation as such. In line with the dominant orientation in educational research after 1900, this was viewed primarily as a problem that had to be dealt with normatively, or in terms of cultural pedagogy (cf. Oelkers 1989). The leading scientific representatives of pedagogy at the time believed that their principal task lay in directing questions of education towards an 'ideal of education' open to national culture (cf. Spranger 1925). For several decades this approach, drawing on sources in the philosophy of life and philosophy of value, remained linked to a pedagogy dedicated to vocation and education. Kipp and Miller-Kipp (1994) note a continuation of cultural-pedagogical premises for vocational pedagogy after the Second World War. Their analysis, which affirms continuity in this regard, suggests that the leading representatives of vocational pedagogy had a concept of education that tended to be functional and oriented to 'integration', based only to a very limited extent on empirical research (ibid.: 740). In view of quite spectacular economic, technological, political and scientific developments, the heavily normative treatment of problems in vocational pedagogy sketched here, which tended to avoid empiricism, proved to be of little use as a disciplinary and theoretical foundation for the field, as will be shown below.

12.2 Vocational pedagogy in the early 1960s

The vocational pedagogy of the 1960s can be viewed as a confrontation and debate with the institutional and scientific tradition described above. The view of the traditionalists will be sketched here first. They wished to adhere to 'classical vocational pedagogy' with its claims to the rigours of systematisation. In their view, Georg Kerschensteiner's work formed the vantage point for all subsequent advancements of educational theory and of vocational education. Therefore, this 'classic' legacy will be briefly presented, followed by the view of the challengers. The work of Friedrich Schlieper and Fritz Blättner can be characterised as indebted to the heritage of traditionalism. Schlieper wanted to create a system for vocational pedagogy integrating Thomism and the humanities, while Blättner saw 'classical vocational pedagogy' as the point of departure for a review in vocational training. In contrast, the attitudes expressed in the publications of Herwig Blankertz and Heinrich Abel in the early 1960s challenged the traditions in vocational pedagogy.

Blättner's *Pädagogik der Berufsschule* (Pedagogy of the Vocational School, 1958) characterised Kerschensteiner's work as a "new school" which had resolutely centred on vocation as a prime focus (Blättner 1965: 24). Blättner argued that Kerschensteiner had helped to free the former schools for further education from their self-conception as a kind of continuation of elementary school instruction. Goethe had already wished to reconcile handicrafts, i.e., vocation, and academic education. Kerschensteiner linked up with this idea and conceived his own "ingenious" solution by closely associating competence in a chosen profession with citizenship (ibid.: 30). These basic principles, which had still been largely valid for Blättner, underwent a certain correction in the analysis by Blättner's friend Eduard Spranger, who differentiated and restructured the theory by placing vocational training in a space between basic education and general academic education. In addition, vocation was to be expanded beyond civic concerns and moulded into a core of an individual's life work. Aloys Fischer, mindful of actual gainful employment and its challenges, stressed the humanising task of vocational training, underscoring a clearly more pronounced role in general education for the vocational school (ibid.: 37 f.). With these comments, Blättner laid out the contours of a tradition by limiting the conceptual foundations of vocational training and the industrial school to a mere triad of authors, i.e., Kerschensteiner, Spranger and Fischer. In his eyes, these thinkers embodied 'classical vocational pedagogy' par excellence.

In this way, vocational training 'on the job' and its theory was linked to a distinctively German discussion that could easily be demarcated in time and space and was adaptable to the reform pedagogy of the turn of the century. By this feat of selective canonisation, thoughts on the complex of vocation, work and education from the Anglo-Saxon world, such as the thoughts of Dewey, Mead and others, who precisely in vigorous debate with contemporaneous German ideas had come to different conclusions, were unfortunately excluded (cf., for example, Knoll 1993). Moreover, from a historical perspective it is somewhat questionable to restrict the theory of vocational training to the authors named above without any more detailed explanation, especially since in the German-speaking countries, far more thinkers could be mentioned who all dealt with these questions, such as the 'Philanthropists' and their opponents, Pestalozzians, and followers of Fellenberg, Fröbel and Herbart (cf. Gonon 1992).

In contrast, a far more systematic view was explicated in Friedrich Schlieper's *Allgemeine Berufspädagogik* (General Vocational Pedagogy, 1963), where he argued that as a relatively young scientific discipline, vocational pedagogy had to be rigorously distinguished from vocational training. In his eyes, the task of vocational pedagogy was to grasp and put in order the phenomena of occupational learning and work. The aim of vocational training was to "perfect" the human being, while the goal of vocational pedagogy as a science was to strive for truth and to stick to the facts (Schlieper 1963: 12). Thoroughgoing reflection on vocational training required various scientific disciplinary aids, appropriated from the toolkits of sociology, psychology and economics. In contrast, vocational *pedagogy* dealt with what was constitutive and typical, "what was really essential in vocational training" (ibid.: 13).

Schlieper legitimated his conception of the field by trying to establish a plausible scientific hierarchy. The vocational pedagogues at the apex were quasi regents who busied themselves with what was essential over and beyond the mere phenomenal. But this conception of course had to be specified more clearly. Schlieper thought the ultimate criterion to be the "generally valid moral norm", springing from the "nature of a person who was vocationally active" and from the "meaning of vocational-professional activity" (ibid.: 19). In contrast to Blättner, he saw no irresolvable conflict between anthropological presuppositions and the social organisation of work. In this he followed the 'classical' approach of Kerschensteiner and Spranger, avoiding any empirical confrontation between the realms of vocation and education and making them accessible to a normative frame. The individual being trained in his or her vocation and the real world of work had to be measured by the ideal of education, which reflects a view also found in the ideas of Kerschensteiner, Spranger and Fischer. Schlieper too basically adhered to the narrowly defined canonisation structures in vocational pedagogy. These were rarely questioned by other pedagogues, or were at best augmented by the addition of another name. Thus, Udo Müllges wrote an article on Theodor Litt's contribution to the problem of vocation and education published in the journal *Die*

Berufsbildende Schule in 1963. In his view the bond between vocation and education had taken on the "classic form of a thoroughly reflected theory of vocational education" as a result of the work of Kerschensteiner, Spranger and Fischer (Müllges 1991: 50). He noted that after the war, Theodor Litt had dealt with questions of vocational training, proceeding from the presupposition that there should be a rethinking as a result of the great "upheaval", and that all concepts, including vocation and education, had to be thought through again, free from any illusions. The person active in his or her vocation should, through a process of reflection, be introduced to human values and history (ibid.: 51).

With the addition of Litt to the triumvirate, the reference points were established for any future vocational pedagogy. Kerschensteiner and Spranger in particular were singled out as thinkers who had established and expanded pedagogical reflection around the central axis of vocation and education. While Kerschensteiner was recognised as having laid the conceptual foundation for the vocational school in particular, Spranger was the theorist who had solidly anchored vocational training in the soil of a theory of values and embedded it in the framework of a general philosophy of culture. In contrast, Kerschensteiner's efforts in this regard had been uncertain and inconclusive. Meanwhile, the more empirical-sociological argumentation of Fischer remained in the background. Litt's contribution in the context of vocational pedagogy was to grasp the difference between pedagogical reflection on the one hand, and industrial development on the other.

Litt had made a name for himself in the 1920s as a critical observer of reform pedagogy, authoring a book *Die Philosophie der Gegenwart und ihr Einfluss auf das Bildungsideal* (The Philosophy of the Present and its Influence on the Ideal of Education, 1925). But it was not until after the Second World War that he turned to questions of vocational training (Litt 1958). Especially influential was his study *Das Bildungsideal der deutschen Klassik und die moderne Arbeitswelt* (The Educational Ideal of German Classicism and the Modern World of Work, 1955), where he accused pedagogy, and especially the canonised representations of vocational pedagogy, of being too exclusively enamoured of German classicism. This preoccupation had blinded them to the needs for the perfection of industrial society. Only

234

as a result of this quasi-instinctive reserve towards change in the workaday world had it been possible for someone like Kerschensteiner to "crown his pedagogical life work with a 'theory of education' whose origins in classical educational theory were undeniable" (ibid.: 67). Although later authors also shared Litt's critique of a kind of immunisation against industrial development, they did not see the remedy to the deficit of theory in vocational pedagogy in the abandonment of the concept of education as *Bildung*. Rather they sought a reinterpretation of this classic conception and its potential, especially as represented by Wilhelm von Humboldt (Blankertz 1985).

If we look at the 'classical' foundations of vocational pedagogy more closely, it is evident that there are some clear limitations. The reason is not merely the small number of authors but can also be found in the text corpus and its content. The authors mentioned were certainly not vocational educational theorists, at least according to today's understanding of what makes a pedagogue. In Spranger's opus as a whole, the topic of vocational education occupies only a modest place. In his collection of essays *Kultur und Erziehung* (Culture and Training), the only striking piece in this regard is his *Grundlegende Bildung, Berufsbildung, Allgemeinbildung* (Basic Education, Vocational Education, General Education, 1925a). Revised and expanded, it appeared as *Berufsbildung und Allgemeinbildung* (Vocational Education and General Education) in Alfred Kühne's *Handbuch für das Berufs- und Fachschulwesen* (Handbook for Vocational and Technical Schools), first published in 1923 (Kühne 1929). In the 1950s, there were other articles by Spranger on the vocational school and its educational tasks. His ideas of tracing vocational education back to the primal vocations of the artisan, farmer and merchant, which were seen as embodying an educative function for the school and world of work, became shakier in his later years, as is evident in his later publication *Ungelöste Probleme der Pflichtberufsschule* (Unresolved Problems of the Compulsory Vocational School, 1970). He candidly confessed to his friend Erwin Jeangros, head of the Office for Vocational Training in Berne, to have thoroughly plundered Jeangros' "maxims on vocational training" before delivering a lecture on this topic. He admitted he needed a lot of imagination in order to address such topics, since he had not really been involved in practical work in the field for many years (Spranger 1978: 290).

In fact, the writings of the least prominent 'classic' thinker, Aloys Fischer, appear more comprehensive and better grounded when dealing with these topics. Although Fischer was primarily interested in questions of psychology and sociology in education, the seven-volume edition of his writings also contains essays on questions of vocation, generally from a sociological point of view. *Wirtschaftsleben und Schulsystem* (Economic Life and the School System) explores vocational training: in his view, such an approach is incomplete since it is cast as economic education without a "true shaping of the human being" (Fischer 1954: 316). In his *Psychologie der Arbeit* (Psychology of Work, 1925), asceticism was stressed as a decisive pedagogical factor (Fischer 1950: 212).

Fischer wished in particular to explore the ethical roots of the modern idea of the vocational school (Fischer 1967: 208). Central for him in this context was "the education of what constitutes the human being in the vocational worker" (ibid.: 210). That is why a vocation was more than the mere satisfaction of some need, indeed he considered it a social service and a "divinely determined fulfilment of duty" (ibid.: 269). In vocational education as *Bildung*, it was important to begin with the idea of vocation. But it should not be forgotten that religious motives were a thing of the past now, and that the order of society based on social estates had been swept away almost completely (ibid.: 285). He considered the separation of work and vocation, as manifested in factory work, to be problematic. Fischer distinguished three ways in which one could get a vocation: through vocational training (which he preferred to the vaguer notion of 'vocational *Bildung*'), through non-school modalities such as existed in handicrafts education, or through school-linked forms for future scholars and officials (ibid.: 481). Fischer considered it important to strengthen the aspect of vocational ethics in particular. That of course should be separated from any social class connections anchored in the old estate system (ibid.: 503). A detailed study *Die Humanisierung der Berufsschule* (Humanising the Vocational School) developed a similar tack, calling for a "new fusion of humanity and work ethos" (Fischer 1950a: 334). Fischer's perspective did not remain limited to the vocational school as such. It was marked by a greater openness to empiricism and avoided excessive metaphysical speculation, which was perhaps precisely why it was deemed less relevant for the field.

Georg Kerschensteiner was another story entirely. His impressive work on school reform and his prominent public engagement for the reform-oriented movement of the activity school predestined him to the role and renown of a 'classic' figure. This was doubtlessly also abetted by the influence of Eduard Spranger, who had early on praised his friend as a worthy successor to Pestalozzi (cf. Chapter 6). Even Kerschensteiner, who throughout his work had faithfully adhered to the importance of the concepts of 'work' and 'vocation' in connection with education, said little that was explicit about vocation-oriented education in the strict sense. It was mainly in his early writings from 1901 to 1908 that he dealt with the question of the vocational school as a concept and its organisation. Later on, he concentrated on the development of a theory of education, grounded on legitimising foundations oriented to work and vocation (cf. Wehle 1966). In this early phase, Kerschensteiner reformed the Munich elementary school system and published essays on the school for further education along with articles on curriculum, school organisation, instruction in drawing and the activity school.

His entire opus is permeated by a rather heterogeneous concept of work. When he ventured beyond methodological and organisational aspects, vocation and education appear in a framework that is explicitly grounded in the theory of values. Central here was not vocation as a socio-economic fact, but rather '*vocatio*' in a clearly religious sense, the so-called 'calling'. In his later years, Kerschensteiner argued against a school with a strong intellectual orientation. This was similar to the typology of Spranger, as developed in his notions of '*Lebensformen*' (Life Forms, 1922), according to which an individual was led to where he or she felt "called by an inner voice". In particular, vocational training is imbued with a teleological function in that it assists the individual in finding what he or she is called to do. This is why general education went "via vocational training", or "the pathway to education through work", school-to-work (Kerschensteiner 1926: 189). In this sense, education for a specific purpose should precede general education (ibid.: 185). In a reversal of the neo-humanistic traditions in education, Kerschensteiner referred to Pestalozzi, noting that vocational education had to become "the gateway to human education" (Kerschensteiner 1930: 167). His reference to Pestalozzi and Dewey – also echoing through his famous Zurich address *Die Schule der Zukunft eine Arbeitsschule* ("The School of the Future. An Activity School") – suggested a certain harmony between the childlike '*Lebenswelt*' and the later occupational or vocational world on the level of didactic method and school organisation. That was to be achieved through an aestheticised concept of work (cf. Chapter 9). In contrast to Dewey, however, it was not the actual vocational or technological development that was crucial. Rather, vocation and work were integrated into a theory of education inspired by Kantian idealism. Yet contemporary admirers of Kerschensteiner viewed this theory with dismay or even rejected it (cf. Dolch 1979; Blättner 1979).

There was only little further critical discussion, not just on the content and scope, but also on the question of coherence and mutual relation in the 'classic' tradition of vocational pedagogy. One such question was how Fischer's approach to a humanistic task for the vocational school could be reconciled and made compatible with Kerschensteiner's idea of general education *through* vocational education. The foundation claimed by Blättner and others could only refer to a small number of relevant passages in Kerschensteiner's, Spranger's and Fischer's works, simply due to the limited space allotted to such questions. The only more comprehensive theory of education which sought to forge a close bond between vocation and education in a consistent manner was that of Kerschensteiner (1926). But down to the present day there has been only scant professional interest in that book. This contrasted with the earlier practical dimension in Kerschensteiner's work which was oriented to improving everyday life. It had preserved him from "the belief that there were some easy common solutions" in the sense of one size fits all. But despite the "monumental work in the theory of education of his later period, as impressive as it is", Theodor Wilhelm wrote in his work on Kerschensteiner with the characteristic subtitle "Legacy and Destiny" (Wilhelm 1957: 20), he found that the late Kerschensteiner was somewhat off the track.

238

The pedagogues, subsequently canonised as 'classic' figures, were at least partly aware that the question of vocational education theory had not been satisfactorily resolved. Fischer pointed out that there were unfortunately no 'systems' in vocational pedagogy, let alone a dominant system. What he could make out in the existing descriptions were questions and problems rather than a theoretical basis for the formulation of solutions (Fischer 1967a: 457). How could a world of work developing in accordance with the laws of technology and the division of labour be harmonised with the concept of vocation and *Bildung*? This discrepancy was also addressed by other thinkers, not just the vocational pedagogues from the ranks of the reform movement who were considered to have the patina of 'classic'. Less distant from the field of industrial technology were Pavel Blonskij, Robert Seidel, and later Anna Siemsen. It was not by chance that all three had leanings towards socialism and viewed industrialism far less as a threat and more as the dawn of a new era.

Those in the 1960s who felt some allegiance to the canon as described above found it evidently quite difficult to relate to the traditional, culture-oriented and inward-looking concept of occupation, as Kerschensteiner and Spranger had delineated it. Fritz Blättner noted that the artisan "who was an artisan both externally and inwardly" had become a rare phenomenon. The person setting out in a vocation was thus greeted "not by a community bound and shaped by custom" but by "specialists". They could only impart their "special knowledge, but beyond that nothing human and manly; there was no relation to life" and how to live it. Work and life were separate spheres, and life, as noted on a dark tone of cultural pessimism, "unfolded in accordance with patterns which today are presented in films and TV, magazines and journals, in a glut of fantasy and wasteful profusion" (Blättner 1965: 57).

This undertone of resignation, resulting from a discrepancy he could no longer overlook between industrial-social development and a community oriented to the ideal of handicrafts creativity, as manifested in cultural pedagogy, opened a window for a new approach among pedagogues who leaned towards tradition. As in the case of Blättner, one can discern a gentle turning toward the empirical registering and analysis of facts involving vocational education. His second revised and expanded edition of the book on vocational school pedagogy, edited by Joachim Münch, focused specifically on these aspects; it included a presentation of the European systems of vocational education and a critical confrontation with the advantages and downsides of the 'Dual System' of vocational-industrial training, or 'school-to-work' as it is known in North America, that encompassed both the school and on-the-job training. Theodor Litt bolstered him in his refusal to continue to adhere to a 'classical' understanding of vocation and education. In the second edition, this cultural-philosophical foundation formed only a point of departure for further observations. Those of course tended to compromise the consistency of the work as a whole.

In Germany in the 1960s, Heinrich Abel's study (1963) on the "problem of vocation" was far more sceptical in thrust. He presented this problem as a discrepancy between vocational thought and vocational reality. Given this point of departure, he was able to sketch the historical development of the educational system since the mid-19th century. This was followed by an analysis of change in the structure of German employment and vocation as a result of industrialisation, based on an evaluation of statistical data and furthermore exploring changes in female work outside the home. Another chapter dealt with questions of changing one's profession within individual economic sectors.

Abel's conclusions were concise. According to him, it was not only crucial to renounce the dogma of a specific image of the human being. "With a similar degree of radicalism", it was also necessary to bid farewell to an "idea of a vocation" (Abel 1963: 185). While it was true that industrialisation led to an ever rising multiplication of vocations, there was no longer a binding ethos of work and vocation in a pluralistic society. That is why there were clear limits to vocational pedagogy when it came to turning gainful employment into something moral in the industrial world of work. Nonetheless, as a foundation for security by means of employment and socialisation, a 'reduced vocation' offered real chances for 'humanisation'. Consequently, it should also be utilised in vocational pedagogy (ibid.: 196). Abel's approach radically questioned the previous tradition in the sense that it was not possible to reflect deductively on vocational pedagogy from the previous definition of an ideal of education. Rather, the definition of a vocation oriented to facts should provide the basis for pedagogical analysis. Similar to an approach sketched by Fischer, this perspective generated ethical postulates which he wished to conceptualise as 'humanisation', and which of course required further elaboration.

In the same year when Abel published his study on the "problem of vocation", Herwig Blankertz offered a new definition for the concept of education. It partly called into question the previous configuration of canonisation in vocational pedagogy. His book *Berufsbildung und Utilitarismus* (Vocational Education and Utilitarianism) is an investigation of the history of a problem that connects with debates in the late 18th and 19th centuries, seeking to do away with the customary dichotomy between general academic education and training for a vocation.

Blankertz wished to take the emancipatory content in the concept of education as developed by Humboldt and the neo-Humanists, and – despite their militant attacks on the Philanthropists – make it fruitful as a tool, applied in the realm of vocational education. Blankertz stressed the importance of an educational concept oriented to universality and individuality over against an "education for industriousness" and its ultimately class-linked implications, as they were associated with the education of the poor (Blankertz 1985: 108). The neo-Humanist goal of general education sprang from *special* education, both vocational and non-vocational. In his view, vocational education could only be justified if it went beyond a utilitarian framework (ibid.: 115). General education in turn could not be reached on its own, but only via some form of special education. With these thoughts, Blankertz raised vocational education from its secondary, or auxiliary, function. Furthermore, the concept of education as *Bildung*, initially viewed with some scepticism by vocational educationists, was thus made accessible and useable for vocational education. He argued that Spranger's interest in imbuing vocational education with a certain 'dignity' should be fostered more consistently. At the same time, it should be freed from the grip of a "historically shaped culture of vocation and life" (ibid.: 113). By reference to Humboldt and a critical-emancipating potential anchored in his concept of education, Blankertz also hoped to avoid what Anna Siemsen had criticised as an ideological entanglement in vocation, i.e., its class orientation. Only then did vocational education reveal education as its inner core, thus leading "educational thought back to itself", as it were (ibid.: 119). The path of education as work on a specific object demanded a formal meaning – as was stressed in reference to Nohl, Weniger and Kerschensteiner – but in such a way that it was tied to a basic content, all the while being differentiated from a content-linked canonisation of general education.

In this way, vocational education in its diversity could be put on a par with the options offered by academically oriented education (ibid.: 122 f.). Although Blankertz' argumentation also builds on classical vocational pedagogy, his approach differs: he seeks to open up the theory of vocational education to extended historical inquiry. Through presentation of the critical debate regarding conceptions of education in the 19th century, these conceptions are themselves historicised. In the process they are thus emptied of their one-sidedly idealistic and cultural-philosophical rationale. In addition, the historical retrospect includes a social and technology-related dimension which must explore the social prerequisites of the respective historically determined understanding of education (Blankertz 1969). Moreover, the consistent approach to forging connections with the humanistic tradition of education binds ideas in vocational pedagogy more powerfully to pedagogy as a discipline. Over against classical vocational pedagogy, the humanistic concept of education is brought into play to serve vocational education itself, and it likewise functions as an instrument for a critique of one's own discipline.

In his book on Humboldt, Spranger aimed at a "modern *German* concept of humanity" which did greater justice to reality (Spranger 1936: 500). Blankertz, in contrast, gives Humboldt credit for going beyond utilitarian ends and orienting education not merely to "naked utility." According to Blankertz it was precisely in this way that the possibility was opened up for a set of didactic methods that responded to and addressed the actual needs of the pupils (Blankertz 1969: 149 ff.). Blankertz furthermore augmented this option by a social-critical and discipline-critical dimension.

12.3 The critique of the theory of vocational education

In terms of these perspectives, espoused by Abel and Blankertz, but already echoed in Litt and Blättner, the central foundations and concepts of vocational pedagogy were subjected to an urgently needed critical examination. The traditional point of departure and basis for reflection on vocational pedagogy were shaken by the works mentioned here; they unveiled cracks in the edifice of thought. Consequently, voices were indeed raised which rejected a disciplinary orientation for vocational pedagogy, or viewed it with great scepticism (cf. Röhrs 1967). Initially, the scepticism was directed against traditional vocational pedagogy, such as the suspicion expressed by Wolfgang Lempert in his preface to Gisela Stütz' *Berufspädagogik unter ideologiekritischem Aspekt* (Vocational Pedagogy: Criticising its Ideology) that German vocational pedagogy had fallen behind the concept of general education and lagged far behind a changing reality in the world of work, so that it represented a "double false consciousness" (Lempert 1970: 1).

Stütz considered her work as a contribution to an emancipating and empowering vocational pedagogy (cf. Stütz 1970). That approach was in turn criticised by Wolfgang Schönharting because – like the classic vocational pedagogues whose thinking had been rejected – it was basically 'functional' in conception. In accordance with Kerschensteiner's approach, this perspective likewise had an important social role, namely to serve in the shaping of a useful citizen, although now in a democratic-socialist frame (Schönharting 1979: 155). Criticism was also levelled against the position taken by Blankertz. Udo Müllges accused his concept of "reflection on education" of being indifferent to the theory and practice of vocational education (Müllges 1991a: 308). Writing in 1975, he noted that the total assessment of the drafts for a scientific vocational pedagogy was "disastrous enough" as a result, and it acted to corroborate Fischer's (1930) view, who was at a loss to see any system in vocational pedagogy whatsoever. This "desolate state of affairs" had not been overcome even decades later, Müllges argued, and no matter how much research was done, no matter how many theories were concocted, they could not blaze a path leading up and out of this dilemma (ibid.: 309). However, Müllges did not say anything about whether such a theory, long a desideratum, was practicable or desirable at all.

Aloys Fischer was not as alarmed as Müllges, so that his criticism of the new attempts to justify and ground the field in the early 1960s can be read at the same time as a form of grieving. What had been lost was a coherent approach such as classical vocational pedagogy seemed to possess. The text corpus that was designated as 'classic', which Müllges and others continued to hold up as an example, proved deficient, and not only with respect to comprehensive theory building. The theoretical assumptions of its representatives were an evident failure when viewed over against the actual ongoing developments in economy and society. Furthermore, its point of departure was too strongly tethered to the institution of the school.

However, even though many agreed, the criticism did nothing to prevent the continued existence of vocational pedagogy and its disciplinary context. On the contrary, discussions on the maladies of vocational pedagogy developed now as an abiding theme in discourse. This acted to spur people on to new efforts to place the conceptual foundations and scientific locus of the field on a sounder footing. The recurrent reflection had a stabilising effect on the discourse in vocational pedagogy in that it helped contribute to a joint treatment of topics. Vital to immediate self-apprehension, these topics were able to mobilise energies, especially if it was a matter of survival. What was important initially, as Harney observed, was to "participate in basal self-descriptions of the system of science with an aim to building a solid foundation for engaged semantics" (Harney 1987: 172).

Perhaps some additional reason for confidence could have been gleaned from Lutz von Werder's habilitation lecture that was published in 1976 in the journal *Deutsche Berufs- und Fachschule*. His thesis was that it was imperative for vocational pedagogy to become more scientific, which in his view meant becoming more social-scientific. Striking a somewhat apodictic tone, he noted that "vocational pedagogy must be made more scientific. This should develop as a theory of the reform of occupational training" (Werder 1976: 324). Here indeed was the expression of a leitmotif which, over the course of the 1970s, emerged into prominence, gaining new impetus by means of the legal reforms in vocational education in West Germany introduced in 1969.

A social-scientific approach and reform in vocational education as a theme appeared in the 1970s as sources of hope for overcoming the theoretical dead end that vocational pedagogy had reached. Of course, not all were able (or wished) to follow that track. After all, vocational pedagogy consisted of a motley assortment of diverse representatives. They had agreed, more tacitly than openly, that they would largely continue to ignore the 'classical' tradition which was a legacy for their own scientific orientation. What conceptual and theoretical references should enter the arena of vocational pedagogy instead was unclear, and there was little consensus about this.

It took a few more clashes, stylised as 'confrontations over paradigm', before a new basis arose for common communication between different scientific standpoints. As Jürgen Zabeck formulated it in retrospect, "after a few irritations lasting about a quarter century", it became possible to establish vocational pedagogy as a sub-discipline in the educational sciences, evident in its strong position and systematic integration into the broader discipline. But also the "internal legitimacy" of this subfield had increased in recent years as a result of a greater readiness to talk and compromise (Zabeck 1992: I f.). This had come about after exponents geared to experiential science, emancipation and critical rationalism had rethought their strategy and had abandoned their skirmishing and struggles in the trenches, thereby opening up space for establishing differing sets of emphasis. These were now viewed as capable of coexistence.

Despite all differences, the upshot of the discussions since the 1960s can be summed up by saying that 'classical' vocational education and its theory had sacrificed some of its aura. In the process, it had come to be viewed as incapable of renewal, at least with respect to how solidly it was anchored in the theory of value and philosophy of culture. Yet the effect was to stop vocation, education and general education from continually being viewed as a bona fide frame of reference.

In particular, Abel and Blankertz were considered representatives who had turned their backs on the 'realistic turn' to a breakthrough in vocational pedagogy. Since then there have been only a small number of attempts to examine the question of a more comprehensive theory building in a broader frame beyond the criticism. It was not until the 1980s that sceptical voices were also raised regarding the approach to a 'realistic' vocational pedagogy, harking back to the earlier question of the theoretical and disciplinary moorings of the field.

The question of the "systematics of vocational pedagogy" is broached as a problem in the journal *Zeitschrift für Berufs- und Wirtschaftspädagogik*, which succeeded the earlier *Deutsche Berufs- und Fachschule*. The renaming of this leading periodical in the field was not accidental; it apparently takes into account the fact that this journal, which initially served teachers and administrative personnel from the sphere of industrial education, had developed into an "organ of disciplinary reproduction" (Harney et al. 1994: 390). As Reinhard Hentke argued in 1982, in contrast to methodology and guiding perspectives oriented to social theory, there had been a "criminal neglect" of the "systematic presentation of statements" as a "constitutive criterion of science" within vocational pedagogy. His sober assessment prompted him to develop a new proposal, namely reordering the field predicated on doing proper justice to the differentiation and total structure of the subject matter (Hentke 1982: 17ff.).

Since the 1980s, Blankertz' emancipatory orientation has also been subjected to increased criticism. With respect to pedagogical and historical questions, to proceed from the "idea of a mature individual" was tantamount to a "contraction of the problem", because it lacked a pedagogical-theoretical basis (Lange 1982: 739). Lisop and Huisinga in turn criticised the strong reliance of vocational pedagogy on sociological theories of social relations in connection with the problem of vocation. Since they had little reflective link with education, these theories served to cast doubt on the very justification of vocational pedagogy as a separate subfield (Lisop/Huisinga 1982: 426f.).

By contrast, the dominant reference point of dissent in vocational pedagogy lay less in the classical tradition as such or in thematic concentrations in content, and more in the general attitude of vocational pedagogy toward society. Vocational pedagogy should not proceed as an 'affirmative' discipline, as the traditionalists and positivists were criticised for doing. Research on vocational training should instead be useful for the reformation of vocational education. Similar to other

246

scientific discourses at the time, both historical and systematic, there was a dominant 'critical' and emancipatory orientation. In the variant in vocational pedagogy within the positivism debate, Harney also saw the possibility of describing the field "as a discipline with a scientific-theoretical base". It could present itself externally in a way that made clear that vocational pedagogy was a bona fide field, also embedded "within the system of science" (Harney 1987: 184).

12.4 Fading out – the paradox legacy of the classics

It seems to be the fate of many classics to disappear from sight, precisely because much of what they introduced has become a matter of course. The curricula of contemporary vocational schools still show the specific design which Kerschensteiner had introduced for his vocational schools in Munich. The particular combination of general education and technical education and the combination of elements of social pedagogy with the intention to develop attitudes and virtues that are relevant for social participation beyond the world of work result in a concept of vocational education that has developed mainly in the German-speaking countries.

It has been one of the aims of this book to demonstrate that a large number of actors had been involved in this development, along with Georg Kerschensteiner also his predecessors and contemporaries. Indeed, Kerschensteiner did not even claim to be particularly original.

In a Hegelian sense we could thus say that Kerschensteiner's idea of combining general with vocational education has been completely adopted in the present-day discourse on vocational education and its reform. The apparent backwardness of his views on the world of work stemmed from a concept of reform that had developed in the Arts and Craft Movement of the 19th century. These views had also been taken up by the Bauhaus movement, which clearly showed in the reform of the industrial world of work based on a return to craftsmanship. It is possible for the craftsman's activity to consist of non-alienated work with a true educational purpose, even under industrial conditions. This idea has recently been put forward again by the sociologist Richard Sennett in his book *The Craftsman* (Sennett 2008).

In the tradition of the classics of vocational pedagogy, the world of work must be organised in such a way as to enable meaningful work and learning experiences. Consequently, the educational system must allow for such an organisation of the world of work through a broad understanding of vocational orientation.

In the 1970s, the concept of vocation as developed by Kerschensteiner and the other classics was considered outdated in view of the technological developments. Today, however, most representatives of the academic discipline of vocational pedagogy agree that by adhering to this concept of vocation a somewhat paradox "modernity of the obsolete" was established (cf. Schütte/Uhe 1998). The vocational orientation in the German system of vocational education guarantees that the aims of the apprentices' education are not limited to mere technical training and the achievement of occupational qualification. In sum, it is therefore justified to conclude that the concepts and ideas of the classics and Kerschensteiner have become so firmly established that they are unconsciously taken for granted and are no longer perceived as particularly remarkable.

Notes on the Chapters

The majority of the chapters in this book are based on papers that have been published previously, mostly in German but some also in English:

Chapter 2: *The Pedagogue Georg Kerschensteiner: A Brief Biography*: revised and translated excerpt from: Gonon, Ph. (2002): Georg Kerschensteiner – Begriff der Arbeitsschule. In: D.-J. Löwisch (ed.): *Werkinterpretationen pädagogischer Klassiker*. Darmstadt: Wissenschaftliche Buchgesellschaft, pp. 121–125.

Chapter 3: *The German Concept of Bildung and School Reform in the 19th Century*: revised version of: Gonon, Ph. (1995): The German concept of 'Bildung' and schools in the 19th century. In: *Nordisk Pedagogik, Journal of Nordic Educational Research* 15 (2), pp. 66–71.

Chapter 4: *Joy in Work – Germany's Educational Debates in the Industrial Age*: revised and translated version of: Gonon, Ph. (1999): Die Arbeit als Thema der öffentlichen Auseinandersetzung. Befindlichkeiten um die Jahrhundertwende und deren pädagogische Bedeutung. In: J. Oelkers and F. Osterwalder (eds.): *Die neue Erziehung – Beiträge zur Internationalität der Reformpädagogik*. Bern, pp. 157–180.

Chapter 5: *Georg Kerschensteiner's Concept of the 'Arbeitsschule' – A Plea for Work as a Foundation for Education*: revised and translated version of: Gonon, Ph. (2002): Georg Kerschensteiner – Begriff der Arbeitsschule In: D.-J. Löwisch (ed.): *Werkinterpretationen pädagogischer Klassiker*. Darmstadt: Wissenschaftliche Buchgesellschaft, pp. 132–159.

Chapter 6: *Kerschensteiner as the 'Pestalozzi of Our Time' – A Pedagogical Hero and His Tragedy*: revised and translated version of: Gonon, Ph. (1995): Kerschensteiner als Pestalozzi unserer Zeit – eine heroologische Betrachtung. In: J. Oelkers and F. Osterwalder (eds.): *Pestalozzi – Umfeld und Rezeption. Studien zur Historisierung einer Legende.* Weinheim, pp. 315–337.

Chapter 7: *School Reform and Pragmatism: John Dewey's Ambiguous Impact on Modernisation in Germany*: revised version of: Gonon, Ph. (2000): Education, not Democracy? The apolitical Dewey. In: *Studies in Philosophy and Education* 19 (1-2), pp. 141–157.

Chapter 8: *Education as Self-guidance – Max Weber's Alternative to Liberal Education*: thoroughly revised and translated version of: Gonon, Ph. (2006): Bildung als Selbstführung. Max Webers Alternative zur geisteswissenschaftlichen Bildungstheorie. In: J. Oelkers, R. Casale, R. Horlacher and S. Larcher Klee (eds.): *Rationalisierung und Bildung bei Max Weber. Beiträge zur historischen Bildungsforschung.* Bad Heilbrunn, pp. 181–208.

Chapter 9: *Georg Simmel's Discourse of Life and Form as a Blueprint for Georg Kerschensteiner's Theory of Education*: revised and translated excerpt of: Gonon, Ph. (1992): *Arbeitsschule und Qualifikation. Arbeit und Schule im 19. Jahrhundert, Kerschensteiner und die heutigen Debatten zur beruflichen Qualifikation.* Bern, pp. 221–231.

Chapter 10: *Apprenticeship, Vocational Education and the Rise of the Dual System*: revised and translated version of: Gonon, Ph. (1998): Berufliche Bildung und Gesellschaft in ökonomischer und pädagogischer Theoriebildung. In: *Zeitschrift für Pädagogik*, 38. Beiheft, pp. 251–266.

Chapter 11: *Efficiency and Vocationalism as Structuring Principles of Vocation-oriented Education in the USA*: slightly modified version of: Gonon, Ph. (2009): "Efficiency" and "Vocationalism" as Structuring Principles of Industrial Education in the USA. In: *Vocations and Learning* 1.

Chapter 12: *The Development of Vocational Pedagogy in Germany*: revised and translated version of: Gonon, Ph. (1997): Berufsbildung. In: R. Fatke (ed.): *Forschungs- und Handlungsfelder der Pädagogik. Beiheft 36 der Zeitschrift für Pädagogik.* Weinheim, pp. 151–184.

References

AKB – [Simmel, G.]: Letter to Georg Kerschensteiner, 15 October 1917. Handwritten manuscript. Handschriftensammlung der Stadtbibliothek München.

AKB 50 – [Zollinger, F.]: Brief an Kerschensteiner vom 23. Dezember 1907. Handwritten manuscript. Handschriftensammlung der Stadtbibliothek München.

AKM 40 – [Kerschensteiner, G.]: Über eine rein soziologische Auffassung des Erziehungsprozesses. Handwritten and stenographic copy. [n.d., n. p.]

AKM 127 – [Kerschensteiner, G.] Pestalozzis angebliche Principien nach P. Natorp. Mit Bemerkungen von mir, herausgehoben aus P. Natorps "Pestalozzi" (Leipzig) und aus P. Natorps "Pestalozzis Princip der Anschauung" (Stuttgart). Archiv der Stadtbibliothek München. [1914]

AKM 177 – [Kerschensteiner, G.]: Zwanzig Jahre im Schulaufsichtsamte. Typewritten manuscript. (Published in: Pädagogische Praxis 1915) [1914]

AKM 359 – [Kerschensteiner, G.]: Kulturproblem und Persönlichkeit. Unpublished typewritten manuscript. [1914a]

Abel, H. (1963): *Das Berufsproblem im gewerblichen Ausbildungs- und Schulwesen Deutschlands (BRD)*. Braunschweig.

Achtenhagen, F. (1990): Vorwort. In: Senatskommission für Berufsbildungsforschung (ed.): *Berufsbildungsforschung an den Hochschulen der Bundesrepublik Deutschland: Situation, Hauptaufgaben, Förderungsbedarf*. Weinheim, pp. I–VIII.

Adrian, R. (1998): *Die Schultheorie Georg Kerschensteiners. Eine hermeneutische Rekonstruktion ihrer Genese*. Frankfurt a. M.

Aebli, H. (1985): *Zwölf Grundformen des Lehrens*. Stuttgart.

Arnold, R. (1992): Universitäre Berufsbildungsforschung "auf dem Prüfstand". Anmerkungen zur Denkschrift der DFG-Senatskommission "Berufsbildungsforschung an den Hochschulen der Bundesrepublik Deutschland". In: *Zeitschrift für Pädagogik* 38, pp. 599–612.

Auerbach, F. (1910): *Die Grundbegriffe der modernen Naturlehre*. Leipzig.

Bader, R. (1994): Lehrerausbildung an Fachhochschulen – keine Lösung. In: *Die berufsbildende Schule* 46, p. 118.

Baker, K. (1988): *Condorcet: from natural philosophy to social mathematics*. Chicago: University of Chicago Press.

Bang, O. (1924): Volkswirtschaft und Volkstum. In: *Friedrich Mann's Pädagogisches Magazin. Abhandlungen vom Gebiete der Pädagogik und ihrer Hilfswissenschaften*. Heft 960. 4th ed. Langensalza.

Barschak, E. (1929): *Die Idee der Berufsbildung und ihre Einwirkung auf die Berufs-erziehung im Gewerbe*. Leipzig.

Bastiat, F. (1858): *Der Classische Unterricht und der Sozialismus*. Hannover.

Bebel, A. (1907): *Charles Fourier – Sein Leben und seine Theorien*. 3. Aufl. Stuttgart.

Beck, K. (1984): Zur Kritik des Lernortkonzepts – Ein Plädoyer für die Verabschie-dung einer untauglichen Idee. In: W. Georg (ed.): *Schule und Betrieb*. Bielefeld, pp. 247–262.

Benner, H. (1977): *Der Ausbildungsberuf als berufspädagogisches und bildungsöko-nomisches Problem*. Hannover.

Bennett, Ch. (1937): *History of Manual and Industrial Education, 1870–1917*. Peoria, IL: Chas. A. Bennett Company.

Bergson, H. (1911): *Creative Evolution*. New York.

Berryman, E. and Bailey T. R. (1992): *The Double Helix of Education & the Econ-omy*. New York: TC.

Best, R. H. and Ogden, Ch. K. (1914): *The problem of continuation schools and its successful solution in Germany*. London.

Beyer, O. W. (1904): Erziehung zur Arbeit. In: W. Rein (ed.): *Enzyklopädisches Handbuch der Pädagogik*. 2. Aufl., Bd. II. Langensalza, pp. 566–577.

Bienfait, A. (1999): *Freiheit, Verantwortung, Solidarität. Zur Rekonstruktion des politischen Liberalismus*. Frankfurt.

Biesenbach, K.-P. (1988): *Subjektivität ohne Substanz. Georg Simmels Individuali-tätsbegriff als produktive Wendung einer theoretischen Ernüchterung*. Diss. (Europäische Hochschulschriften Reihe XI, Pädagogik, Vol. 371). Frankfurt a. M.

Blankertz, H. (1969): *Bildung im Zeitalter der großen Industrie*. Hannover.

Blankertz, H. (1985): *Berufsbildung und Utilitarismus. Problemgeschichtliche Unter-suchungen*. Weinheim/Munich.

Blättner, F. (1965): *Pädagogik der Berufsschule*. 2nd ed. Heidelberg.

Blättner, F. (1979): Ist Theorie der Bildung als Wissenschaft überhaupt möglich? In: G. Wehle (ed.): *Georg Kerschensteiner*. Darmstadt, pp. 148–174.

Blossfeld, H.-E. (1993): Die berufliche Erstausbildung Jugendlicher im internationa-len Vergleich. In: P. Diepold and A. Kell (eds.): Entwicklungen in der Be-rufsausbildung. Deutsche Berufsausbildung zwischen Modernisierung und Mo-dernitätskrise im Kontext der Europäischen Integration. *zbw*, Beiheft 11. Stutt-gart, pp. 23–40.

Bohnenkamp, H., Dirks, W. and Knab, D. (eds.) (1966): *Empfehlungen und Gutach-ten des Deutschen Ausschusses für das Erziehungs- und Bildungswesen 1953– 1966. Gesamtausgabe*. Stuttgart.

Bohnsack, R. (1976): *Erziehung zur Demokratie. John Deweys Pädagogik und ihre Bedeutung für die Reform unserer Schule*. Maier, Ravensburg.

Boldt, H. (2001): „Den Staat ergänzen, ersetzen oder sich mit ihm versöhnen?" As-pekte der Selbstverwaltungsdiskussion im 19. Jahrhundert. In: E. Hanke and W. J. Mommsen (eds.): *Max Webers Herrschaftssoziologie. Studien zu Entstehung und Wirkung*. Tübingen, pp. 139–165.

Bouillon, H. (1991): *Ordnung, Evolution und Erkenntnis. Hayeks Sozialphilosophie und ihre erkenntnistheoretische Grundlage*. Tübingen.

Bourdieu, P. (1985): Sozialer Raum und "Klassen". In: P. Bourdieu: *Sozialer Raum und "Klassen". Leçon sur la leçon – Zwei Vorlesungen*. Translated by Bernd Schwibs. Frankfurt a. M.

Brand, W. and Brinkmann, D. (1978): Theoretische und praktische Maßstäbe für die Berufserziehung zwischen Dogmatismus und Skeptizismus. Anmerkungen zu Lempert, W. and Franzke, R.: Die Berufserziehung. In: W. Brand and D. Brinkmann (eds.): *Tradition und Neuorientierung in der Berufs- und Wirtschaftspädagogik. Beiträge zur Theorie und Praxis beruflicher Bildungsprozesse in der Gegenwart*. Hamburg, pp. 197–208.

Brentano, L. (1875): Gutachten VII. In: Verein für Socialpolitik (ed.): *Die Reform des Lehrlingswesens. Sechzehn Gutachten und Berichte*. Leipzig, pp. 49–71.

Brentano, L. (1893): *Über das Verhältnis von Arbeitslohn und Arbeitszeit zur Arbeitsleistung*. 2nd ed. Leipzig.

Brentano, L. (1897): *Die Stellung der Studenten zu den sozialpolitischen Aufgaben der Zeit*. Munich.

Brentano, L. (1901): *Die Schrecken des überwiegenden Industriestaats*. Berlin.

Brentano, L. (1902): *Ethik und Volkswirtschaft in der Geschichte. Rektoratsrede gehalten am 23. November 1901*. Munich.

Brentano, L. (1931): *Mein Leben im Kampf um die soziale Entwicklung Deutschlands*. Jena.

Breuer, S. (1991): *Max Webers Herrschaftssoziologie*. Frankfurt.

Brezinka, W. (1972): *Von der Pädagogik zur Erziehungswissenschaft*. Weinheim.

Brezinka, W. (1978): *Metatheorie der Erziehung*. Munich: Reinhardt.

Bücher, K. (1896): *Arbeit und Rhythmus*. Leipzig.

Campbell, J. (1989): *Joy in Work, German Work*. New Jersey: Princeton University Press.

Campbell, J. (1989a): *Der deutsche Werkbund 1907–1934*. Munich.

Campbell, J. (1995): *Understanding John Dewey*. Chicago: Open Court.

Campe, J. (1979): *Allgemeine Revision des gesamten Schul und Erziehungswesens von einer Gesellschaft praktischer Erzieher*. 16 vols. Vaduz: Topos.

Carlyle, T. (1843): *Past and Present, Book II*. London.

Carlyle, T. (n.d.): *Über Helden, Heldenverehrung und das Heldentümliche in der Geschichte – Sechs Vorlesungen*. Translated by R. v. Erdberg. Berlin.

Christinger, J. (1877): Die Fortbildungsschulen in Süddeutschland. In: *Schweizerische Zeitschrift für Gemeinnützigkeit XVI*, pp. 232–272.

Cioran, E. M. (1990): *Das Buch der Täuschungen*. Bukarest. Frankfurt.

Condorcet, M. (1981): *Esquisse d'un tableau historique des progrès de l'esprit humain*. Reprint. Hildesheim.

Condorcet, M. (1989): *Cinq mémoires sur l'instruction publique*. Paris: Edilig.

Condorcet, M. (1989a): Premier mémoire. Ecrits sur l'instruction publique. Volume premier. In: M. Condorcet: *Cinque mémoires sur l'instruction publique*. Paris: Edilig, pp. 35–80.

Cooley, E. (1912): *Vocational Education in Europe. Report to the Commercial Club of Chicago*. Chicago: CCC.

Copa, G. and Bentley, C. B. (1991): Vocational Education. In: P. W. Jackson (ed.): *Handbook of Research on Curriculum*. New York: Mac Millan, pp. 891–944.

Cornelius, H. (1897): *Psychologie als Erfahrungswissenschaft*. Leipzig.

Crusius, R., Lempert, W. and Wilke, M. (1974): *Berufsausbildung – Reformpolitik in der Sackgasse?* Reinbek b. Hamburg.

Dahms, H.-J. (1994): *Positivismusstreit. Die Auseinandersetzung der Frankfurter Schule mit dem logischen Positivismus, dem amerikanischen Pragmatismus und dem kritischen Rationalismus*. Frankfurt a. M.

Danneberg, J. F. H. (1872): *Das deutsche Handwerk und die sociale Frage*. Leipzig.

Danner, S. (1991): *Georg Simmels Beitrag zur Pädagogik*. Bad Heilbrunn.

Davenport, E. (1914): *Education for Efficiency. A discussion of certain phases of the problem of universal education with special reference to academic ideals and methods*. Revised Edition. Boston: D.C. Heath (EA 1909).

De Man, H. (1927): *Der Kampf um die Arbeitsfreude. Eine Untersuchung auf Grund der Aussagen von 78 Industriearbeitern und Angestellten*. Jena.

Deissinger, T. (1992): *Die englische Berufserziehung im Zeitalter der industriellen Revolution*. Markt Schwaben.

Dewey, J. (1905): *Schule und öffentliches Leben* (translated by Else Gurlitt). Berlin.

Dewey, J. (1907): *The School and the Society*. New York: Macmillan.

Dewey, J. (1910): *How We Think*. New York: Heath.

Dewey, J. (1911): Culture and Culture Values. In: P. Monroe (ed.): *A Cyclopedia of Education*, Volume l, pp. 238–239.

Dewey, J. (1927): *The Public and its Problems*. Ohio: University Press.

Dewey, J. (1929): *The Quest for Certainty. A Study of the Relation between Knowledge and Action*. New York: Minton, Balch.

Dewey, J. (1948): *Reconstruction in Philosophy*. Boston: Beacon Press.

Dewey, J. (1951): *Wie wir denken*. Zurich.

Dewey, J. (1963): *Experience and Education*. New York: Macmillan.

Dewey, J. (1997): *Democracy and Education. An Introduction to the Philosophy of Education*. New York: Free Press.

Dewey, J. and Kilpatrick, W. H. (1935): *Der Projekt-Plan. Grundlegung und Praxis*. Weimar.

DFG (Deutsche Forschungsgemeinschaft) (1990): *Berufsbildungsforschung an den Hochschulen der Bundesrepublik Deutschland. Situation – Hauptaufgaben – Förderungsbedarf. Denkschrift*. Weinheim.

Diepold, P. and Ziegler, H. (1993): *Literaturdokumentation Berufliche Bildung. Expertise im Auftrag des Bundesministers für Bildung und Wissenschaft*. Göttingen.

Dolch, J. (1979): Georg Kerschensteiners Bildungstheorie (1927). In: G. Wehle (ed.): *Georg Kerschensteiner*. Darmstadt, pp. 128–147.

Drost, W. (1967): *David Snedden and Education for Social Efficiency*. Madison: University of Wisconsin Press.

Dubs, R. (1992): Die Führung einer Schule. In: *zbw* 88, pp. 442–460.

Dubs, R., Metzger, C. and Seitz, H. (1977): Modell einer lernzielorientierten Unterrichtsplanung. In: *DtBFsch* 73, pp. 564–591.

Durden, W. G. (1996): The Academics of School-To-Work. Looking at the German Model. In: *Wisconsin Interest* 5 (1), pp. 43–50.

Durkheim, E. (1989): *Education et Sociologie*. Paris: Quadrige, Presses Universitaires de France.

Ebner, H. G. (1996): Vorstudien zur Grundlegung eines für die Didaktik bedeutsamen Handlungsbegriffs. In: K. Beck et al. (eds.): *Berufserziehung im Umbruch*. Weinheim, pp. 11–26.

Einsiedler, W. (1995): Unterricht, schülerorientierter. In: D. Lenzen (ed.): *Enzyklopädie Erziehungswissenschaft*, Volume 3. Stuttgart, pp. 628–632.

Eliot, Ch. W. (1906): *Education for Efficiency and the New Definition of the Cultivated Man*. Boston: Houghton Mifflin.

Eucken, R. (1921): *Der Sinn und Wert des Lebens*. Leizpig.

Ferber, Ch. v. (1959): *Arbeitsfreude. Wirklichkeit und Ideologie. Ein Beitrag zur Soziologie der Arbeit in der industriellen Gesellschaft*. Stuttgart.

Ferguson, A. (1988): *An Essay on the History of Civil Society*. Hildesheim.

Fernau-Kerschensteiner, G. (1954): *Georg Kerschensteiner oder „Die Revolution der Bildung"*. Munich.

Fischer, A. (1950): Psychologie der Arbeit. In: K. Kreitmair (ed.): *Aloys Fischer – Leben und Werk*. Vol. 2. Munich, pp. 171–243.

Fischer, A. (1950a): Die Humanisierung der Berufsschule. In: K. Kreitmair (ed.): *Aloys Fischer – Leben und Werk*. Vol. 2. Munich, pp. 315–384.

Fischer, A. (1954): Wirtschaftsleben und Schulsystem. In: K. Kreitmair (ed.): *Aloys Fischer – Leben und Werk*. Vols. 3/4. Munich, pp. 301–317.

Fischer, A. (1957): Die Krisis der Arbeitsschulbewegung (1924). In: K. Kreitmair (ed.): *Aloys Fischer – Leben und Werk*. Vols. 5/6. Munich, pp. 425–478.

Fischer, A. (1967): Die sozialpädagogische Bedeutung der Berufsschule. In: K. Kreitmair (ed.): *Aloys Fischer – Leben und Werk*. Vol. 7. Munich, pp. 201–234.

Fischer, A. (1967a): Beruf und Berufserziehung. In: K. Kreitmair (ed.): Aloys Fischer *– Leben und Werk*. Vol. 7. Munich, pp. 441–458.

Fischer, A. and Spranger, E. (eds.) (1924): *Jugendführer und Jugendprobleme. Festschrift zu Georg Kerschensteiners 70. Geburtstag*. Leipzig/Berlin.

Fischer, A. and Spranger, E. (1924a): Vorwort. In: A. Fischer and E. Spranger (eds.): *Jugendführer und Jugendprobleme. Festschrift zu Georg Kerschensteiners 70. Geburtstag*. Leipzig, pp. I–VIII.

Flitner, E. (2001): Grundmuster und Varianten von Erziehung in modernen Gesellschaften. Eine erziehungswissenschaftliche Lektüre der herrschafts- und religionssoziologischen Schriften Max Webers. In: E. Hanke and W. J. Mommsen (eds.): *Max Webers Herrschaftssoziologie. Studien zu Entstehung und Wirkung*. Tübingen, pp. 265–281.

Foucault, M. (1991): Governmentality. In: G. Burchell, C. Gordon and P. Miller (eds.): *The Foucault Effect. Studies in Governmentality*. Chicago: The University of Chicago Press, pp. 87–104.

Fourier, Ch. (1847): *De l'Anarchie industrielle et scientifique*. Paris: Librairie Phalanstérienne.

Fourier, Ch. (1925): *Der sozietäre Reformplan*. Basel.

Freud, S. (1993): *Abriss der Psychoanalyse. Das Unbehagen in der Kultur*. Frankfurt a. M.

Frey, K. (1998): *Die Projektmethode*. 5th revised edition. Weinheim.

Freyer, H. (1921): *Die Bewertung der Wirtschaft im philosophischen Denken des 19. Jahrhunderts*. Leipzig.

Freyer, H. (1966): *Die Bewertung der Wirtschaft im philosophischen Denken des 19. Jahrhunderts*. Hildesheim.

Fuchs, M. (2002): *Hans Aebli zwischen Psychologie und Pädagogik*. Aarau.

Garrison, J. (1999): The Political Theory of John Dewey and the importance of Listening in Education. In: J. Oelkers and F. Osterwalder (eds.): *Die neue Erziehung. Beiträge zur Internationalität der Reformpädagogik*. Bern, pp. 371–394.

Gaudig, H. (1982): Der Begriff der Arbeitsschule. In: G. Wehle (ed.): *Georg Kerschensteiner. Ausgewählte pädagogische Schriften Band 2: Texte zum pädagogischen Begriff der Arbeit und Arbeitsschule*. Paderborn, pp. 39–45.

Geissler, K.-H. (1996): Kerschensteiner: Ein Erfolg der zu denken gibt. In: *Zeitschrift für Berufs- und Wirtschaftspädagogik* 92 (1), pp. 19–30.

Georg, W. (1993): *Berufliche Bildung des Auslands: Japan. Zum Zusammenhang von Qualifizierung und Beschäftigung im Japan im Vergleich zur Bundesrepublik Deutschland*. Baden-Baden.

Gerhardt, U. (2001): *Idealtypus. Zur methodischen Begründung der modernen Soziologie*. Frankfurt a. M.

Goldman, H. (2005): The Revision of Webers' Ethics. In: Ch. Camic, P. Gorski and D. Trubek (eds.): *Max Weber's Economy and Society*. Standford: University Press, pp. 47–69.

Gonon, P. (1992): *Arbeitsschule und Qualifikation. Arbeit und Schule im 19. Jahrhundert, Kerschensteiner und die heutigen Debatten zur beruflichen Qualifikation*. Bern.

Gonon, P. (1994): Kerschensteiner and Education. In: T. Husen and T. N. Postlethwaite (eds.): *The international Encyclopedia of Education*. Vol. 6, 2nd ed. Oxford: Pergamon, pp. 3133–3138.

Gonon, P. (1997): Kohlberg statt Kerschensteiner, Schumann und Kern statt Spranger, Habermas, Heydom und Luhmann statt Fischer: Zum prekären Status der berufspädagogischen ‚Klassik'. In: R. Arnold (ed.): *Ausgewählte Theorien zur beruflichen Bildung*. Hohengehren, pp. 3–24.

Gonon, P. (1998): *Das internationale Argument in der Bildungsreform. Die Rolle internationaler Bezüge in den bildungspolitischen Debatten zur schweizerischen Berufsbildung und zur englischen Reform der Sekundarstufe II*. Bern.

Gonon, P. (2005): Dewey and James in Germany – Missed Opportunities in German Pedagogy for Creative Encounter with American Pragmatism. In: D. Tröhler and J. Oelkers (eds.): *Pragmatism and Education*. Rotterdam: Sense Publishers, pp. 69–94.

Gonon, P. (2008): Berufsbildung von heute als Alternative zur gewerblichen Berufslehre. In: T. Bauder and F. Osterwalder (eds.): *75 Jahre eidgenössisches Berufsbildungsgesetz*. Bern, pp. 69–89.

Gonon, P. (2008a): Apprenticeship, Vocationalism and Opposing VET-Reform Trends in Europe. In: V. Aarkrog and Ch. H. Jorgensen (eds.): *Divergence and convergence in education and work*. Bern, pp. 57–76.

Gonon, P. and Müller, A. (1982): *Öffentliche Lehrwerkstätten im Berufsbildungssystem der Schweiz*. Luzern.

Graberg, F. (1894): *Die Erziehung in Schule und Werkstätte*. Zürich.

Greinert, W.-D. (1990): Das Verhältnis von politischer und beruflicher Bildung. In: Bundeszentrale für politische Bildung (ed.): *Umbrüche in der Industriegesellschaft*. Bonn, pp. 401–413.

Greinert, W.-D. (2002): Die europäischen Berufsbildungssysteme (unpublished manuscript).

Groddeck, N. (1995): Unterricht, offener. In: D. Lenzen (ed.): *Enzyklopädie Erziehungswissenschaft*, Vol. 8. Stuttgart, pp. 621–625.

Groth, G. (1995): Methodisch-mediales Handeln im Lernbereich Technik – Wirtschaft – Gesellschaft. In: D. Lenzen (ed.): *Enzyklopädie Erziehungswissenschaft*, Vol. 4. Stuttgart, pp. 307–327.

Grottker, D. (1990): Erziehung und Berufsethik – Ideengeschichtliche Grundlagen berufspädagogischen Denkens im Werk von Max Weber. In: *Zeitschrift für Berufs- und Wirtschaftspädagogik* 86 (5), pp. 387–401.

Grubb, N. W. (1999): *Honored but invisible. An Inside Look at Teaching in Community Colleges*. New York: Routledge.

Grüner, G. (1976): Problemfeld Berufstheorie. In: *DtBFsch* 72, pp. 335–345.

Grüner, G., Kell, A. and Kutschka, G. (1987): Neue Technologien und Bildung. In: *Zeitschrift für Pädagogik*, Beiheft 21. Weinheim, pp. 119–129.

Gudjons, H. (1997): *Pädagogisches Grundwissen*. Bad Heilbrunn.

Gundolf, F. (1918): *Goethe*. Berlin.

Habel, W. (1990): *Bildungstheorie des 19. und 20. Jahrhunderts*. Köln.

Habermas, J. (1981): *Theorie des kommunikativen Handelns*. 2 vols. Frankfurt a. M.

Habermas, J. (1996): Georg Simmel on Philosophy and Culture: Postscript to a Collection of Essays. Translated by Mathieu Deflem. In: *Critical Inquiry* 22 (3), pp. 403–414.

Häfeli, K. (2001): Berufsbildung USA – Mythen und Fakten. In: *Panorama* 4, pp. 48–49.

Hamer, E. U. (1983): *Die historischen Anfänge der Handfertigkeitsunterrichts- bzw. der Arbeitsschulbewegung in Deutschland in den Jahren 1880/1881 bis 1886 mit einem Ausblick auf die nachfolgende Entwicklung*. Frankfurt.

Hanke, E. (2001): Max Webers „Herrschaftssoziologie". In: E. Hanke and W. J. Mommsen (eds.): *Max Webers Herrschaftssoziologie. Studien zu Entstehung und Wirkung*. Tübingen, pp. 19–46.

Harney, K. (1987): Kritische Theorie als Bestandteil berufspädagogischer Selbstformierung im Wissenschaftssystem. In: F. H. Paffrath (ed.): *Kritische Theorie und Pädagogik der Gegenwart. Aspekte und Perspektiven der Auseinandersetzung*. Weinheim, pp. 171–191.

Harney, K., Bormann, K. and Wehrmeister, F. (1994): Das Berufsbildungssystem als Erschwernis der Berufs- und Wirtschaftspädagogik: Strukturelle Dilemmata und Möglichkeiten der Zeitschrift für Berufs- und Wirtschaftspädagogik (ZBW). In: K. Strattmann (ed.): *Berufs- und wirtschaftspädagogische Zeitschriften. Aufsätze zu ihrer Analyse*. Frankfurt a. M., pp. 383–395.

Haufe, E. (1896): *Die Erziehung zur Arbeitstüchtigkeit, eine Hauptforderung an die moderne Schule*. Znaim.

Hayek, F. A. v. (1959): *Missbrauch und Verfall der Vernunft. Ein Fragment*. Frankfurt a. M.

Hayek, F. A. v. (1971): *Die Verfassung der Freiheit*. Tübingen.

Helmer, K. (1995): Interesse. In: D. Lenzen (ed.): *Enzyklopädie Erziehungswissenschaft*, Volume 3. Stuttgart, pp. 488–495.

Hennis, W. (1996): *Max Webers Wissenschaft vom Menschen. Neue Studien zur Biographie des Werks*. Tübingen.

Hentke, R. (1982): Zur Systematik der Berufs- und Wirtschaftspädagogik. In: *zbw* 78, pp. 17–30.

Herbst, J. (1996): *The Once and Future School. Three Hundred and Fifty Years of American Secondary Education*. New York, London: Routledge.

Herders Konversationslexikon (1902): *Arbeit*. Freiburg.

Herkner, H. (1894): *Die Arbeiterfrage. Eine Einführung*. Berlin.

Herkner, H. (1905): Die Bedeutung der Arbeitsfreude in Theorie und Praxis der Volkswirtschaft. In: *Neue Zeit- und Streitfragen* 3, pp. 1–36.

Horkheimer, M. (1967): *Zur Kritik der instrumentellen Vernunft*. Frankfurt a. M.

Humboldt, W. v. (1987): *Ideen zu einem Versuch, die Grenzen der Wirksamkeit des Staats zu bestimmen*. Stuttgart: Reclam.

Hume, D. (1988): *Politische und ökonomische Essays*. Hamburg.

Hunziker, O. (1872): Die Fortbildungsschulen mit besonderer Berücksichtigung der im Kanton Zürich bestehenden Verhältnisse. In: *Schweizerische Zeitschrift für Gemeinnützigkeit* XI, pp. 219–241.

Hyland, T. (2001): Vocationalism, Work and the Future of Higher Education (Review Article). In: *Journal of Vocational Education and Training* 53 (4), pp. 677–684.

Hylla, E. (1949): Vorwort des Herausgebers. In: E. Hylla (ed.): *John Dewey – Demokratie und Erziehung – eine Einleitung in die philosophische Pädagogik*. Braunschweig, pp. 7–10.

Jank, W. (1995): Unterricht, erfahrungsbezogener. In: D. Lenzen (ed.): *Enzyklopädie Erziehungswissenschaft*, Volume 3. Stuttgart, pp. 594–600.

Jegelka, N. (1992): *Paul Natorp. Philosophie Pädagogik Politik*. Würzburg.

Jeismann, K.-E. (1974): *Das preussische Gymnasium in Staat und Gesellschaft.* Stuttgart.

Jodl, F. (1909): *Was heisst Bildung? Vortrag gehalten anlässlich der Eröffnung des vom Wiener Volksbildungsverein erbauten Volksbildungshauses.* Wien.

Jung, W. (1990): *Georg Simmel zur Einführung.* Hamburg.

Kantor, H. and Tyack, D. (1982): *Work, Youth and Schooling. Historical Perspectives on Vocationalism in American Education.* Stanford: Stanford University Press.

Kern, H. and Schumann, M. (1984): *Das Ende der Arbeitsteilung? Rationalisierung in der industriellen Produktion.* Munich.

Kerschensteiner, G. (1899): *Betrachtungen zur Theorie des Lehrplans.* Munich.

Kerschensteiner, G. (1901): *Die gewerbliche Erziehung der deutschen Jugend.* Festvortrag. Darmstadt.

Kerschensteiner, G. (1901a): *Beobachtungen und Vergleiche über Einrichtungen für gewerbliche Erziehung ausserhalb Bayern.* Munich.

Kerschensteiner, G. (1901b): *Der erste naturkundliche Unterricht. Ein Beitrag zur Unterrichtsmethode aller Schulgattungen* (Einzelabdruck des Anhanges zur 2. Auflage der "Betrachtungen zur Theorie des Lehrplanes"). Munich.

Kerschensteiner, G. (1905): *Die Entwicklung der zeichnerischen Begabung.* Munich.

Kerschensteiner, G. (1908): Redebeitrag. In: Deutscher Werkbund (ed.): *Die Veredelung der gewerblichen Arbeit im Zusammenwirken von Kunst, Industrie und Handwerk. Verhandlung zu München am 11. u. 12. Juli 1908.* Leipzig, pp. 137–143.

Kerschensteiner, G. (1910): *Grundfragen der Schulorganisation.* 2nd ed. Leipzig.

Kerschensteiner, G. (1910a): Das Problem der Volkserziehung. In: G. Kerschensteiner (ed.): *Grundfragen der Schulorganisation.* 2nd ed. Leipzig, pp. 1–22.

Kerschensteiner, G. (1910b): Berufs- oder Allgemeinbildung? In: G. Kerschensteiner (ed.): *Grundfragen der Schulorganisation.* 2nd ed. Leipzig, pp. 23–43.

Kerschensteiner, G. (1910c): Produktive Arbeit und ihr Erziehungswert. In: G. Kerschensteiner (ed.): *Grundfragen der Schulorganisation.* 2nd ed. Leipzig, pp. 44–73.

Kerschensteiner, G. (1910d): Die Schule der Zukunft eine Arbeitsschule. In: G. Kerschensteiner (ed.): *Grundfragen der Schulorganisation.* 2nd ed. Leipzig, pp. 97–114.

Kerschensteiner, G. (1911): *Three lectures on Vocational Education.* Chicago: University Press.

Kerschensteiner, G. (1912): *Begriff der Arbeitsschule.* 1st ed. Leipzig.

Kerschensteiner, G. (1912a): *Der Begriff der staatsbürgerlichen Erziehung.* Leipzig.

Kerschensteiner, G. (1912b): Das Fach- und Fortbildungsschulwesen. In: P. Hinneberg (ed.): *Die allgemeinen Grundlagen der Kultur der Gegenwart.* Teil I, Abteilung 1. 2nd ed. Berlin, pp. 258–297.

Kerschensteiner, G. (1913): *The Idea of the Industrial School.* New York.

Kerschensteiner, G. (1914): *The Schools and the Nation.* Authorised translation by C. K. Ogden. London: Macmillan.

Kerschensteiner, G. (1916): *Deutsche Schulerziehung in Krieg und Frieden*. Leipzig/Berlin.

Kerschensteiner, G. (1917): *Das Grundaxiom des Bildungsprozesses und seine Folgerungen für die Schulorganisation*. Berlin.

Kerschensteiner, G. (1921): *Die Seele des Erziehers und das Problem der Lehrerbildung*. Leipzig.

Kerschensteiner, G. (1922): *Begriff der Arbeitsschule*. 5th ed. Leipzig.

Kerschensteiner, G. (1926): *Theorie der Bildung*. Leipzig.

Kerschensteiner, G. (1926a): Georg Kerschensteiner. In: E. Hahn (ed.): *Die Pädagogik der Gegenwart in Selbstdarstellungen*. Leipzig, pp. 45–96.

Kerschensteiner, G. (1927): *Ansprache am Pestalozzi-Todestag in der Kirche zu Birr*. Handschriftlicher Redebeitrag. (Pestalozzianum Zürich: P II 441).

Kerschensteiner, G. (1928): *Theorie der Bildung*. 2nd ed. Leipzig.

Kerschensteiner, G. (1929): *Charakterbegriff und Charaktererziehung*. 4th ed. Leipzig.

Kerschensteiner, G. (1930): *Begriff der Arbeitsschule*. 8th ed. Leipzig.

Kerschensteiner, G. (1932): Die Prinzipien der Pädagogik Pestalozzis. In: A. Buchenau, E. Spranger and H. Stettbacher (eds.): *Pestalozzi-Studien*. Band 2. Leipzig, pp. 1–14.

Kerschensteiner, G. (1933): *Theorie der Bildungsorganisation*. Leipzig.

Kerschensteiner, G. (1949): *Die Seele des Erziehers und das Problem der Lehrerbildung*. 4th ed. Munich.

Kerschensteiner, G. (1959): *Das Grundaxiom des Bildungsprozesses und seine Folgerungen für die Schulorganisation*. Final rev. ed. Munich.

Kerschensteiner, G. (1963): *Wesen und Wert des Naturwissenschaftlichen Unterrichtes*. Munich.

Kerschensteiner, G. (1966): Staatsbürgerliche Erziehung der deutschen Jugend (1901). In: G. Wehle (ed.): *Georg Kerschensteiner. Ausgewählte pädagogische Schriften Band 1: Berufsbildung und Berufsschule*. Paderborn, pp. 5–88.

Kerschensteiner, G. (1966a): Letter Dated March 21, 1915. In: L. Englert (ed.): *Georg Kerschensteiner – Eduard Spranger. Briefwechsel 1912–1931*. Stuttgart, pp. 32–35.

Kerschensteiner, G. (1966b): Kerschensteiner to Spranger, February 1, 1931. In: L. Englert (ed.): *Georg Kerschensteiner – Eduard Spranger. Briefwechsel 1912–1931*. Munich, pp. 306–308.

Kerschensteiner, G. (1982): Der pädagogische Begriff der Arbeit. In: G. Wehle (ed.): *Georg Kerschensteiner. Ausgewählte pädagogische Schriften Band 2: Texte zum pädagogischen Begriff der Arbeit und Arbeitsschule*. Paderborn, pp. 46–62.

Kerschensteiner, G. (1982a): Selbstdarstellung. In: G. Wehle (ed.): *Georg Kerschensteiner. Ausgewählte pädagogische Schriften Band 2: Texte zum pädagogischen Begriff der Arbeit und Arbeitsschule*. Paderborn, pp. 110–149.

Kerschensteiner, G. (1987): Wie ist unsere männliche Jugend von der Entlassung aus der Volksschule bis zum Eintritt in den Heeresdienst am zweckmäßigsten für die bürgerliche Gesellschaft zu erzielen? (Faksimiledruck der Erstausgabe 1901)

In: A. Kunze (ed.): *Die Arbeiterjugend und die Entstehung der berufsschulischen Arbeiterausbildung. Sechs Schriften, 1890–1938.* Quellenschriften Band 2. Vaduz, pp. 1–78.

Kerschensteiner, G. and Spranger, E. (1966): *Briefwechsel 1912–1931.* Ed. by Ludwig Englert. Munich/Wien/Stuttgart.

Kerschensteiner, M. (1939): *Georg Kerschensteiner. Der Lebensweg eines Schulreformers.* Munich.

Kett, J. (1994): *The Pursuit of Knowledge under Difficulties. From Self-Improvement to Adult Education in America, 1750–1990.* Stanford: Stanford University Press.

Kilpatrick, W. H. (1935): Erziehung für eine sich wandelnde Kultur. In: J. Dewey and W. H. Kilpatrick (eds.): *Der Projekt-Plan. Grundlegung und Praxis.* Weimar, pp. 7–84.

King, I. (1913): *Education for Social Efficiency. A Study in the Social Relations of Education.* New York: Appleton.

Kipp, M. and Miller-Kipp, G. (1994): Kontinuierliche Karrieren – diskontinuierliches Denken? Entwicklungslinien der pädagogischen Wissenschaftsgeschichte am Beispiel der Berufs- und Wirtschaftspädagogik nach 1945. In: *Zeitschrift für Pädagogik* 40, pp. 727–144.

Kipp, M. and Seubert, R. (1975): Einige Klärungsversuche zur Qualifikationsproblematik. In: *DtBFsch* 71, pp. 161–178.

Klages, L. (1929–1932): *Der Geist als Widersacher der Seele.* 4 vols. Leipzig.

Kliebard, H. (1986): *The Struggle for the American Curriculum 1893–1958.* Boston, London: Routledge.

Kliebard, H. (1999): *Schooled to Work. Vocationalism and the American Curriculum 1876–1946.* New York: Teachers College.

Knoll, J. (1993): Dewey versus Kerschensteiner. Der Streit um die Einführung der Fortbildungsschule in den USA 1910–1917. In: *Pädagogische Rundschau* 47, pp. 131–145.

Knox, B. M. W. (1964): *The Heroic Temper. Studies in Sophoclean Tragedy.* Berkeley/Los Angeles: University of California Press.

Koch, R. (1998): *Duale berufliche Ausbildung zwischen Bildungsnachfrage und Qualifikationsbedarf.* Bielefeld.

Koch, R. and Reuling, I. (eds.) (1993): *Modernisierung, Regulierung und Anpassungsfähigkeit des Berufsausbildungssystemes der Bundesrepublik Deutschland.* Berlin.

Köhnke, K. Ch. (1996): *Der junge Simmel in Theoriebeziehungen und sozialen Bewegungen.* Frankfurt a. M.

Konrad, F.-M. (1998): Dewey in Deutschland (1900–1940). Rezeptionsgeschichtliche Anmerkungen. In: *Pädagogische Rundschau* 52, pp. 23–46.

Kost, F. (1984): Die Projekt(-ions-)methode. Zur Geschichte und Kritik des didaktischen Projektbegriffs. In: *Bildung und Erziehung* 37 (1), pp. 29–36.

Kramer, W. and Schlafke, W. (eds.) (1994): *Studierfähigkeit qualifizierter Berufspraktiker.* Köln.

261

Kühne, A. (ed.) (1929): *Handbuch für das Berufs- und Fachschulwesen.* 2nd ed. Leipzig.

Kutscha, G. (1975): Qualifikationsbestimmung und Bezugssysteme in der didaktischcurricularen Theorie. In: *DtBFsch* 71, pp. 189–212.

Kutscha, G. (1992): Das duale System der Berufsausbildung in der Bundesrepublik Deutschland – ein auslaufendes Modell? In: *Die Berufsbildende Schule* 44, pp. 145–156.

Kutscha, G. (1992a): „Entberuflichung" und „Neue Beruflichkeit" – Thesen und Aspekte zur Modernisierung der Berufsbildung und ihrer Theorie. In: *zbw* 88, pp. 535–548.

Landauer, G. (1978): *Aufruf zum Sozialismus.* (Nachdruck der 2. Aufl. 1923). Wetzlar.

Lange, F. A. (1879): *Die Arbeiterfrage. Ihre Bedeutung für Gegenwart und Zukunft.* Winterthur.

Lange, H. (1982): Das Verhältnis von Berufsbildung und Allgemeinbildung in der erziehungswissenschaftlichen Diskussion. In: *zbw* 78, pp. 733–748.

Lasserre, R. and Lattard, A. (1994): *Berufliche Bildung in der Bundesrepublik Deutschland. Spezifika und Dynamik des dualen Systems aus französischer Sicht.* Villingen.

Lauglo, J. (1993): *Vocational training: analysis of policy and modes. Case studies of Sweden, Germany and Japan.* Paris: UNESCO – IIEP.

Lazerson, M. and Grubb, N.W. (1974): Introduction. In: N. W. Grubb and M. Lazerson: *American Education and Vocationalism. A Documentary History 1870–1970.* New York: Teachers College Press, pp. I–XII.

Leake, A. H. (1913): *Industrial Education. Its Problems, Methods and Dangers.* Boston: Houghton Mifflin.

Leixner, O. v. (1882): *Unser Jahrhundert. Ein Gesamtbild der wichtigsten Erscheinungen auf dem Gebiete der Geschichte, Kunst, Wissenschaft und Industrie der Neuzeit. 1. Bd.* Stuttgart.

Lempert, W. (1970): Vorwort. In: G. Stütz: *Berufspädagogik unter ideologiekritischem Aspekt.* Frankfurt a. M., pp. 1–9.

Lempert, W. and Thomssen, W. (1974): *Berufliche Erfahrung und gesellschaftliches Bewusstsein.* Stuttgart.

Lenhart, V. (1998): *Protestantische Pädagogik und der „Geist" des Kapitalismus.* Frankfurt a. M.

Lenzen, D. (ed.) (1995): *Enzyklopädie Erziehungswissenschaft, Handbook and Lexicon of Education in 11 Volumes with one Index Volume.* 2nd unchanged ed. Stuttgart.

Lerche, J. (1919): *Arbeiter unter Tarnkappen.* Stuttgart.

Lexis, W. (1912): Das Wesen der Kultur. In: P. Hinneberg (ed.): *Die Kultur der Gegenwart – Ihre Entwicklung und ihre Ziele.* 2nd ed. Berlin, pp. 1–53.

Lhotzky, H. (1919): *Arbeiten, nichts als arbeiten!* Stuttgart.

Lisop, I. and Huisinga, R. (1982): Das Berufsproblem und die Berufs-, Arbeits- und Wirtschaftspädagogik – Dargestellt am Beispiel der „subjektbezogenen Theorie der Berufe" von Ulrich Beck und Michael Brater. In: *zbw* 78, pp. 415–428.

Litt, T. (1925): *Die Philosophie der Gegenwart und ihr Einfluss auf das Bildungsideal.* Leipzig/Berlin.

Litt, T. (1955): *Das Bildungsideal der deutschen Klassik und die moderne Arbeitswelt.* Bonn.

Litt, T. (1958): *Berufsbildung, Fachbildung, Menschenbildung.* Bonn.

Löwith, K. (1989): *Mein Leben in Deutschland vor und nach 1933.* Frankfurt a. M.

Lukacs, G. (1965): *Die Theorie des Romans. Ein geschichtsphilosophischer Versuch über die Formen der grossen Epik.* Darmstadt.

Lukacs, G. (1971): *Die Seele und die Formen. Essays.* Berlin.

Lukacs, G. (1984): *Die Zerstörung der Vernunft. Der Weg des Irrationalismus von Schelling zu Hitler.* Berlin.

Mandeville, B. de (1980): Eine Abhandlung über Barmherzigkeit, Armenpflege und Armenschulen. In. B. de Mandeville: *Die Bienenfabel oder Private Laster, öffentliche Vorteile.* Frankfurt a. M., pp. 286–353.

Mandeville, B. de (1988): *The Fable of the Bees or Private Vices, Publick Benefits. 2 vols. With a Commentary Critical, Historical, and Explanatory by F.B. Kaye.* Indianapolis: Liberty Fund.

Markus, G. (1977): Die Seele und das Leben. Der junge Lukacs und das Problem der "Kultur". In: A. Heller et al. (eds.): *Die Seele und das Leben. Studien zum frühen Lukacs.* Frankfurt a. M., pp. 54–98.

Martinak, E. (1924): Georg Kerschensteiners Charakterlehre und die innere Gesundung unseres Volkes. In: A. Fischer and E. Spranger (eds.): *Jugendführer und Jugendprobleme. Festschrift zu Georg Kerschensteiners 70. Geburtstag.* Leipzig/Berlin, pp. 67–81.

Mertens, D. (1974): Schlüsselqualifikation. Thesen zur Schulung für eine moderne Gesellschaft. In: *Mittelungen aus der Arbeitsmarkt- und Berufsforschung* 7, pp. 36–43.

Meyer, H. (1987): *Unterrichtsmethoden II: Praxisband.* Frankfurt a. M.

Michels, R. (1928): *Die Verelendungstheorie.* Leipzig.

Mill, J. (1921): *Grundsätze der politischen Ökonomie mit einigen Anwendungen auf die Sozialphilosophie.* Jena.

Millar, J. (1967): *Vom Ursprung des Unterschieds der Rangordnungen und Stände der Gesellschaft.* Frankfurt a. M.

Mommsen, Wolfgang J. (1974): *Max Weber und die deutsche Politik 1890–1920.* Tübingen.

Monar, J. (1988): Philosophische Kultur. In: F. Volpi and J. Nida-Rümlein (eds.): *Lexikon der Philosophischen Werke.* Stuttgart, p. 557.

Monroe, P. (1913): Vocational Education. In: P. Monroe (ed.): *Cyclopedia of Education.* Vol. V. New York: MacMillan, p. 740.

Monshheimer, O. (1968): *Erziehung für Übermorgen. Erziehung für die technisierte Welt der amerikanischen Leistungsgesellschaft.* Weinheim.

Müller, G. (1952): Dewey, John. In: H. Kleinert et al. (eds.): *Lexikon der Pädagogik, in 3 volumes*. Vol. 3. Bern, pp. 105–106.

Müller, H.-P. (2003): Kultur und Lebensführung durch Arbeit? In: G. Albert, A. Bienfait, S. Sigmund and C. Wendt (eds.): *Das Weber-Paradigma. Studien zur Weiterentwicklung von Max Webers Forschungsprogramm*. Tübingen, pp. 271–297.

Müllges, U. (1991): Theodor Litts Beitrag zum Problem von Beruf und Bildung. In: J. Justin (ed.): *Udo Müllges – Berufspädagogik*. Mannheim, pp. 50–65.

Müllges, U. (1991a): Berufstatsachen und Erziehungsaufgabe – das Grundproblem einer Berufspädagogik als Wissenschaft. In: J. Justin (ed.): *Udo Müllges – Berufspädagogik*. Mannheim, pp. 294–315.

Müllges, U. (1991b): Das literarische Erbe Georg Kerschensteiners und seine wissenschaftliche Aufnahme. In: J. Justin (ed.): *Udo Müllges – Berufspädagogik*. Mannheim, pp. 149–175.

Münch, J. (1994): *Das Berufsbildungssystem in der Bundesrepublik Deutschland*. Berlin.

Münk, D. (2001): Tendenzen und Entwicklungsperspektiven der beruflichen Aus- und Weiterbildung im Kontext der europäischen Integrationspolitik. In: H. Reinisch et al. (eds.): *Modernisierung der Berufsbildung in Europa*. Opladen, pp. 155–164.

Musil, R. (2003): *Der Mann ohne Eigenschaften*. Reinbek bei Hamburg.

Muthesius, H. (1908): Redebeitrag. In: Deutscher Werkbund (ed.): *Die Veredelung der gewerblichen Arbeit im Zusammenwirken von Kunst, Industrie und Handwerk. Verhandlung zu München am 11. u. 12. Juli 1908*. Leipzig, pp. 143–150.

Myers, P. (2002): *The Double-Edged Sword. The Cult of Bildung, its Downfall and Reconstitution in Fin-de-Siècle Germany (Rudolf Steiner and Max Weber)*. Austin: University of Texas Press.

Myers, P. (2004): Max Weber – Education as Academic and Political Calling. In: *German Studies Review* 27 (2), pp. 269–288.

Natorp, P. (1903): Über die Grundlagen der Sozialpädagogik Pestalozzis. In: *Schweizerische Pädagogische Zeitschrift* XIII (I), pp. 27–45.

Natorp, P. (1904): *Sozialpädagogik. Theorie der Willenserziehung auf der Grundlage der Gemeinschaft*. Stuttgart.

Natorp, P. (1912): *Pestalozzi. Sein Leben und seine Ideen*. 2nd ed. Leipzig.

Natorp, P. (1922): Herbart, Pestalozzi und die heutigen Aufgaben der Erziehungslehre. In: P. Natorp: *Gesammelte Abhandlungen zur Sozialpädagogik*. Zweites Heft. 2nd ed. Stuttgart.

Natorp, P. (1922a): Kant oder Herbart? Eine Gegenkritik. In: P. Natorp: *Gesammelte Abhandlungen zur Sozialpädagogik*. Anhang. Zweites Heft. 2nd ed. Stuttgart.

Natorp, P. (1922b): Pestalozzi unser Führer. In: P. Natorp: *Gesammelte Abhandlungen zur Sozialpädagogik*. Erstes Heft. 2nd ed. Stuttgart.

Naumann, F. (1902): *Kunst und Volk. Vortrag gehalten in Neumünster am 28. September 1902*. Berlin.

Naumann, F. (1907): *Die Erziehung zur Persönlichkeit im Zeitalter des Grossbetriebs.* Berlin.

Naumann, F. (1964): Die Kunst im Zeitalter der Maschine. In: H. Ladendorf (ed.): *Friedrich Naumann. Werke.* 6th Vol. Köln, pp. 186–201.

Neubert, S. (1998): *Erkenntnis, Verhalten und Kommunikation. John Deweys Philosophie des "experience" in interaktionistisch-konstruktivistischer Interpretation.* Münster.

Nicklis, W. (1962): Das Verhältnis der Pädagogik G. Kerschensteiners zu Pestalozzi. Monographische Studie über Wirkungen und Nachwirkungen Pestalozzis im XX. Jahrhundert. In: *Paedagogica Historica* II (2), pp. 255–286.

Nieser, B. (1992): *Aufklärung und Bildung.* Weinheim.

Niethammer, F. (1968): *Der Streit des Philantropismus und Humanismus in der Theorie des Erziehungs-Unterrichts unserer Zeit.* Jena.

Nietzsche, F. (1988): Die Geburt der Tragödie. In: G. Colli and M. Montinari (eds.): *Friedrich Nietzsche – Sämtliche Werke.* Munich/Berlin/New York, pp. 9–156.

Nohl, H. (1976): Pädagogische Menschenkunde. In: D. Höltershinken (ed.): *Das Problem der pädagogischen Anthropologie im deutschsprachigen Raum.* Darmstadt, pp. 39–47.

Nordau, M. (1909): *Die conventionellen Lügen der Kulturmenschheit.* Leipzig.

Nostitz, H. v. (1900): *Das Aufsteigen des Arbeiterstandes in England. Ein Beitrag zur socialen Geschichte der Gegenwart.* Jena.

Oakshott, M. (1989): Education – The Engagement and its Frustration. In: T. Füller (ed.): *Michael Oakshott on Education.* New Haven: Yale University Press, pp. 63–94.

Oelkers, J. (1989): *Reformpädagogik – Eine kritische Dogmengeschichte.* Weinheim/Munich.

Oelkers, J. (1993): Dewey in Deutschland – ein Missverständnis. Epilogue to the new edition. In: J. Oelkers (ed.): *John Dewey: Demokratie und Erziehung.* Weinheim, pp. 497–517.

Oelkers, J. (2000): John Deweys Philosophie der Erziehung: eine theoriegeschichtliche Analyse. In: H. Joas (ed.): *Philosophie der Demokratie. Beiträge zum Werk von John Dewey.* Frankfurt a. M., S. 280–315.

Offe, C. (1984): *„Arbeitsgesellschaft": Strukturprobleme und Zukunftsperspektiven.* Frankfurt a. M.

Offe, C. (2004): *Selbstbetrachtung aus der Ferne. Tocqueville, Weber und Adorno in den Vereinigten Staaten.* Frankfurt a. M.

Osthaus, K. E. (1920): *Van de Velde. Leben und Schaffen des Künstlers.* Hagen.

Paulsen, F. (1897): *Geschichte des gelehrten Unterrichtes auf den deutschen Schulen und Universitäten.* 2nd Vol. Leipzig.

Pestalozzi, J. H. (1943): Geist und Herz in der Methode. In: A. Buchenau, E. Spranger and H. Stettbacher (eds.): *Pestalozzi. Sämtliche Werke. Schriften aus der Zeit von 1805–1806.* Bd. XVIII. Berlin, pp. 1–52.

Petersen, P. (1935): Nachwort. Entwicklung eines eigenen Schulwesens in USA. In: J. Dewey and W. H. Kilpatrick (eds.): *Der Projekt-Plan. Grundlegung und Praxis.* Weimar, pp. 206–212.

Picavet, F. (1972): *Les idéologues. Essai sur l'histoire des idées et des théories scientifiques, philosophiques, religieuses etc. en France depuis 1989.* Hildesheim.

Pleiss, U. (1986): Berufs- und Wirtschaftspädagogik als wissenschaftliche Disziplin. Eine wissenschaftstheoretische und wissenschaftshistorische Modellstudie. In: R. Lassahn and B. Ofenbach (eds.): *Arbeits-, Berufs-, und Wirtschaftspädagogik im Übergang.* Frankfurt a. M., pp. 79–130.

Prange, K. (1996): *Bauformen des Unterrichts.* Bad Heilbrunn.

Prantl, R. (1925): Dewey als Pädagog. In: *Vierteljahresschrift für wissenschaftliche Pädagogik* 1, pp. 287–300, 387–400 and 572–637.

Putnam, H. and Putnam, R. A. (1999): Erziehung zur Demokratie. In: *Deutsche Zeitschrift für Philosophie* 47 (1), pp. 39–57.

Radkau, J. (1989): *Technik in Deutschland. Vom 18. Jahrhundert bis zur Gegenwart.* Frankfurt.

Radkau, J. (2005): *Max Weber. Die Leidenschaft des Denkens.* Munich.

Raffe, D. (1991): Scotland vs. England: The place of "Home Internationals" in comparative research. In: P. Ryan (ed.): *International Comparisons of Vocational Education and Training for Intermediate Skills.* London, pp. 47–67.

Ratz, U. (1980): *Sozialreform und Arbeiterschaft. Die Gesellschaft für Soziale Reform und die sozialdemokratische Arbeiterbewegung von der Jahrhundertwende bis zum Ausbruch des Ersten Weltkrieges.* Berlin.

Rehm, A. (1924): Individuelle Bildung und Schulbildung. In: A. Fischer and E. Spranger (eds.): *Jugendführer und Jugendprobleme. Festschrift zu Georg Kerschensteiners 70. Geburtstag.* Leipzig/Berlin, pp. 98–120.

Reich, K. (1995); Arbeit – Bildung. In: D. Lenzen (ed.): *Enzyklopädie Erziehungswissenschaft.* Vol. 8. Stuttgart, pp. 383–389.

Reichwein, G. (1979): Georg Kerschensteiners "Theorie der Bildung". In: G. Wehle (ed.): *Georg Kerschensteiner.* Darmstadt, pp. 111–127.

Reid, Th. (2007): *On Practical Ethics.* Edinburgh: University Press.

Rickert, H. (1920): *Die Philosophie des Lebens. Darstellung und Kritik der philosophischen Modeströmungen unserer Zeit.* Tübingen.

Rickert, H. (1921): *Allgemeine Grundlegung der Philosophie. Part I.* Tübingen.

Riehl, W. H. (1861): *Die deutsche Arbeit.* Stuttgart.

Riehl, W. H. (1883): *Die deutsche Arbeit.* 3rd ed. Stuttgart.

Riehl, W. H. (1907): *Die bürgerliche Gesellschaft.* Stuttgart.

Ringer, F. (2004): *Max Weber. An Intellectual Biography.* Chicago: The University of Chicago Press.

Rissmann, R. (1911): Warum ich die Herbartsche Pädagogik ablehne. In: R. Rissmann: *Volksschulreform: Herbartianismus – Sozialpädagogik – Persönlichkeitsbildung.* Leipzig, pp. 24–25.

Röhrs, H. (ed.) (1967): *Die Wirtschaftspädagogik – eine erziehungswissenschaftliche Disziplin?* Frankfurt a. M.

266

Röhrs, H. (1977): *Die Reformpädagogik als Internationale Bewegung. Die progressive Erziehungsbewegung. Verlauf und Auswirkung der Reformpädagogik in den USA.* Berlin.

Röhrs, H. (1989): Die Erneuerung des Bildungswesens im Geiste Georg Kerschensteiners. In: *Pädagogische Rundschau* 43 (1), pp. 3–15.

Ross, I. (1995): *The Life of Adam Smith.* Oxford: Claredon Press.

Rossi, P. (1988): Diskussionsbeitrag. In: Ch. Gneuss and J. Kocka (eds.): Max Weber – Ein Symposion. In: *Max Weber und die Welt von heute – Eine Diskussion mit Wilhelm Hennis, Wolfgang J. Mommsen und Pietro Rossi.* Munich, pp. 195–214.

Rothschild, E. (2001): *Economic sentiments. Adam Smith, Condorcet and the Enlightment.* Cambridge.

Rust, A. (1996): Pragmatismus und Erziehung bei John Dewey. In: E. Angehrn and B. Bertschi (eds.): *Philosophie und Erziehung.* Bern, pp. 225–259.

Ryan, A. (1995): *John Dewey and the High Tide of American Liberalism.* New York: Norton.

Saupe, E. (1927): Georg Kerschensteiner. In: E. Saupe (ed.): *Deutsche Pädagogen der Neuzeit – Ein Beitrag zur Geschichte der Erziehungswissenschaft zu Beginn des 20. Jahrhunderts.* Osterwieck a. Harz, pp. 57–69.

Scheffler, K. (1917): *Der Geist der Gotik.* Leipzig.

Scheffler, K. (1932): *Der neue Mensch.* Leipzig.

Scheffler, K. (n.d.): *Die Zukunft der deutschen Kunst.* Berlin.

Scheibner, O. (1928): *Zwanzig Jahre Arbeitsschule in Idee und Gestaltung.* Leipzig.

Schenckendorff, E. v. (n.d.): *Die Ausgestaltung der Volksschule nach den Bedürfnissen der Gegenwart.* (n.p.)

Schlieper, F. (1963): *Allgemeine Berufspädagogik.* Freiburg.

Schluchter, W. (1988): *Religion und Lebensführung. Band 1. Studien zu Max Webers Kultur- und Werttheorie.* Frankfurt.

Schluchter, W. (1998): *Die Entstehung des modernen Rationalismus. Eine Analyse von Max Webers Entwicklungsgeschichte des Okzidents.* Frankfurt a. M.

Schluchter, W. (2003): Handlung, Ordnung und Kultur. Grundzüge eines weberianischen Forschungsprogramms. In: G. Albert, A. Bienfait, S. Sigmund and C. Wendt (eds.): *Das Weber-Paradigma. Studien zur Weiterentwicklung von Max Webers Forschungsprogramm.* Tübingen, pp. 42–74.

Schmitz, E. L. (1995): Erwachsenenbildung als lebensweltlicher Erkenntnisprozess. In: D. Lenzen (ed.): *Enzyklopädie Erziehungswissenschaft.* Vol. 11. Stuttgart, pp. 95–123.

Schmoller, G. (1875): *Über einige Grundfragen des Rechts und der Volkswirtschaft. Ein offenes Sendschreiben an Herrn Professor Dr. Heinrich von Treitschke.* 2nd ed. Jena.

Schmoller, G. (1918): *Die soziale Frage. Klassenbildung, Arbeiterfrage, Klassenkampf.* Munich.

Schnädelbach, H. (1983): *Philosophie in Deutschland 1831–1933.* Frankfurt a. M.

Schönharting, W. (1979): *Kritik der Berufsbildungstheorie. Zur Systematik eines Wissenschaftszweiges*. Weinheim/Basel.

Schorer, F. (1986): *Berufliche Bildung – Menschenbildung gestern und heute. Aktuelle Lösungsversuche bei Pestalozzi und Kerschensteiner*. 2nd ed. Bern: Lang.

Schulze-Gaevernitz, G. (1890): *Zum socialen Frieden. Eine Darstellung der socialpolitischen Erziehung des englischen Volkes im neunzehnten Jahrhundert*. 2 Vols. Leipzig.

Schumann, M., Baethge-Kinsky, V., Kuhlmann, M. and Neumann, U. (1994): *Trendreport Rationalisierung. Automobilindustrie, Werkzeugmaschinenbau, Chemische Industrie*. Berlin.

Schütte, F. (2001): Die Arbeit am "Projekt der Moderne" – Der berufspädagogische Wissenstransfer zwischen Deutschland und der USA 1906–1998. In: H. Reinisch et al. (eds.): *Modernisierung der Berufsbildung in Europa*. Opladen, pp. 173–182.

Schütte, F. and Uhe, E. (eds.) (1998): *Die Modernintät des Unmodernen. Das deutsche System der Berufsausbildung zwischen Krise und Akzeptanz*. Berlin.

Schwarte, N. (1980): *Schulpolitik und Pädagogik der deutschen Sozialdemokratie an der Wende vom 19. zum 20. Jahrhundert*. Köln.

Seidel, R. (n.d.): *Lichtglaube und Zukunftssonnen*. Berlin.

Sennett, R. (2008): *The Craftsman*. New Haven: Yale University Press.

Sieferle, R. P. (1984): *Fortschrittsfeinde? Opposition gegen Technik und Industrie von der Romantik bis zur Gegenwart*. Munich.

Siemsen, A. (1926): *Beruf und Erziehung*. Berlin.

Simmel, G. (1888): Einige Bemerkungen über Goethes Verhältnis zur Ethik. In: *Zeitschrift für Philosophie und philosophische Kritik*. Neue Folge 92, pp. 101–106.

Simmel, G. (1905): *Sechzehn Vorlesungen gehalten an der Berliner Universität*. Berlin.

Simmel, G. (1906): *Kant und Goethe*. Berlin.

Simmel, G. (1908): *Soziologie. Untersuchungen über die Formen der Vergesellschaftung*. Leipzig.

Simmel, G. (1913): *Goethe*. Leipzig.

Simmel, G. (1916): *Rembrandt. Ein kunstphilosophischer Versuch*. Leipzig.

Simmel, G. (1918): *Lebensanschauung. Vier metaphysische Kapitel*. Munich/Leipzig.

Simmel, G. (1922): *Schulpädagogik. Vorlesungen, gehalten der der Universität Strassburg*. Osterwieck/Harz.

Simmel, G. (1983): Der Begriff und die Tragödie der Kultur. In: G. Simmel: *Philosophische Kultur. Über das Abenteuer, die Geschlechter und die Krise der Moderne. Gesammelte Essais*. Berlin, pp. 183–206.

Simmel, G. (1987): Der Konflikt der modernen Kultur. In: M. Landmann (ed.): *Das individuelle Gesetz. Philosophische Exkurse*. Frankfurt a. M., pp. 148–173.

Simmel, G. (1989): Über soziale Differenzierung. In: O. Rammstedt (ed.): *Georg Simmel – Gesamtausgabe*. 2nd Vol. Frankfurt a. M., pp. 109–296.

Simmel, G. (1989a): *Philosophie des Geldes*. Frankfurt a. M.

Simmel, G. (1991): *Schopenhauer and Nietzsche*. Urbana: University of Illinois Press.

Simons, D. (1966): *Georg Kerschensteiner – his thought and relevance today*. London.

Smith, A. (1904a): *Inquiry into the Nature and Causes of the Wealth of Nations*. Edited with an Introduction, Notes, Marginal Summary and an Enlarged Index by Edwin Cannan. Vol. 1. London: Methuen.

Smith, A. (1904b): *Inquiry into the Nature and Causes of the Wealth of Nations*. Edited with an Introduction, Notes, Marginal Summary and an Enlarged Index by Edwin Cannan. Vol. 2. London: Methuen.

Snedden, D. (1910): *The Problem of Vocational Education*. Boston: Houghton Mifflin Company.

Snedden, D. (1931): *American High Schools and Vocational Schools in 1960*. New York: Teachers College, Columbia University.

Sombart, W. (1911): Technik und Kultur. In: Deutsche Gesellschaft für Soziologie (ed.): *Verhandlungen des Ersten Deutschen Soziologentages vom 19.–22. Oktober 1910 in Frankfurt*. Tübingen, pp. 63–83.

Spengler, O. (1923): *Der Untergang des Abendlandes*. 2 Vols. Munich.

Spengler, O. (1933): *Der Mensch und die Technik. Beitrag zu einer Philosophie des Lebens*. Munich.

Spranger, E. (1922): *Lebensformen. Geisteswissenschaftliche Psychologie und Ethik der Persönlichkeit*. 3rd ed. Halle.

Spranger, E. (1924): Die Generationen und die Bedeutung des Klassischen in der Erziehung. In: A. Fischer and E. Spranger (eds.): *Jugendführer und Jugendprobleme. Festschrift zu Georg Kerschensteiners 70. Geburtstag*. Leipzig/Berlin, pp. 307–332.

Spranger, E. (1925): Die Bedeutung der wissenschaftlichen Pädagogik für das Volksleben. In: E. Spranger: *Kultur und Erziehung. Gesammelte Pädagogische Aufsätze*. 3rd ed. Leipzig, pp. 138–158.

Spranger, E. (1925a): Grundlegende Bildung, Berufsbildung, Allgemeinbildung. In: E. Spranger (ed.): *Kultur und Erziehung. Gesammelte Pädagogische Aufsätze*. 3rd ed. Leipzig, pp. 159–177.

Spranger, E. (1936): *Wilhelm von Humboldt und die Humanitätsidee*. Berlin: Gruyter.

Spranger, E. (1949): Geleitwort. In: G. Kerschensteiner: *Die Seele des Erziehers und das Problem der Lehrerbildung*. Munich, pp. 7–11.

Spranger, E. (1966): (Letter) Spranger an Kerschensteiner 14.1.1912. In: L. Englert (ed.): *Georg Kerschensteiner – Eduard Spranger. Briefwechsel 1912–1931*. Munich, pp. 23–24.

Spranger, E. (1966a): Letters Dated March 22, 1915 and March 14, 1915. In: L. Englert (ed.): *Georg Kerschensteiner – Eduard Spranger. Briefwechsel 1912–1931*. Stuttgart, pp. 30 and 35–38.

Spranger, E. (1970): Ungelöste Probleme der Pflichtberufsschule. In: L. Englert (ed.): *Eduard Spranger. Gesammelte Schriften*. Vol. 3. Heidelberg, pp. 393–405.

Spranger, E. (1978): An Dr. Erwin Jeangros. In: H. Bahr (ed.): *Eduard Spranger. Gesammelte Schriften*. Vol. 7. Tübingen, p. 290.

Stein, L. v. (1846): Der Begriff der Arbeit und die Principien des Arbeitslohnes in ihrem Verhältnisse zum Socialismus und Communismus. In: *Zeitschrift für die gesamte Staatswissenschaft* 3, pp. 233–290.

Steinbeis, F. (1879): Fortbildungsschule, Fachschule, Lehrwerkstätte. Gutachten für den Verein für Socialpolitik. In: Verein für Socialpolitik (ed.): *Das Gewerbliche Fortbildungswesen.* Leipzig, pp. 1–23.

Stewart, D. (1994): *Lectures on Political Economy II.* (Reprint). Bristol: Thoemmes Press.

Stratmann, K. (1983): Berufs-/Wirtschaftspädagogik. In: H. Blankertz, J. Derbolav, A. Kell and G. Kutscha (eds.): *Enzyklopädie Erziehungswissenschaft.* Vol. 9.2. Stuttgart, pp. 186–189.

Stratmann, K. (1992): *"Zeit der Gärung und Zersetzung". Arbeiterjugend im Kaiserreich zwischen Schule und Beruf.* Weinheim.

Stratmann, K. (1999): Georg Kerschensteiner – kritische Analyse seiner Pädagogik. In: G. Pätzold and M. Wahle (eds.): *Karlwilhelm Stratmann – Berufserziehung und sozialer Wandel.* Frankfurt, pp. 631–645.

Stratmann, K. (1999a): Technik und Technikkritik in der Reformpädagogik – das Beispiel Georg Kerschensteiner. In: G. Pätzold and M. Wahle (eds.): *Karlwilhelm Stratmann – Berufserziehung und sozialer Wandel.* Frankfurt, pp. 647–671.

Stütz, G. (1970): *Berufspädagogik unter ideologiekritischem Aspekt.* Frankfurt a. M.

Suchanski, M. W. (1947): *Der Begriff der Arbeit im Erziehungswerke Pestalozzis, seiner Nachfolger und Anhänger.* (Diss.) Zürich.

Suhr, M. (1994): *John Dewey zur Einführung.* Hamburg: Junius.

Szakolczai, A. (1998): *Max Weber and Michel Foucault. Parallel life-works.* London: Routledge.

Tenbruck, F. (1999): Die Genesis der Methodologie Max Webers. In: H. Homann (ed.): *Das Werk Max Webers. Gesammelte Aufsätze zu Max Weber.* Tübingen, pp. 1–58.

Tessaring, M. (1993): Das duale System der Berufsausbildung in Deutschland. Attraktivität und Beschäftigungsperspektiven. In: *Mitteilungen aus der Arbeitsmarkt- und Berufsforschung* 26, pp. 131–161.

Tönnies, F. (2001): *Community and Civil Society.* Cambridge: CUP.

Treitschke, H. v. (1859): *Die Gesellschaftswissenschaft. Ein kritischer Versuch.* Leipzig.

Treitschke, H. v. (1874): Der Socialismus und seine Gönner. In: H. v. Treitschke: *Zehn Jahre Deutscher Kämpfe 1865–1874. Schriften zur Tagespolitik.* Berlin, pp. 458–555.

Treitschke, H. v. (1907): Die Freiheit. In: H. v. Treitschke: *Ausgewählte Schriften.* 1st vol., 3rd ed. Leipzig, pp. 1–47.

Tyack, D. and Justice, B. (2003): Vocational Education in the U.S. – Some Historical Perspectives. In: J. Oelkers (ed.): *Futures of Education II – Essays from an Interdisciplinary Symposium.* Bern, pp. 179–196.

Tymister, H. J. (1995): Projektunterricht. In: D. Lenzen (ed.): *Enzyklopädie Erziehungswissenschaft*. Vol. 8. Stuttgart, pp. 524–527.

Verein für Socialpolitik (1875): *Die Reform des Lehrlingswesens. Sechzehn Gutachten*. Leipzig.

Voigt, W. (1975): *Einführung in die Berufs- und Wirtschaftspädagogik*. Munich.

Walder, F. (1992): *Georg Kerschensteiner als Hochschullehrer und Bildungstheoretiker*. Bad Heilbrunn.

Weber, A. (1913): Der soziologische Kulturbegriff. In: Deutsche Gesellschaft für Soziologie (ed.): *Verhandlungen des Zweiten Deutschen Soziologentages vom 20.–22. Oktober 1912 in Berlin*. Tübingen, pp. 1–20.

Weber, A. (1914): Ernst Haeckel und sein Einfluss auf die technische Kultur der Gegenwart. In: H. Schmidt (ed.): *Was wir Ernst Haeckel verdanken*. Leipzig, pp. 96–114.

Weber, L. (1936). *Schichtung und Vermittlung im pädagogischen Denken Georg Kerschensteiners*. (Unpublished Diss.).

Weber, M. (1911): Geschäftsbericht. In: Deutsche Gesellschaft für Soziologie (ed.): *Verhandlungen des Ersten Deutschen Soziologentages vom 19.–22. Oktober 1910 in Frankfurt*. Tübingen, pp. 39–62.

Weber, M. (1984): Das preussische Wahlrecht. In: H. Baier, M. R. Lepsius, W. J. Mommsen, W. Schluchter and J. Winckelmann (eds.): Max Weber Gesamtausgabe. MWG I/15: W. J. Mommsen (ed.): *Zur Politik im Weltkrieg. Schriften und Reden 1914–1918*. Tübingen, pp. 224–235.

Weber, M. (1985): *Wirtschaft und Gesellschaft*. 5th ed. Tübingen.

Weber, M. (1988): Politik als Beruf. In: J. Winckelmann (ed.): *Gesammelte Politische Schriften*. Tübingen, pp. 505–560.

Weber, M. (1988a): Roscher und Knies und die logischen Probleme der historischen Nationalökonomie. In: J. Winckelmann (ed.): *Gesammelte Aufsätze zur Wissenschaftslehre*. Tübingen, pp. 1–145.

Weber, M. (1988b): Der Sinn der „Wertfreiheit" der soziologischen und ökonomischen Wissenschaften. In: J. Winckelmann (ed.): *Gesammelte Aufsätze zur Wissenschaftslehre*. Tübingen, pp. 489–540.

Weber, M. (1988c): Wissenschaft als Beruf. In: J. Winckelmann (ed.): *Gesammelte Aufsätze zur Wissenschaftslehre*. Tübingen, pp. 582–613.

Weber, M. (1988d): Die Wirtschaftsethik der Weltreligionen. In: M. Weber: *Gesammelte Aufsätze zur Religionssoziologie I*. Tübingen, pp. 237–573.

Weber, M. (1998): Bemerkungen über R. Blank, Soziale Zusammensetzung. In: H. Baier, M. R. Lepsius, W. J. Mommsen, W. Schluchter and J. Winckelmann (eds.): Max Weber Gesamtausgabe – MWG I/8: W. Schluchter (ed.): *Wirtschaft, Staat und Sozialpolitik*. Tübingen, pp. 122–199.

Weber, M. (1998a): The Relations of the Rural Community to Other Branches of Social Science. In: H. Baier, M. R. Lepsius, W. J. Mommsen, W. Schluchter and J. Winckelmann (eds.): Max Weber Gesamtausgabe – MWG I/8: W. Schluchter (ed.): *Wirtschaft, Staat und Sozialpolitik*. Tübingen, pp. 212–227.

Weber, M. (2005): Das antike Judentum. Schriften und Reden 1911–1920. In: H. Baier, M. R. Lepsius, W. J. Mommsen, W. Schluchter and J. Winckelmann (eds.): Max Weber Gesamtausgabe – MWG I/21, 2. Halbband: O. Eckart (ed.): *Die Wirtschaftsethik der Weltreligionen*. Tübingen, pp. 707–830.

Wehle, G. (ed.) (1966): *Georg Kerschensteiner. Ausgewählte pädagogische Schriften Band 1: Berufsbildung und Berufsschule*. Paderborn.

Wehle, G. (1966a): Georg Kerschensteiners Beitrag zur Begründung der modernen Berufsschule. In: G. Wehle (ed.): *Georg Kerschensteiner. Ausgewählte pädagogische Schriften Band 1: Berufsbildung und Berufsschule*. Paderborn, pp. 188–199.

Wehle, G. (1966b): Bemerkungen zur Textauswahl, Textgeschichte und Textwiedergabe. In: G. Wehle (ed.): *Georg Kerschensteiner. Ausgewählte pädagogische Schriften Band 1: Berufsbildung und Berufsschule*. Paderborn, pp. 202–207.

Wehle, G. (ed.) (1979): *Georg Kerschensteiner*. Darmstadt.

Wehle, G. (ed.) (1982): *Georg Kerschensteiner. Ausgewählte pädagogische Schriften Band 2: Texte zum pädagogischen Begriff der Arbeit und Arbeitsschule*. Paderborn.

Wehle, G. (1982a): Georg Kerschensteiner und die reformpädagogische Bewegung seiner Zeit. In: G. Wehle (ed.): *Georg Kerschensteiner. Ausgewählte pädagogische Schriften Band 2: Texte zum pädagogischen Begriff der Arbeit und Arbeitsschule*. Paderborn, pp. 184–199.

Werder, L. v. (1976): Zur Verwissenschaftlichung der Berufspädagogik – einige Thesen. In: *DtBFsch* 72, pp. 323–335.

Westbrook, R. B. (1991): *John Dewey and American Democracy*. Ithaca: Cornell University Press.

Wiget, Theodor (1914): *Grundlinien der Erziehungslehre Pestalozzis*. Leipzig.

Wilhelm, Th. (1957): *Die Pädagogik Kerschensteiners. Vermächtnis und Verhängnis*. Stuttgart.

Wilhelm, Th. (1967): *Pädagogik der Gegenwart*. Stuttgart.

Wilhelm, Th. (1975): Pragmatische Pädagogik. In: *Erziehungswissenschaftliches Handbuch*. Vol. IV. Berlin, pp. 147–198.

Winch, Ch. (2006): Georg Kerschensteiner – founding the dual system in Germany. In: *Oxford Review of Education* 37 (3), pp. 381–396.

Witte, J. H. (1889): Über Berufsbildung des Kaufmanns. In: J. H. Witte: *Sinnen und Denken. Gesammelte Abhandlungen und Vorträge aus den Gebieten der Literatur, Philosophie und Pädagogik*. Halle-Saale, pp. 179–250.

Wolf, F. (1835): *Über Erziehung, Schule und Universität (Concilia scholastica)*. Leipzig.

World Bank (1991): *Vocational and Technical Education and Training. A World Bank Policy Paper*. Washington D.C.

Wright, J. C. and Allen, Ch. R. (1929): *Efficiency in Education. A study of the applications of the principles of efficiency to educational administration, supervision and methods of teaching*. New York: J. Wiley & Sons.

Zabeck, J. (1992): *Die Berufs- und Wirtschaftspädagogik als erziehungswissenschaftliche Teildisziplin.* Baltmannsweiler.

Zabeck, J. (2003): Goethe im Lichte der Berufs- und Wirtschaftspädagogik. In: A. Bredow, R. Dobischat and J. Rottmann (eds.): *Berufs- und Wirtschaftspädagogik von A–Z.* Baltmannsweiler, pp. 67–82.

Zillig, P. (1907): Darf der Altruismus zur Grundlegung des Bildungsideals und damit des Lehrplans für die Volksschule genommen werden? In: *Jahrbuch des Vereins für wissenschaftliche Pädagogik* 39, pp. 1–59.

Ziman, J. M. (1994): *Prometheus Bound. Science in a Dynamic Steady State.* Cambridge: Cambridge University Press.

Zimmer, J. (1995): Der Situationsansatz als Bezugsrahmen der Kindergartenreform. In: D. Lenzen (ed.): *Enzyklopädie Erziehungwissenschaft.* Vol. 6. Stuttgart, pp. 21–38.

Zschokke, H. (1859): *Volksbildung ist Volksbefreiung. Eine Rede gehalten in der Versammlung des schweizerischen Volksbildungsvereins zu Lausen d. 10. April 1836.* Aarau.

Zymek, B. (2000): Domination, Legitimacy and Education: Max Weber's Contribution to Comparative Education. In: J. Schriewer (ed.): *Discourse formation in comparative education.* Frankfurt a. M., p. 133–151.

Index of Names

Abel, H. 233, 242, 243, 245, 247
Achtenhagen, F. 230
Adler, A. 86
Aebli, H. 129–131
Allen, Ch. R. 213
Arnold, M. 212
Avenarius, R. 83

Bailey, T. 213
Barschak, E. 231, 232
Bastiat, F. 195, 204, 205, 208
Baumgarten, E. 124
Bebel, A. 55
Bennett, Ch. 216
Bergson, H. 173
Berryman, S. 213
Bismarck, O. v. 18, 79, 97, 107, 153
Blankertz, H. 41, 233, 243–245, 247, 248
Blättner, F. 111, 233–235, 240, 241, 245
Blonskij, P. 61, 241
Bohnsack, F. 132
Bourdieu, P. 145
Brentano, L. 50–52, 206, 207, 208, 210
Brezinka, W. 133
Bücher, K. 50

Cabanis, P.-J.-G. 36
Campe, J. H. 39
Carlyle, T. 50, 51, 61, 77, 107, 181
Cassirer, E. 175
Condorcet, Marquis de 34–38, 189, 198
Cornelius, H. 84, 186

D'Alembert, J. le R. 39
Davenport, E. 216
Degerando, J.-M. 36
Dewey, J. 21, 70, 71, 81, 83, 85, 86, 91, 93, 107, 108, 117–137, 141, 167, 212, 214, 215, 217, 218, 220, 223, 224, 234, 240
Diderot, D. 39
Diesterweg, A. 91
Dilthey, W. 72, 91, 154, 174, 180, 182
Durden, R. F. 230
Durkheim, É. 183

Eisner, K. 31
Eliot, Ch. W. 214
Engels, F. 51, 79, 209
Eucken, R. 173

Fellenberg, Ph. E. 235
Fénelon, F. 206
Ferguson, A. 197
Fernau-Kerschen-steiner, G. 27, 29
Fichte, J. G. 153
Fischer, A. 19, 70, 88, 89, 93, 234–236, 238, 240, 241, 243, 245, 246
Flitner, E. 146
Flitner, W. 111
Foerster, F. W. 71, 151
Fourier, Ch. 54, 55
Freinet, C. 132
Freud, S. 173
Frey, K. 127
Freyer, H. 46, 61
Fröbel, F. 95, 96, 106, 235

Gaudig, H.	70, 87–89, 93, 108	Kipp, M.	233
Gessner, H.	98	Klages, L.	174
Goethe, J. W.	23, 45, 53, 55, 60, 91, 97, 106, 108, 143, 144, 153, 156, 168–172, 179, 180, 234	Kliebard, H. M.	220
		Krüsi, H.	91
		Landauer, G.	31, 55
Graberg, F.	59	Langbehn, J.	169
Groos, K.	108	Lange, F. A.	44
Gundolf, F.	168	Leake, A. H.	219
		Lempert, W.	245
Habermas, J.	173	Lerche, J.	53
Harney, K.	246, 249	Lietz, H.	70
Haufe, E.	59	Lippmann, W.	135
Hayek, F. A. v.	195, 204–206	Lisop, I.	248
Hegel, G. W. F.	40, 106	Litt, T.	42, 45, 61, 106, 111, 174, 175, 235 –237, 242, 245
Hentke, R.	248		
Herbart, J. F.	77, 81, 83–85, 92, 94, 96, 100, 102, 106, 108–110, 129 –131, 235	Locke, J.	39
		Löwith, K.	148
		Lukacs, G.	133, 173, 174
Herkner, H.	45, 53	Mach, E.	83
Heuss, T.	30	Mandeville, B. de	195–197, 203, 204
Horkheimer, M.	133	Marcuse, H.	133
Huisinga, R.	248	Marx, K.	51, 79
Humboldt, A. v.	39	Matthias, A.	108
Humboldt, W. v.	30, 34–39, 41, 92, 143	Mead, G. H.	234
		Meyer, H.	126, 127
Hume, D.	197, 198	Mieses, L. v.	204
Hylla, E.	134, 135	Mill, J. S.	205
		Millar, J.	198
James, W.	122	Miller-Kipp, G.	233
Jeangros, E.	237	Monroe, P.	212, 213
Jodl, F.	140	Montesqieu, Baron de	206
Jung, C. G.	86	Montessori, M.	73
		Morris, W.	57
Kant, I.	84, 85, 90, 99–102, 104, 108, 156, 169, 183	Müller, S.	29
		Müllges, U.	235, 245, 246
		Münch, J.	242
Kantor, H.	222	Musil, R.	139
Kehr, C.	84	Muthesius, H.	60, 62, 106
Kerschensteiner, A.	29		
Kerschensteiner, M.	27, 31, 97	Napoleon	36
Kilpatrick, W. H.	123–126	Natorp, P.	18, 70, 84, 98–106, 167, 175
King, I.	215		

Naumann, F. 30, 58, 62, 142
Newton, I. 27, 37
Nicklis, W. 103, 105
Niederer, J. 95
Niethammer, F. I. 40, 41
Nohl, H. 111, 112, 174, 175, 244
Nordau, M. 43, 44
Nostitz, H. v. 51, 62, 63, 79, 80, 209

Oedipus 110
Oelkers, J. 135

Paulsen, F. 39
Pestalozzi, J. H. 18, 21, 27, 33, 41, 42, 53, 66–70, 81, 83–85, 91, 92, 95–114, 118–122
Petersen, P. 111, 124, 125, 127
Picavet, F. 36
Planck, M. 28
Plato 18, 30, 67, 79, 83, 85
Prange, K. 130

Reichwein, G. 111
Reid, T. 197
Rein, W. 53, 102
Rembrandt 144, 169
Rickert, H. 70, 141, 144, 169, 176, 183, 185
Riehl, W. H. 47–49, 52, 55, 62
Ringer, F. 146
Rissmann, R. 96
Robespierre 206
Röhrs, H. 113, 124
Rousseau, J.-J. 39, 206
Ruskin, J. 53, 56, 57, 61

Saint-Just, L.-A. de 206
Scheffler, K. 56, 58
Scheibner, O. 88
Schelling, F. W. J. 173
Schlieper, F. 233, 235
Schmoller, G. 48, 49, 51, 62, 206

Schnädelbach, H. 171, 172
Schönharting, W. 245
Schulze-Gaevernitz, G. 50
Seidel, R. 62, 67, 241
Sennet, R. 250
Siemsen, A. 45, 241, 243
Simmel, G. 21, 91, 92, 111, 141, 144, 167–179, 182–190
Simons, D. 19
Smith, A. 23, 48, 195, 197–208, 210, 221
Snedden, D. 217, 218, 220, 223, 224
Sombart, W. 144, 156
Sophocles 110, 112
Spengler, O. 174
Spranger, E. 18, 27, 91, 92, 96, 97, 103, 105–112, 121, 141–144, 149, 154, 156, 165, 167, 172, 179, 181–187, 190, 234–237, 239–241, 243, 244
Stein, L. v. 52
Steinbeis, F. 208
Stern, W. 108
Stewart, D. 198, 199
Stratmann, K. 229
Stütz, G. 245
Tönnies, F. 144, 173
Tracy, D. de 36
Trapp, Ch. H. 39
Treitschke, H. v. 47–49, 51, 52, 58, 62, 77, 208
Trotzki, L. 149
Türk, K. Ch. W. v. 95
Tyack, D. 222
Tymister, H. J. 125, 126
Van de Velde, H. 57, 58
Weber, A. 144
Weber, L. 190

Weber, M.   21, 114, 139–152, 157–165
Wehle, G.   19, 105
Weniger, E.   244
Werder, L. v.   246
Wiget, T.   102
Wilhelm, T.   108, 109, 134, 240
Willmann, O.   102
Wilson, W.   221
Winch, Ch.   20
Wolf, F. A.   39

Wollestonecraft, M.   39
Wright, J. C.   213
Zabeck, J.   247
Zeller, C. A.   95
Ziller, T.   81, 83, 99, 101, 102, 129
Zillig, P.   83
Zollinger, F.   97
Zschokke, J. H.   15
Zymek, B.   146

studies in vocational and continuing education

edited by
philipp gonon & anja heikkinen

The aim of this series is to present critical, historical and comparative research in the field of vocational and continuing education and human research development, seen from a pedagogical, organisational, economic and societal perspective. It discusses the implications of latest research to contemporary reform policies and practices. One central issue reflected in all publications is gender. A basic feature of all volumes is their cross-cultural approach.

The series has a firm basis in the international research network "VET and Culture" (Vocational Education and Training and Culture; www.peda.net/veraja/uta/vetculture) and the editors invite distinguished researchers from Europe and other continents to contribute to the series. Studies in vocational and continuing education include monographs, collected papers editions, and proceedings.

Vol. 1   Antony Lindgren & Anja Heikkinen (eds)
          Social Competences in Vocational and Continuing Education
          2004. 256 S. ISBN 3-03910-345-8 / US-ISBN 0-8204-7013-9

Vol. 2   Liv Mjelde
          The Magical Properties of Workshop Learning
          2006. 230 S. ISBN 3-03910-348-2 / US-ISBN 0-8204-7014-7

Vol. 3   Liv Mjelde & Richard Daly (eds)
          Working Knowledge in a Globalizing World
          From Work to Learning, from Learning to Work
          2006. 406 S. ISBN 3-03910-974-X / 0-8204-8364-8

Vol. 4   Philipp Gonon, Katrin Kraus, Jürgen Oelkers & Stefanie Stolz (eds)
          Work, Education and Employability
          2008. 324 S. ISBN 978-3-03911-294-4

Vol. 5   Olav Eikeland
          The Ways of Aristotle
          Aristotelian Phrónêsis, Aristotelian Philosophy of Dialogue,
          and Action Research
          2008. 560 S. ISBN 978-3-03911-471-9

Vol. 6   Vibe Aarkrog & Christian Helms Jørgensen (eds)
          Divergence and Convergence in Education and Work
          2008. 441 S. ISBN 978-3-03911-505-1

Vol. 7   Anja Heikkinen & Katrin Kraus (eds)
          Reworking Vocational Education. Policies, Practices and Concepts
          2009. 230 S. ISBN 978-3-03911-603-4

Vol. 8   Markus Weil, Leena Koski & Liv Mjelde (eds)
          Knowing Work. The Social Relations of Working and Knowing
          2009. 252 S. ISBN 978-3-03911-642-3

Vol. 9   Philipp Gonon
          The Quest for Modern Vocational Education – Georg Kerschensteiner
          between Dewey, Weber and Simmel.
          2009. 278 S. ISBN 978-3-0343-0026-1